Watching Shakespeare
on Television

Watching Shakespeare on Television

H. R. Coursen

Rutherford ● Madison ● Teaneck
Fairleigh Dickinson University Press
London and Toronto: Associated University Presses

© 1993 by Associated University Presses, Inc.

Associated University Presses
440 Forsgate Drive
Cranbury, NJ 08512

Associated University Presses
25 Sicilian Avenue
London WC1A 2QH, England

Associated University Presses
P.O. Box 338, Port Credit
Mississauga, Ontario
Canada L5G 4L8

The paper used in this publication meets the requirements of the American National Standard for Permanence of Paper for Printed Library Materials Z39.48-1984.

Library of Congress Cataloging-in-Publication Data

Coursen, Herbert R.
    Watching Shakespeare on television / H.R. Coursen.
        p.   cm.
    Includes bibliographical references and index.
    ISBN 0-8386-3521-0 (alk. paper)
    1. Shakespeare, William, 1564–1616—Film and video adaptations.
    2. English drama—Film and video adaptations.   3. Television
    adaptations.   I. Title.
    PR3093.C68   1993
    791.45′75—dc20   92-55123
                                                                               CIP

PRINTED IN THE UNITED STATES OF AMERICA

Contents

Acknowledgments   7

1. Some Problems, Some Responses   11
2. Style in *Dream:* The ART Version   33
3. "Alas, Poor Yorick!"   57
4. Gertrude's Story   70
5. Playing Space: The Kline *Hamlet*   80
6. Editing the Script   93
7. Closure in *Hamlet*   113
8. The Case for a Black Othello   126
9. "'Tis Nudity": Peter Greenaway's *Prospero's Books*   163
10. Epilogue: The Stage in the Global Village   177

Notes   183
Works Cited   186
Index   193

This book is for Jim Bulman.

Acknowledgments

Thanks to Pamela Mount for so cheerfully putting this manuscript on the computer, and to Bill Watterson for a variety of assists, tangible and spiritual, as the manuscript took shape. Many people have helped me show tapes of live performances, and from such sessions my own insights have developed. Thanks, then, to Jim Andreas, Jim Bulman, Karen Bush, Ann Jennalie Cook, Sam Crowl, Alan Dessen, Peter Donaldson, David Evett, Carmen Greenlee, Jim Hissom, Nancy E. Hodge, Dick Hornby, Bob Johnson, Alan Kimbrough, Harry Keyishian, Michael Manheim, Tom Marcus, Ken Mason, Paul Merrix, Dee Pearson, Meredith Price, Ray Rutan, Jerry Schiffhorst, Hassell Sledd, Patrick Spottiswoode, Ed Taft, David Thorberg, John Velz, Sam Wanamaker, and Bob Willson. For assistance beyond the call of duty, thanks to Alan Butland, Tom Lederer, and Andy Mydellton.

Thanks to coconspirators Sharon Beehler, Kathleen Campbell, and Barbara Hodgdon. Editors who have given great encouragement along the way include Bruce Brandt, Maurice Hunt, Bernice Kliman, Jim Lusardi, Ken Rothwell, and June Schlueter. A few of the fine students who have sharpened my own powers of observation include Barbara Armstrong, Noel Austin, Lisa Belisle, Michael Berry, Rosemary Blake, Ann Catherine Bonis, Patrick Brackley, David Bradshaw, Marshall Carter, C. Mae Clement, Joe Dane, Stephen Dickey, Moose Gorman, Glyde Hart, Laura Heer, Andrea Henrichon, Peter Honchaurk, Pat Horgan, Matt Hornbeck, Douglas Kennedy, James Kohn, Amy Kunhardt, Emily Lenz, Tracey Levitt, Amy Lewis, Tom Pennington, Curt Perrin, Amy Carlisle Sanderson, Sarah Sargeant, Toni Schrader, Jill Seymour, Stefanie Sirc, Laurie Smith, Doug Stenberg, Meredith Sumner, Jennifer Tews, Anne Britting Tobey, and Alice Waugh. I have enjoyed the blessing that comes to too few teachers—superb students.

Photo credits: American Repertory Theatre, *A Midsummer Night's Dream:* A.R.T. "Taping the Ghost," 1980: BBC-TV; BBC, *A Midsummer Night's Dream,* 1981: BBC-TV; "Hamlet the Dane!": J. Arthur Rank, Maximilian Schell, 1960: Kurt Gewissen; Stellen

Scarsgaard, 1984: WNYC-TV; Herlie and Burton, 1964: Alexander H. Cohen; Bloom and Stewart, 1980: BBC-TV; Kevin Kline, 1990: Nancy LeVine; Jacobi and Swan, 1980: BBC-TV; Chamberlain, 1970: Hallmark, Inc.; Hopkins and Hoskins, 1981: BBC-TV; Welles and Cloutier, 1952: Mogador Films; Kani and Weinberg: Janet Suzman; McKellen, 1990: Thames Television.

Watching Shakespeare
on Television

1

Some Problems, Some Responses

Shakespeare wrote his plays for his stage, indeed, explored the possibilities of his stage with his plays. When Hamlet points at "this brave o'erhanging firmament," he is pointing to the ceiling over the stage of the Globe Theatre, and to the sky above the Globe as well. Shakespeare created worlds within his Globe, but he asked for help with his creations:

> Piece out our imperfections with your thoughts:
> Into a thousand parts divide one man
> And make imaginary puissance.
> Think when we talk of horses, that you see them
> Printing their proud hoofs i' th' receiving earth
> For 'tis your thoughts that now must deck our kings . . .
> And eke out our performance with your mind.

Perhaps the central fact of Shakespeare's theater was its demand that the spectator complete the imaginative equation by providing a visual equivalent for the language. This was a theater that required an energetic give-and-take, as opposed to the "fourth-wall" stage which permits us, by removing one wall of a room, to look in upon "reality." Anyone who has ever experienced a superb live performance of a Shakespeare script has also experienced a powerful building-up of communal energy as the production developed, along with a profound sense of personal involvement in what is being half-perceived and half-created.

Shakespeare's stage had its heaven and hell as well as several levels and several proximities to, or distances from, the audience in which human conflict occurred. His stage conveyed the built-in symbolism of the conventional worldviews, and could incorporate or challenge that worldview with just a word or a gesture. Hamlet does both simultaneously when he describes man as merely a "quintessence of dust."

Our modern equivalent for Shakespeare's infinitely suggestive stage is the film. But the film, or more precisely, the camera, does our seeing for us. The camera is an instrument other than the human eye and is linked up with an intelligence other than ours, that of the director. While a stage director or an actor on stage will pull our attention to where he wants us to look, our eyes are aware of the frame, that which creates an overarching and inclusive context for whatever it is that voice, gesture, lighting, or blocking may insist that we observe at any given moment of a play. The camera zooms or booms, tracks or pans, jump cuts or dissolves, obliterating frames with the magician's ease that delighted its early practitioners and thrilled its early audiences. What we "observe" is the imagination of a director, and it is to that that we respond as critics of a film—to Eisenstein, Welles, and Fellini.

If the basis of a play by Shakespeare is language that elicits our imaginative response, the basis of film is the image. Films began in silence—the rattle of the reel, the piano reinforcing the action excepted—and needed no voices for three decades. "Dialogue? We had faces!" as Gloria Swanson says in *Sunsest Boulevard*. Film does the visualizing for us—we need not interact with language to complete the sensory transaction. Film can evoke an emotional response in us—fear when a shadow looms behind the heroine, relief when the hero arrives in the nick of time—but that response is the result of a set of images already fixed on a light-sensitive medium, as opposed to theater, where images are created in a moment of kinesis that asks us to visualize a glooming or a blood-red morning, a starlit or a hellishly murky night. At any given moment in our experience of a Shakespeare play we must integrate the linear movement—the development of the narrative line, of character and relationships, the linkages between what we have already learned and heard, and what is happening at that instant *and* the vertical—the precise image of the line being spoken, the facet of character, conflict, and relationship being reflected at that instant. All of this is *framed* for us, as I shall suggest, as neither film nor TV is. The unsigned but real contract that the theater-goer makes is far more complex and demanding than any made by the film-goer or TV-auditor. TV, as Sheldon Zitner suggests, incorporates no ceremony (Zitner, p. 31).

Unlike stage or film, television is "about" something, as Thomas Berger suggests:

Television is many things. One of the things it is is rooms. It is the squad room of "Hill Street Blues" and "You'll Never Get Rich"; it is the flight deck of the starship *Enterprise;* it is the Long Branch Saloon of "Gunsmoke"; it is the tent of Hawkeye Pierce; it is the barroom of "Cheers";

and it is the composite living room of Ozzie and Harriet Nelson, Rob and Laura Petrie, and Cliff and Claire Huxtable. But most of all it is the kitchen of Ralph and Alice Kramden. (Berger, 238)

It is, then, about families in rooms; one could add the Andersons of "Father Knows Best," "The Waltons," and the Bunkers of "All in the Family." The scale of TV, of course, demands the room as the space it depicts, but so does the purpose of TV. It is about things that go *into* rooms: toothpaste and tissue for the bathroom, beer and cornflakes for the kitchen, detergents for the laundry room; cars for the garage, and, of course, a TV in every room (exclusive of the "entertainment center"). We the audience, are ourselves sold to advertisers via ratings. We "have become commodities," as Gerry Spence says (Spence, p. 302), delivered to those who move commodities, and even the noncommercial segment of American television is compromised by commercial and political interests.[1] Obviously, what goes between the commercials sells a "life-style" merely rendered specific by the commercials. TV has yet to develop a sitcom featuring a homeless mother and child living in a welfare hotel in Detroit.

Television reflects our own comfortable space; it "creates an intimacy between two rooms, ours and that of the screen," as Gary Waller says (Waller, p. 23). We watch in a room, surrounded by our own familiar objects and perhaps accompanied by people who also inhabit our rooms. We watch people in rooms sorting out issues that may have a more dramatic shape and pressure than our own, that may be a generation out-of-date,[2] and that, with the exception of an eternal soap, probably achieve more clarification than our own problems. We no more know how to *watch* television than we know how to watch a room. Some people, in fact, have televisions to watch rooms for them.

Courses in film, theater, and how to read texts are manifold, but not "How to Watch Television." Good reasons exist for this vacuum, reasons built into the medium. It is no accident that "TV" is both the machine and the event the machine delivers. Any distinction between the two seems irrelevant. Television emerges from the latter years of the twentieth century and from certain assumptions and manipulations of those assumptions. The assumptions have been managed into invisibility, as successful items on any "hidden agenda" always are. Or, perhaps, the assumptions are as obvious as Poe's letter and therefore just as invisible. Shakespeare "bodies forth the form of things unknown," as one of his skeptical Dukes says. Shakespeare makes all things visible, including the mind behind the TV camera that would translate word and image into a mindlessness designed for that oxymoron known as "popular culture." It is not necessarily objectionable for that unusual entity known as "Shakespeare on television" that we cannot observe the techniques of television. If we try, the observation soon lapses as the skillful and predictable editing of the three-camera format erases our effort. The problem here is the *lulling* effect of TV. Does the erasure of our effort to observe techinque permit Shakespeare's language to emerge as the primary datum of our experience? At times it does, and for reasons inherent in the medium, as I shall suggest. For most television, however, what Teresa de Lauretis says applies: "masters are made as we . . . accept their answers or their metaphors" (de Lauretis, p. 3). TV's mastery is absolute once we turn the set on. Even its blank-faced silence mocks us. The metaphor it makes—the viewer as consumer—is always true.

One of the popular clichés of current criticism talks of the "site" of an event. The jargon is useful, however, in describing where "the event" of a medium occurs. The site of film is the large screen. If we are not "pulled into it," we are certainly dominated by it as we sit in a large dark room with (mostly) strangers under a widening cone of light that penetrates a million motes of dust a millisecond before it becomes an image. The site of the event of a Shakespeare play on a thrust stage, as opposed to a fourth-wall proscenium format, is in the exchange of energy between stage and audience and therefore somewhere *between* the two points. Word, gesture, characterization, and the concatenation of imagery and conflict in every moment of the Shakespeare play evoke a response. The spectator of a play may be still—and should be—but is hardly passive. The site of television is a "living" room. The TV is a piece of equipment in a space that reflects our space, whether the machine is turned on or not. (It is accidental but appropriate that the set when turned off, forms a sort of murky mirror.) Unless we are watching a sporting event, our role as viewers is passive, and even with a game we have instant replay in case we were not watching the first time. On television even our laughing is done for us. Our own participation is minimal and it is meant to be, the better to lull us into the robotism of consumption. We look down on TV, often literally in a physical sense, as we may also look down on that portion of our persona that is merely consumer.

Given this reduced dimension, "televised Shakespeare" becomes an oxymoron. But since television evolved from radio and thus has a heritage wholly different than film, indeed has a heritage based entirely on sound—as radio and film developed independently of each other in the 1920s—Shakespeare can work on TV, as some productions have proved. As Sheldon Zitner says, "it is wholly *un*reasonable to deplore as theoretically impossible television productions that have been successful indeed" (Zitner, p. 34). The question, then, is how do we watch *Shakespeare* on TV, or, to put it another way, how does Shakespeare body forth the mind behind the TV camera which the techniques of television render invisible? Zitner offers this analysis:

> Shakespeare's plays were written for Shakespeare's theatre. And what his theatre provided most often was humanity seen not in the all-defining close-up of psychology or at the far and narrowed distance of sociology or through the historical retrospect of montage but in the open middle distance of social relation. Shakespeare's is a relational not an essentializing or ideologizing stage: not a stage pre-empted by convictions that must focus on one causal chain, psychological or sociological, but a stage closer to the tenor of encountered experience in which causes and motives of all sorts jostle. It offers whole human figures disposed in patterns that exhibit what is primarily a social (often familial) meaning in space that can—when the meaning dictates—be both Rome and Egypt, and on occasion convert up and left to heavenward and sinister. The solitariness of his characters onstage is generally painful and undesired; their immersion in crowds violent, fearful, or silly. For this sort of stage his plays were meant. What the camera can instantly suggest—enclosing sociology with a long shot, defining private states with a close-up—Shakespeare must do by other, more elaborate, means, and usually does not do at all. In sum, the simplicity and flexibility of the Elizabethan stage do not provide encompassing environments. But film and, more emphatically, television—despite the two-dimensional screen—give a priority to time, place, and objects, and so create environments in which human actors are expressions of a context rather than its creators. To re-define the locus of dramatic action, its characters, its size, its depth, the angle from which it is viewed, is thus to tamper with the conceptual foundations of the Elizabethan text. It is also to create a new medium, one that will certainly demand different kinds of words, at times even no words at all. But if one wants to preserve the old words, one has to discover in the medium some equivalents of the old. This, rather than the conventional problems of interpretation, is the challenge of televising Shakespeare's plays. (Zitner, pp. 38–39)

No doubt other media—even different types of stages—tamper with the assumptions of Shakespeare's stage. Shakespeare's stage itself changed during his career. We must account for the radical translation that film and television impose upon the Shakespearean script. Shakespeare does provide the close-up of psychology in his plays, often via the soliloquy. Psychology as an underlying contributor to conflicts in the relationships of a script is not just an invention of Freud and his followers. While an overtly Freudian interpretation can rob a production of its suggestiveness, that does not erase the subtle homosexual resonance in *The Merchant of Venice,* the Oedipal energy working within Prince Hamlet, or the repressed sexuality of Angelo and Isabella. These energies are part of the matrix of relationships the scripts insist that we consider as, in turn, those relationships force us to consider our own singular role in them. The encompasing viewpoint of sociology is also present in Shakespeare's plays, although I would shift the terms a bit and call it the sociology of politics, that is, the way people and their groupings are defined by their relationship to power, to the party in power, and by their half-understood grasp on the forces working independent of the decisions of the great men, forces more powerful than, and often contradictory to, what kings would do. Shakespeare leaves the interpretation of a play's politics up to the director of a modern production. The spectrum of emphasis can make the same script pro- or antiwar, pro- or anticolonialist, sexist or feminist.

Shakespeare did not have to italicize his meanings on his stage. He could indeed, let motives jostle without definition or explanation. A physical frame around *King Lear* gave the play a focus and containment, even if the words themselves challenge any inherited set of beliefs. Perhaps the stage or "Wooden O"—the structure and its implicit heaven, hell, and earth—merely told its audience that the event within it was a fiction, a construct, something resembling a cosmic nightmare perhaps, but held within a visible set of limits and controlled by a well-established set of assumptions about drama and conventions of performance, including, of course, the fact that Goneril, Regan, and Cordelia would have been played by boy-actors. One factor in Shakespeare's apparently infinite capacity for being reshaped and reexperienced in different times and new media is his escape from the defining structure of the stage within which his plays occurred.

It may be that *King Lear*'s "once upon a time" auspices—the old King decides to divide his old kingdom—also distanced spectator from content. Regardless of the play's content, Shakepeare's audience tended to believe, as I take it we do not, that beyond the Globe and above it an unseen spectator observed the audience and each individual within it.[3] That fact tended to be the truth of the audience, even if the play they heard may have challenged their assumptions. Shakespeare could depict "the frame of things" as "disjoint," but the frame was there. The "Elizabethan World Picture" was being

challenged consistently by Shakespeare and by "the new philoso-
phy," but the challenge could be mounted because the norm was
there. Shakespeare's audience were "fellows . . . crawling between
earth and heaven . . . passing through nature to eternity," and his
visual stage captured that process automatically.

We cannot, obviously, re-create the Shakespearean world, nor
should we attempt to define production values on what we take to
be Elizabethan value-systems. What we must do is to recognize the
limitations that Zitner outlines, the ways in which Shakespeare's
scripts tend to overcome those limits, and the problem that William
Worthen defines:

> Perhaps because TV performances are transmitted by the camera,
> across a visibly domestic space, TV acting rarely tests its fictive bound-
> aries. *King Lear* constitutes a certain kind of role for the spectator by
> requiring a range of response from him, a response both to the drama
> and to the acting of it. The TV camera requires different responses—
> more "receiving" and less "doing"—and so constitutes a rather different
> role for us, one that seems partly incompatible with the challenges of
> the play.
> By protecting us from the particular kind of challenge that *Lear*—and
> perhaps any stage play—creates in performance, the camera constitutes
> an inadequate role for the TV viewer. The challenge to feeling remains,
> but the difficult challenge to presence, the challenge that the theatrical
> spectator shares with and experiences through the actor, is simply not a
> part of the play. (Worthen, p. 11)

I suggest that even the challenge to feeling is unlikely on television,
though not impossible, as I shall argue. Shakespeare's stage and television are both linguistic media, or, in the case of TV, "a visual,
iconic sign system with strong but supplemental aural-verbal support" (Waller, p. 23). In Shakespeare's dramaturgy, word is fitted
to action and action to word, so that a constant and simultaneous
reinforcement of each by the other occurs.

Television stands between film and theater. Its image is smaller
than that of film, and requires words to complete it. If TV occurs
without sound we expect an immediate "Do Not Adjust Your Set"
notice. The problem for TV is that when it does Shakespeare, word
and image can *compete* with each other. The filmmaker eliminates
language. The TV director, confronted by Shakespeare, must keep
moving his camera in ways that may not be motivated by the language. Shakespeare was not writing a shooting script. Stephen Hearst
suggests one of the major problems in translating Shakespeare to television:

a written text on the right-hand side of any script page which makes complete sense by itself is a bad text. What are the pictures there for? . . . The words, except in exceptional circumstances, need to follow the pictures. . . . Pictures have their own grammar, their own logic . . . and cannot easily be kept waiting. . . . To such a picture you could speak no more than about 25 words. . . . Language seems to play a secondary role in television. (Hearst, pp. 4–5)

If we apply Hearst's analysis to Shakespeare, we may recognize that language does not play a secondary role but struggles with the image for primacy. The fact of a script-in-being is not necessarily an advantage for the director of Shakespeare. What does he do with his three-camera format when the script has not been written for that set of conventions or scaled down to that dimension?

Even efforts to transcend the assumptions behind modern television are usually undercut by its physical dimensions, as Jerry Mander suggests:

Programs concerned with the arts . . . are distorted by television's inability to convey their several aspects. . . . Some people argue that television delivers a new world of art to people in, say, Omaha, who might otherwise never see the Stuttgart Ballet or the New York Philharmonic. They say this stimulates interest in the arts. I find this very unlikely. . . . On television the depths are flattened, the spaces edited, the movements distorted and fuzzed-up, the music thinned and the scale reduced. . . . Seeing the Stuttgart Ballet performing on television leaves one with such a reduced notion of ballet as to reduce the appeal of Ballet itself. The result is likely to be boredom and switched channels. To say that such a program stimulates new interest in the arts is to believe, as Howard Gossage put it, "That it's possible to convince an eight-year-old that making love is more fun than ice cream cones." (Mander, pp. 280–81)

Such a diminution seems inevitable. Two apparent exceptions should be noted, however—the television coverage of the John Kennedy funeral and the recent *Civil War* series on Public Television.

For Marshall McLuhan, the Kennedy funeral showed television at its most powerful and flexible. I would suggest that the event was unusual in the national history and unique in television's history. Television derived a transitory greatness from the event. It was, of course, noncommercial. It was ubiquitous. All sets were on. The only variety was provided by the different commentators on the different networks. It was an event of images, augmented only occasionally by sound. We remember the bloodstained suit that Jackie wore at LBJ's swearing-in; John Jr.'s salute, the soon-to-die lieutenant in charge of the bearers lending a hand as the coffin went up the steps to the Capitol; the nurse who had ridden out in the ambulance-hearse getting bounced by the Secret Service and told that she must find her own way back into the city; the precise staging of Oswald's murder by Ruby; and, for a line, Kendall Merriam, the senior White House correspondent, with his shocking "Good morning, Mr. President," directed at LBJ the morning after. It was a sequence of montages shot from middle distance. If a sense of "the monumental" came through, it did so because the streets were empty, so that the columns and steps of the great buildings came right down to the gutters just as the cortege swung into the camera. A city devoid of traffic projected an appropriate sense of doom and was abetted by the reiterated Chopin, and by the restless, riderless horse—Blackjack—which punctuated the procession. Our own emotional involvement with the events of November 1963 gave energy to the medium that it had not received before nor has since. We did more than automatically integrate the image. We provided an emotion equal to the current running in at the back of the set. At that rare moment, television and audience met on a plane higher than just commercial.

The *Civil War* series picks up some intrinsic energy from its audience. Like the Kennedy event it issues a "challenge to feeling," likely to be reciprocated by those who watch it. Real divisions still exist between North and South in social attitudes, economics, and concepts of justice. The war is as close historically to the United States in the 1990s as were the Wars of the Roses to Elizabethan England. The American Civil War was the first war to be photographed, so that it has something in common with the first televised war, Vietnam, and thus evokes at least a retina memory of the latter event for many Americans. The series creates a fine balance between photograph and narrative. The few sound effects are superb—the massed rifle fire is more frightening than the rattle of machine guns because one knows that the sound is the product of thousands of individual trigger fingers. We are forced to imagine, as in old-time radio, what was happening to the men trapped in the maelstrom of lead. In another instance, a mournful trumpet sounds over a beseiged town, a haunting metonymy for which television seldom reaches.

The *Civil War* is a good example of McLuhan's "cool medium," that is, a medium low in sensory data. Both that series and the Kennedy funeral were in black-and-white. Color TV renders the viewer even more passive than black-and-white by doing the sensory job. More important, however, is that black-and-white is the "documentary" color. The Kennedy funeral was an instant documentary in which the cameras pursued a format prescribed by ceremonial patterns some of which derived from the death of Lincoln. In this instance, history had archetypes to provide energy to what usually is a "disposable moment." The assassination of Oswald reminded us of the chaos from which the ceremonial had emerged, the chaos that ceremony is designed to placate and propitiate. The Civil War series is also a documentary and is again a noncommercial production. Word and image encourage a participatory response from the auditor and fulfill McLuhan's optimistic assessment of television: "It engages you. You have to be with it" (McLuhan, p. 312). The series creates an appeal to feeling, as opposed to the appeal to fact and contextual pattern that we expect of "history." The series is not "educational," but perhaps serves as an invitation to study and research.[4]

One reason why documentaries work well on television is that they do not ask us to "suspend our disbelief." Shakespeare's drama, however, makes that demand of us, insisting that we believe that those actors moving and speaking in that sector of the world that happens to be turned toward us, are something other than just actors playing Brutus or Caesar, Hamlet or Gertrude, Prospero or Cleopatra. We do not believe that the actors *are* those personages, but we believe in the *mimesis*, and we participate in and complete the imitation of an action. Television tends to be a realistic medium. Part of that tendency is a function of the mechanics of camera, magnetic tape, transmission, and reproduction of image, and part of it is a product of our own expectations for the medium. The latter dictate to some extent what can occur within the frame. Unlike Shakespeare's stage—and even that stage as experienced in modern formats—TV's frame is not mimetic. It does not ask that we participate in an imitation that becomes an emotional and psychological reality. On the other hand, television, like Shakespeare's language, insists upon our participation, as McLuhan suggests. TV is a "cool medium" demanding "participation or completion by the audience. . . . And speech is a cool medium of low definition [i.e., not well-filled with sensory data] because so little is given and so much has to be filled in by the listener" (McLuhan, pp. 22, 23). The difference is that Shakespeare's language demands a sensory response *and* an immediate linkup with the imagination. TV seldom asks us to take that second step.

Television directors, Alan Dessen argues, tend to avoid "anything smacking of things beyond man." The "emphasis" falls "upon the psychological rather than the otherworldly," an approach that "suits prevailing interpretations . . . and sidesteps effects that may strike television viewers as questionable, even laughable" (Dessen, pp. 1, 8). With the exception of a kindly and very human ghost or two or a playful genie, TV is a "normative" medium. And we the consumers are the norm. If we see insanity, it is "The Munsters," who live in a mildly macabre environment, filled with the props of horror films, that they take for granted. We smile, if we smile, because we discern the discrepancy between their mildly distorted world and our own scrubbed and conventional zones of being.

Shakespeare's stage asks us not merely to suspend our disbelief but to provide the energy of our imaginations to complete the dramatic transaction. Thus are our meager existential formats challenged into the transcendence of mere ego that good theater can engender.

TV is already "real," all by itself. It needs no help from us. We are reduced to passivity by a specialist in reduction. The exceptions to TV's version of "reality" are themselves normative—MTV, Saturday morning cartoons, and television's rare successful venture into fantasy, the presidential news conference. A play on TV has already been recorded by a camera onto tape. The event is in the past. We do not participate in a sequence created by and for us within that intensity known as the present. TV is a fourth-wall medium. The wall is permeable only by ratings, that is, only by its ability to make our walls open into its walls.

TV, as Dessen argues, denies the possibility of agencies larger than man. To render the unknown as psychological is to reduce the unknown to the space of a single brainpan and to enclose "meaning" within the narrow mode of "realism." Thus in the 1954 Schaefer *Macbeth,* the second set of prophecies comes to Maurice Evans in a bad dream. The possibility of a real evil abroad in the world is reduced to the image-making of an infected psyche. The effort to go the other way, however, won't work. In Schaefer's 1960 *Tempest,* Prospero's crystal ball reduces him to a minor-league wanderer in Kansas, and Ariel's miniaturization is, as Dessen suggests, "laughable," merely reminding us of the reduction already inherent in the medium.

The scale of TV insists upon a diminution of the image and an erasure of any background. It lacks any depth of field. When the TV image is enlarged to the size of a small movie screen, the picture is usually distorted, not enhanced. This problem may resolve itself as pictures become accommodated to larger screens. Film provides the dimensions essential to fantasy, and perhaps the best way to grasp the difference between film and television is to recognize how film's larger—deeper and wider—frame can incorporate special effects. Atlanta burns convincingly in the huge darkened space where we sit. Those twisters churn dangerously as Dorothy yanks at the implacable storm door. The icons exploding at us from *Raiders of the Lost*

Ark threaten our space. On TV, the twisters in *Wizard* look like a documentary on tornadoes, but Arnold Gillespie had more than that in mind when he matched ominous background and swirling foreground on his large screen. The Wicked Witch of the West is scarcely a threat to our home space, and the effects of *Raiders* are trivialized when they pop and crackle on nineteen diagonal inches in the domestic and domesticated space of our playroom. TV is Disney World. We need provide no imaginary puissance. The experiencing is done for us.

By "definition" TV is a medium on which special effects are "questionable, even laughable," as Dessen says. Do directors of scripts that incorporate the supernatural have any choice but to translate it into the psychological? TV is a medium that does not call attention to itself. It is not the product but the way of selling the product. Film is an egotistic medium, forever showing off, as Woody Allen demonstrates in satirizing filmic virtuosity in *Annie Hall.* TV, by nature as well as scale, has a hard time being "filmic." When it calls attention to itself it subverts its purpose.

The question, then, is how to establish a scale and a style for Shakespeare on television. It is like playing with toy soldiers. Everything must fit, at least it had to for me as a child. I had two types of soldiers—the British boxed version and the cast-lead, made-in-the-USA Manoil variety. The former were precisely painted and parade-ready, with rifle arms that swung. The latter were larger, olive-drab, and in combat. While I had no grasp of anachronism, I had a sure grip on matters of scale. My elegant British soldiers were for display. The workaday grunts were deployed on the playroom floor. They fought and died even as the guard changed peacefully at the Palace.

Obviously, the acting of Shakespeare on TV must balance elegance with the everyday; it must be microacting where the words are tamed to "naturalness," as in the playful chatter of Joan Plowright's Portia and Angela Carteret's Nerissa in Miller's *Merchant* and the vicious banter of Janet Suzman's Cleopatra and Richard Johnson's Antony in Trevor Nunn's *Antony and Cleopatra.* In each case we get tricked into the mythology—of the beautiful princess frozen on her mountain and of the epic hero's quest for the fabulous creature. "Heavy" acting—American actors playing Hamlet—induces boredom and fulfills negative expectations of "what Shakespeare is like." Histrionic acting on TV—as if the actor were on a stage in a large auditorium— drives us back from the set in embarrassment or laughter, that is, unless the style is built in to the role. Falstaff playacting in the tavern, or the First Player reading a speech before an audience in Elsinore, know they are being theatrical.

Robert Willson challenges Zitner by asserting that "sensitive direction and virtuoso acting can overcome the limitations of the acting space" (Willson, p. 8). While that is true, the limitations are not merely those of the acting space. The questions are, how do directors help actors become "believable" when the latter are speaking Shakespearean verse on television? And, how does acting space integrate with our space? It is a matter of *style*. One style seems far superior to any other. It is the style that most approximates Shakespeare's "intention," and one that can, in the hands of a superb practitioner, challenge television's inability to induce a suspension of disbelief.

Michele Willems defines three difference conceptions of production for the BBC Shakespeare Series: the naturalistic, the pictorial, and the stylized. The first dominated the early years of the BBC Series as produced by Cedric Messina. The second characterized the Miller and Moshinsky productions, and the third typified the Jane Howell versions of the *First Henriad* and *the Winter's Tale*. Willems finds the latter, "where the visual element is used as functional or suggestive preferable to one in which it is referential ['naturalistic'] or decorative ['pictorial']" (Willems, p. 100).

The naturalistic approach tends to resemble the Hollywood "period pieces" of the 30s and 40s, laden with costumes and furniture but light on anything but cliché villains and lovers. The complexity of Shakespeare's exploration of politics in the *Second Henriad*, for example, tends toward simplistic close-ups of "character." The effort to depict battles fall between film's sweep and depth and Shakespeare's technique of keeping the battle just out of sight while the stage becomes a zone into which survivors stagger, across which retreats and pursuits are conducted, or in which two combatants go *mano-a-mano*. Mark Crispin Miller delivers an accurate indictment of the naturalistic approach as it was applied to the *Richard II—Henry V* cycle:

> These adaptations are desperately "Shakespearean" and entirely meaningless, turning the plays into empty antiquarian spectacles.
> Their emphasis, in other words, is the opposite of Shakespeare's. The actors at the Globe performed on an empty stage, expecting their audience to listen with imagination: "Think, when we talk of horses, that you see them / Printing their proud hoofs i' th' receiving earth." Shakespeare's language was evocative enough to make backdrops and props redundant. In order to let that language do its work, the best directors of Shakespearean film and television—Olivier, Brook, Welles, Kozintsev, Hall—have tried to stylize their productions. Each has avoided historical literalism,

using his medium not to bolster vulgar notions of the past but to convey a certain set of meanings derived from personal study of the text. "Shakespeare Plays," on the other hand, reflects the corporate approach, hiring lots of "experts," spending too much money, and making something deadly out of something good. Each play is just another useless product, meant for quick consumption.

Struggling to create the proper aura, the BBC has blown a wad on later medieval bric-a-brac; hogsheads, cross-bows, goblets, scrolls—everything but ye kitchen sink. These irrelevant items clutter irrelevant sets, all those dungeons and taverns and banquet halls which Shakespeare only mentions, but which the BBC has meticulously reconstructed. Such "realism" is supposed to lend these shows an atmosphere at once authentic and colorful, but it only distracts us from the verse, and has the further ill effect of implying a certain condescension, both to the plays and to the past. This literalism becomes hilarious when the action moves "outdoors," that is, onto a studio set covered with fake knolls and plastic trees. While the film studio can present a credible illusion of the natural world, the nails and plaster are always obvious on television. (Using the real thing is no less of an error, as last year's *As You Like It*, set disconcertingly amid actual woods, made very clear.) This fact of video adds a touch of humor to the BBC's battle scenes, in which small groups of uneasy men try to roughhouse on fields of Astroturf. (Miller, pp. 261–62)

That is not to say, however, that these plays were unmitigatedly disastrous. Some fine moments come through, as when the heartbroken Duke of York and the courageous Bishop of Carlisle are brought into a relationship by the camera that the script does not suggest, the series of dissolves through which Richard II's long prison soliloquy meanders, and the opening of *Henry V*, in which Canterbury and Ely posture at prayer while discussing politics. This conflict between pose and agenda might have been carried forward as a metaphor for the production but is instead, like so much else in this sequence, just an isolated moment.

The pictorial approach—what I would call the painterly—creates beautiful pictures. The emphasis is on color, tonality, and composition, as in Miller's use of Vermeer for his *Shrew*, and Veronese for his *Antony and Cleopatra*. Dramatic issues are buried somewhere beneath the pictures. A play is not a painting. What we get is surface. This tendency is augmented by Miller's insistence on "normalizing" his characters, so that Kate becomes domesticated within a Puritan household, Antony a middling-good rugby player ten years from his last scum with a provincial club, and Othello a King Hussein. While such a reduction might seem to be dictated by the medium, it represents a surrender-in-advance *to* the medium. I and others have discussed the pictorial approach at length.[5] One of the values of these productions, for me, is that they force us back to the scripts, not only for their range of possible interpretations, but also for their potentially televisual values. These productions, then, reinforce the continuum between production as manifestation of the text, and the text as print, where it retains its enormous potentiality.[6]

What Willems calls the "stylized," I would rename the "theatrical." In this category we find productions televised in front of live audiences, often with the audience in view. While some of these suffer from the weaknesses that can plague any stage production, many seem to pick up energy from the fact that they are performed before an audience and at least imitate the concept of "suspension of disbelief." Not only does the energy of the audience transmit itself to the television viewer, but some of the excesses of the stage that suffer from a close-up technique—projection and gesture, for example—can work within a frame that simulates the presence of theater. Bad acting is bad acting anywhere, of course, and television is merciless with acting that might just get by on stage. Some of the live productions that have appeared on television are the energetic American Conservatory Theatre's *Shrew,* Joseph Papp's *King Lear,* and *Dream,* a number of productions from Stratford, Canada, Sarah Caldwell's *Macbeth,* and Nunn's *Comedy of Errors.* A variation of this technique, where the camera observes a stage and all angles are as if from a spectator's position, are the Bard productions of, for example, *Macbeth, Antony and Cleopatra,* and *The Tempest,* the BBC's *Winter's Tale,* and the Renaissance Theatre's *Twelfth Night.* The absence of an audience can create the feeling of an empty theater. Even though rehearsals scarcely off-book can be very exciting, as the actors make discoveries among themselves, the effect of an empty theater tends to deaden these productions, as does the static stance from which we watch. One production of this type that I find effective, however, is the Bard version of *Othello,* with William Marshall and Ron Moody.

Another variation of the "theatrical" mode is the production redesigned for TV after appearing on stage. Some of Derek Jacobi's characterizations of Hamlet—his doning of a skull-mask before the Play Scene, for example—derives from his Old Vic stage performance. The excellent RSC *Macbeth* and *Antony and Cleopatra,* perhaps the two best television versions of Shakespeare ever, emerge from a stage history, as do the recent RSC *Othello,* Miller's *Merchant* with Olivier, and the Kline *Hamlet.* Such productions partake of all that the actors have learned and worked out in front of live audiences. Not only are they not underrehearsed, as some of the BBC versions seem to be, but the actors' familiarity with the roles permits them to relax into the lower-key style demanded by TV. In the instances of *Macbeth* and *Antony and Cleopatra,* the director creates a minimal context in which superb acting can work, that of Judi Dench, Ian McKellen, Janet Suzman, and Richard Johnson. *Antony and Cleopatra* contrasts the black-and-white of Rome, with its metallic surfaces, harsh angles, hard columns, and purposeful movement with the languid pace of molten Egypt, swept by slow fans and Cleopatra's eyelashes. Egypt is a place of pillows on which to lean and lie and filmy curtains that open onto more curtains as Cleopatra enticingly reveals this or that fraction of her infinite variety. The style is consistent with a play that encompasses two worlds and their radically divergent worldviews and the scale of television. Why the BBC did not "go to school" with this production baffles me. *Macbeth* comes from the studiolike dimensions of The Other Place and The Warehouse. On television it uses stark contrasts and tight framing to create a claustrophobic intensity.

Another successful approach within the theatrical model is the set that works like a stage. In Desmond Davis's *Measure for Measure,* for example, the brothel and the convent are the same set with different paint, so that the linear movement of television tape permits us to experience the same set as emblem of both purity and the licentiousness which overzealous purity may repress. Given its theatrical premises, this production employs a technique that would have seemed like a continuity glitch in other "perfected" TV productions. The sound of a previous scene continues into the next scene or the image of the previous scene overlays the sound of a new scene. This interplay of sound and picture is a televisual equivalent of the simultaneous exit/entrance of the Shakespearean stage. In Peter Brook's 1953 *King Lear,* with Orson Welles, Lear, having dragged the dead Cordelia in, slumps onto the throne from which he had commanded the opening sequence. Cordelia lies on the steps where she had knelt earlier to be auctioned off to France or Burgundy. As the frame expands, we see the pedestals on which Lear's daughters had stood so long before, prize dolls in the King's collection. Brook does not pursue Albany's order to "Produce the bodies," one that permits the final tableau to mirror in death the opening scene, so deceptively vibrant with life and new beginnings, and which gives us a gestaltian glimpse of all that has happened between those moments. The "staging" of the final scene, however, reminds us that the silence and emptiness of the ending are directly attributable to the fulsomeness of the opening. The link between beginning and ending is the continuing silence of Cordelia, as Lear leans forward for a word from her. At the end, he gets nothing. Earlier, Cordelia's asides had been voice-overs, with Cordelia occasionally mouthing the words. She speaks her "Nothing, my lord," making it remarkably powerful and permitting it to carry over into the silence of the finale.

More successful, I feel, than her unit set and geometric shapes for her *Winter's Tale* is Jane Howell's stage set for *The First Henriad,* in this case, a unit set with ramps, doors, balconies, curtained areas, and a central space which word and lighting can translate into throne room, street, or battlefield. As she says,

> Some sets you find in your head, some sets are in books. I knew this one was in the street. I did not know what it was. Then one day I was out in a car, and suddenly I saw the top of an adventure playground which had been crudely painted in medieval colours by the kids. It was lovely. I was in such a hurry that I couldn't stop, but I knew I had solved it. It was some strange area in which you could play, in which you could pretend, which is an equivalent of Shakespeare's stage. (Howell, p. 82)

Howell's set becomes a place for exploration, a space in which the relatively unknown dimensions of these plays can be charted, and it works superbly, as critics note. "The paradox was that of television accommodating a self-consciously staged production, rougher and more pantomimic than anything to be found in the theatre itself" (Ackroyd, *S on T,* p. 292); "the production and setting managed to contain both the kindergarten babyishness and the noble savagery of the work" (Jones, *S on T,* p. 292). Another device that Howell deploys in her refusal to yield to television's normative "realism" is the use of doubling—David Burke as Gloucester, and Dick the Butcher and Antony Brown as Whitmore and Iden, for example. I and others have discussed these productions at length.[7]

While television tends to hide its techniques the better to sell us something, *Shakespeare on Television* demands that we pay attention *to* technique. Watching Shakespeare on television may not be like "watching Shakepeare," but it is not like watching television either.

One of the possible fallacies of any discussion of Shakespeare and television is the assumption that television is subject to rational evaluation, that is, that it conveys "meanings" in ways that can be described in language. We are lulled into such an assumption by the predictable pattern of the camera—close-up, two-shot, reaction shot—a rhythm employed even in "newsmaker" interviews. The consistency and straightforwardness of the camera does not necessarily convey the same attributes to the content. We are meant to believe so, but, as David Marc says, "Television is American dada, Charles Dickens on LSD, the greatest parody of European culture since *The*

Dunciad. . . . Art or not art? This is largely a lexographical quibble for the culturally insecure. Interesting? Only the hopelessly genteel could find such a phantasmagoria flat" (Marc, p. 35). Some aspect of Revelation—Christ or anti-Christ?—must be at hand. Certainly Marc makes the conventional critiques of, for example, "the new fall lineup on NBC" wonderfully irrelevant as delivered by those who take TV on its own terms.*

Marc may also make a discussion of Shakespeare on television irrelevant, unless the discussion accounts for the parodic nature of the medium itself, consciously realized in shows like "Monty Python" and "Black Adder." Can the potentially subversive "underscript" of the script emerge from television, or does TV subvert depth so that "serious" Shakespeare on television becomes a parody of theater? Howell manages the "fit" superbly in her *II Henry IV,* a script whose phantasmagoria suits the tube, if a director lets the play's parody of politics emerge via a stylization that some directors claim cannot work on television. A director must account for and overcome the potentially generic and tonal distortions that the medium itself is likely to impose on "serious" drama.

Don De Lillo's character Murray, in *White Noise*, suggests that

> TV is a problem only if you've forgotten how to look and listen. My students and I discuss this all the time. . . . I tell them they have to learn to look as children again. Root out the content. Find the codes and messages. [To them] television is just another name for junk mail. But I tell them I can't accept that. I tell them I've been sitting in this room for more than two months, watching TV into the early hours, listening carefully, taking notes. A great and humbling experience, let me tell you. Close to mystical. I've come to understand that the medium is a primal force in the American home. Sealed-off, timeless, self-contained, self-referring. It's like a myth being born right there in our living room, like something we know in a dream-like and preconscious way. You have to learn how to look. You have to open youself to the data. It opens ancient memories of world birth, it welcomes us into the grid, the network of little buzzing dots that make up the picture pattern. There is light, there is sound. I ask my students, "What more do you want?" Look at the wealth of data concealed in the grid, in the bright packaging, the jingles,

---

*Perhaps the *reductio ad absurdum* of television to commercial premises is a Lite Beer commercial that shows a fellow calling his TV repairperson because the TV has filled with beer. The repairperson suggests a party, so a group of yuppies gather to drink TV, or Lite Beer, as the TV has become. Why fool around with an intermediate soporific like television when the tube has become beer *per se*? In this case, the medium is the *product.* Come over and drink TV—and watch some beer.

the slice-of-life commercials, the products hurtling out of darkness, the coded messages and endless repetitions, like chants, like mantras. "Coke is it, Coke is it." The medium practically overflows with sacred formulas if we can remember how to respond innocently and get past our irritation, weariness, and disgust. (De Lillo, pp. 50–51)

Murray answers the question asked by a man in a recent *New Yorker* cartoon. "Sure, we all *watch* television—but how many of us really *see* television?" Murray sees it as a regression back to infancy. The problem is that no return can occur *from* infancy. The seer is fixated in a precognitive, almost nonverbal stasis. Myths are dynamic. The myth of Eden as an energy system derives its strength not from the symbiotic relationship that Adam and Eve had with God, but in the Fall, from which everything follows, for better or for worse. A useful regression is a return to a source of energy and a return from it into a renewed existential rhythm. Murray spaces out and then claims that half-truths are great insights.

Murray's excited sense that TV is somehow religious is clarified by Martin Esslin:

The rational culture of the Gutenberg Galaxy never extended beyond the very narrow confines of an educated minority elite . . . the vast majority of mankind, even in the developed countries, and even after the introduction of universal education and literacy, remained on a fairly primitive level of intellectual development. The limits of the rational culture are shown only too clearly in the reliance on pictorial material and highly simplified texts by the popular press that grew up in the period between the spread of literacy and the onset of the electronic mass media. Even the Christianity of more primitive people, relying as it did on a multitude of saints, each specializing in a particular field of rescue, was basically animistic. And so was—and is—the literalism of fundamentalist forms of puritan protestantism. Television has not created this state of affairs, it has merely made it more visible. . . . Ultimately the dramaturgy and content of the TV commercial universe is the outcrop of the fantasies and implied beliefs of [the] masses themselves; it is they who create the scenarios of the commercials through the continuous feedback of reactions between the makers of the artifacts concerned and the viewers' responses. (Esslin, p. 106)

But Murray does define a central issue—how do we get back to the myth that "hurtles out of the darkness" of a Shakespearean script? How do we get the words to mean more than "Coke is it," a mantra perhaps, but a repeated set of syllables that, when repeated, becomes nonsense. Some of the BBC productions of the early 1980s provide a stillborn, conventionally packaged Shakespeare that receives polite, bored, pro forma response from people who know already that "Shakespeare is dull." Unfortunately, BBC convinced some of us who believe otherwise. Such may be the power of the medium. "The aim of television is to be normal," says Marc (Marc, p. 35). If, as Marc claims, "the medium leaves behind a body of dreams that is, to a large extent, the culture we live in" (Marc, p. 34), then it may be that it *must* reflect a normative Shakespeare, one shaped to our diminished cultural expectations and to the product-filled cupboards of our "dreams." Since Shakespeare *has* succeeded on television, however, to claim that he cannot on the basis of a theoretical construct is ridiculous. The point is not success or failure, Shakespeare versus television. If the act of measurement changes what is measured, as Heisenberg suggests, the act of producing Shakespeare on television involves a transition that obviously "changes" Shakespeare. It can also, but not inevitably, change the medium.

Certainly television changes our relation to the event it depicts. Film does so also, of course, but we know, unless we are watching a documentary, that we are not watching an *event*. When, for example, we see Ronald Coleman as the actor playing Othello, or Richard Burton as Edwin Booth on stage as Hamlet, or Albert Finney as Wolfit playing Lear, we know that the audience in the film is made up of actors. If the film "moves" us it does so through the quality of its fictions, and we, the sophisticated film-goers, never forget that they *are* fictions. It moves us in a different way to learn the actress (Maggie McNamara) playing opposite Burton in "Prince of Players" never got another role and died young.

Shakespeare in the television studio *is* an event. This fact derives from television's early days of live drama and from television's inability to do much sophisticated camera work, to create special effects, or to do more than rudimentary editing based on standardized conventions of shots.

Perhaps the best way to suggest how the *event* changes because of television is to look briefly at televised sports.

I can remember being disturbed when, in the 1960s, I heard, "CBS Presents the National Football League." A network could present a variety show or a live drama—but "The National Football League"? I had naively seen television as a neutral window through which to watch the Giants. A few ads, sure, but they provided time to get to and from the fridge. But suddenly the medium was as important as the event. More important, the event was suddenly a function of entertainment. My assumptions were jarred. I was experiencing a "package," not a sports event that dragged along some inevitable and necessary sponsors.

Beyond that, however, the medium changed a viewer's relationship to the game, a fact not well captured via football, with its fixed scrimmage line and cliché vocabulary, where point of view is "fixed" for the beginning of each shooting sequence and the commentary predictable. Let a great but unformatted and nonscoring play occur—Joe Theisman knocking a deflected pass from the hands of an opposing lineman—and it won't make the halftime highlights, even as Theisman will remember it as the best play he ever made. Football assumes a fifty-yard line seat with variables. Baseball television, however, moves us from place to place and fundamentally disturbs our relationship to the game. At the park we watch from a fixed position and adjust to this angle of vision. What we see, what we miss, what we imagine, is defined by the seat we have purchased and by the expertise of the sitter—although the replay screen means that we now lose one of the former benefits of being there at "real" live sporting events: the necessity of seeing it right the first time. That function now is reserved for the umpires. We get a center fielder's telephoto shot from behind the pitcher, a shot of the pitcher on the mound as either the first or third baseman would see him, a shot of the batter as the man crouched in the on-deck circle might see him, and, occasionally, a high-angle shot from behind the batter's box, the latter one of the few angles that puts us in the position of being a spectator at an actual game. We see more, perhaps, but the experience is fragmented in the name of inclusiveness, and the responsibilities of observing and evaluating are no longer ours. They belong to the camera and to the "experts." Occasionally, an expert *is* helpful. "What is Casey telling him, Phil? . . . Your guess is as good as mine. I never understood a word he said." The camera gives us a series of points of view, like Browning's "The Ring and the Book," but the camera defines and redefines, leaving us no space for inference. Being at the game permits us to see many different things from *our* point of view. A portion of that viewpoint is formed by the variable of the crowd, of course, and by those around us in Section 8. TV necessarily robs the event of any grandeur. Baseball is subtle, but never intimate. It is fortunate that we have Babe Ruth on film, inevitable that we have Roger Maris on television.

The camera and commentary are meant to compensate for the small scale of the screen and for our not "being there." A single camera sitting on a box seat and doing what a normal set of eyes would be doing would not substitute for someone sitting in that seat. The camera would not know why it was watching the outfielders warm up between innings, why it was watching the on-deck hitter time the pitcher with his bat, why it watched the third baseman charge in on an expected bunt even as it swung to see the pitch go high and outside, why it was listening to a home-run roar as it stepped out of the men's room, or stared from time to time at that woman behind the Red Sox dugout.[8]

A single camera set on a theater seat would have the same nonhuman effect, as would a single camera set in the front of a television studio. Television, obviously, modifies the Shakespearean script to its unique requirements. The script insists on modifying the medium. The script, for example, dictates scene lengths seldom tailored to televisual segments. The script may insist that television try to escape from its "up close and personal" format, but is that possible on a small screen? Can TV shift our position—which is attitude in a couple senses of the word—so as to make "big scenes" work? If so, are those scenes edited to fragments of insight and reaction that serve as a synecdoche for the scope of a forum, throne room, or battlefield? Since TV makes no request that we "piece out its imperfections with our thoughts," we sense a crucial way in which the medium may believe it must perform—that is, as a "realistic" translator of stage fictions. Can a big scene work on TV in the twentieth century without its ever-present frame of heaven, Globe, and hell? Perhaps—if the theatrical metaphor is permitted to suggest its formative power behind the fiction.

Finally, I want to address a couple of discrepancies having to do with the medium of TV. It tends to be "disposable," except for old *I Love Lucy* and *Car 54, Where Are You?* and, of course, the aforementioned *Civil War* series. I am making perhaps more of TV than it deserves, suggesting that televised Shakespeare is worthy of attention that we might give to a stage production or a film but that television seldom warrants. The best of televised Shakespeare does deserve this kind of study. Second, I will commit the occasional fallacy of treating film as TV. The Richardson *Hamlet* was originally disseminated as a film, but it is, as Bernice Kliman argues, primarily a television production with its emphasis on the close-up and its lack of any deep-field camera work (Kliman, p. 167). The Branagh *Henry V* was distributed as a film, of course, but with an inevitable eye on the cassette market. The media of film and TV seem to be merging in some ways, a fact perhaps unfortunate for film but promising for Shakespeare. As I write, the Zeffirelli *Hamlet*, with Mel Gibson and Glenn Close, has yet to appear. I will, however, deal with that production later in these pages. How well will that film translate to TV? It may already contain that translation within its production design.

2

Style in *Dream:* The ART Version

The linear movement of television tape tends to follow the movement of the Shakespeare script, which is usually forward in time, with the occasional wedging back into time by Bolingbroke (*II Henry IV:* III.1.57 ff.), Mowbray the Younger (*II Henry IV:* IV.1.113 ff.), King Hamlet (I.5.35 ff.), and Prospero (I.2.53 ff.). The latter two moments, at least, are capable of a "flashback" technique, as in the Olivier film, which shows King Hamlet identifying Claudius, as well as Prince Hamlet's encounter with the pirates, and as in the Shaeffer TV *Tempest,* where Maurice Evan's Prospero has a crystal ball at his disposal. Film, obviously, can be much more flexible with time than can TV. The latter's relationship to time is also conditioned by its use as a killer of time. When we go to a film, our purpose is not to waste time, since we are aware of the money we are spending. A rented cassette fits a middle position, costing some money but coming at us from our own TV, which, presumably, has nothing else we consider worth watching that night. In most cases, TV is, as Duke Theseus says, something that will "wear away this long age of three hours / Between our after-supper and bedtime" (*Dream:* V.1. 33–34). The linear movement of the tape through a small space in front of us demands a simplified image and tends to collapse the techniques that filmmakers can employ, or that novelists use for their geographies. How does television re-create the thickness of Hardy's countryside through which Tess must walk, or Tony Hillerman's Navaho country, where mountains block radio transmissions, or Hawthorne's wild forest beyond the tight strictures of town?

Film can create a sense of the spontaneity of events and the generation of events. Fiction can restructure the chronological order of narrative, thereby enhancing our involvement in the story. TV can suggest coherent generative forces behind the depicted events in a number of simple ways. Seldom do these methods involve the building of a detailed set—for Shakespeare. An exception—Miller's *Mer-*

chant of Venice, with Olivier and Plowright, uses detail as theme—the lazy susan on which the caskets revolve, for example, evidence of affluent leisure, a Victorian upper class which corresponds to the Renaissance opulence of Belmont. That production had the incalculable advantage of a stage history behind it. In most cases, televised Shakespeare works best with minimalist sets, as in the contrast that Nunn creates for his *Antony and Cleopatra:* pillows, billowing curtains, the bronze color of heat, a wrinkled foil mirror, flabby eunuchs, the laughter of women poising their languid energies against columns, helmets, clenched male faces, and purposeful movement through shadows. Jane Howell's strategy for the *Henry VI—Richard III* sequence involves a versatile, "playground" set, with various doors and levels, altered by a meticulous control of light and enhanced by a consistent sense of metadramatic reference. At one point when Peter Benson's Henry VI comes shambling in, he turns, startled, at the fanfare that has announced his arrival.

TV must "re-center" the script, forcing the medium to involve us consistently and constantly, that is, to generate in us the response which a good stage production invariably evokes. Something must work underneath or behind the events themselves to suggest that the images are also archetypes, as opposed to merely an attractive surface, as in the painterly approach of Miller's *Antony and Cleopatra* for BBC, or the heavy medieval detail of BBC's *Second Henriad.* David Giles, who directed this sequence, says of the Trial by Combat in *Richard II:*

> It was an absolute swine. You can't do it realistically in a television studio and yet we didn't want it to get too stylized; that's why we used real horses. If we had gone too stylized with the list scene we would have had to stylize the play all the way through, and stylization on television is very difficult. In the theatre as soon as the curtain goes up one gets the total picture: If it's a stylized picture then that's it. (Fenwick, p. 20)

It usually is a stylized picture for the stage and *can* be for television. The issues conflate when we discuss, as I will do here, a televised stage production.

A Midsummer Night's Dream offers a remarkable challenge for television. It is an anachronistic script, ranging from the deep mythology of "Hercules and Cadmus" (IV.1.109) to the shops of Elizabethan artisans, and absorbing Ovid, Chaucer, Huon de Bordeaux, Apeuleius, and Reginald Scot with breathless ease as the script develops, juxtaposes, and combines its various worlds. The presence of those worlds, of course, invites a "concept," nor have modern directors been reluctant to provide one:

The time is "now" and the place is "the shopping mall and the forest," the two locales in Appalachia that best represent the new and the old, the commercial, acquisitive, socialized spirit and the earth-spirit, the ancestral spirit of mysterious forces and solitary individualism. [This] blending revealed some of the odd contrasts offered by contemporary Appalachian life. (French, p. 16)

Having not seen this production, I reserve judgment about what it may have revealed about *Dream.* My own inclination is not to modernize into contemporary times, since the analogies often smother the script. I prefer, for example, an updating into an era that is definitely in the past, as when Lysander becomes a young Tennyson, jotting some of his better lines in an ever-ready notebook, an affectation that can play against Demetrius's membership in a good regiment. Here we are invited to make an enjoyable historical jump to the time of Balaclava, where blunder in battle could still be redeemed by rhyme (Theater at Monmouth, 1982). To seek a contemporary resonance, as opposed to using a current setting and costuming, can be powerful, as Thomas Clayton describes the Ciulei production at the Guthrie in 1985, which I saw in another manifestation later at the Arena: "the feelings on display and in action [are] primarily possessiveness, resentment or desire . . . in this particular mid-eighties vision" (Clayton, p. 234).

It may be that "productions [of *Dream*] where all four centers of interest vie for equal attention are few and far between" (Smith, p. 416), and thus our attention to the play resembles our reading of a novel—we tolerate Mary Garth but we are really eager to get back to Dorothea, or Lydgate. But *Dream* is forever being re-created and reshaped in search of a unifying principle which was the Elizabethan stage itself, if we believe W. Moelwyn Merchant, a thesis itself doubtful in view of the limited number of scenes, the necessity for leaving characters asleep on stage, because entrances and exits require only two doors behind the playing area, and because the script does not call for the inner or upper stages prominent in Shakespeare's early plays and obviously available in his theater. Some internal evidence exists, then, for a "great hall" performance. The script does seem to reach outward from a paucity of technical structure toward the definition of reinforcing formats, where lighting can augment the lines and where the music the page calls for can actually sound, or toward the translation into ballet, opera, or into film or TV, and, perhaps inevitably, into some conformance with a zeitgeist other than Elizabethan.

To some extent, a production must decide which of the play's worlds is normative and what the norm is. Clearly, the world of the play is not that in which "Pyramus and Thisbe" occurs, a world literally as threatening as Quince and Company think their play will be, a nightmare Babylonian zone from which one cannot awake, "a world whose purposeless driving forces afford accidental coincidences that trick imaginative man into interpreting them as part of a play wrought and sustained by a cosmic intelligence" (Herbert, p. 110), where "animist lovers [wander through] a soul-less world" (Herbert, p. 114). The vision of most directors will move in the direction of Hippolyta, if given the choice of rhetorics described by Howard Nemerov: "The poetry of Theseus is rational, civic-minded, discursive, and tends constantly to approach prose. The poetry of Hippolyta is magic, fabulous, dramatic, and constantly approaches music. The excess of Theseus is to declare that art is entertainment; the excess of Hippolyta, to declare that art is mystery" (Nemerov, pp. 23–24).

The intuitive Hippolyta can glimpse a gestalt "of great constancy" (V.1.26) and, as modern theater has evolved, a director must glimpse the gestalt of the play. He will do so in various ways, of course, not just because he partakes of a unique psychology of perception, but also because the signals from the script are themselves variable, as if Shakespeare intended to launch this spaceship into time to be inhabited and controlled by different crews at different moments in time. Wilhelm Hortman claims, rightly I think, that it is the forest world which, when interpreted, defines the "rare [or mundane] vision" that informs a particular production:

> Apparently what kind of *Dream* a given production is going to be depends on an initial decision about the nature of the forces at work in Athens wood. Is it the domain of creative Eros, stormily, even grotesquely upsetting, but finally life-enhancing, optimistic, and regenerative? Or is Athens wood the place of ultimate self-confrontation, where we are made to recognize the human depravity which no manner of magic can gloss? A further factor that makes for diversity would seem to be what kind of lovers errant (roues or ingenues, contemporaries or historical figures) and what sort of strolling players the director decides to send into Athens wood to be transformed. [A director has great] freedom of choice . . . for the introduction of a variety of social, emotional, and temperamental types. . . . (Hortman, pp. 217–18)

Two extremes of vision were established for stage by Brook (1970) and Barton (1977), with Luivi Ciulei's mid-and-late 80s productions taking Brook's vision a few steps further toward Brechtian "alienation." The famous Brook version moved with the speed, variety, and minute but significant choices that the greatest of the racquet games—squash—demands. Whether that is why Brook placed the production *in* a squash court I do not know. The production was influenced, of course, by Jan Kott's *Shakespeare, Our Contemporary* (1964) and featured the blatant phallicism of David Waller's Bottom, a fairy's arm tumescent between Bottom's legs as he was carried triumphantly off to Titania's bower. The play did, however, end with festivity in the Brook version for all of its rampant sexuality at the core. The Ciulei version took Brook a step further and did *not* provide the "unequivocally festive ending," but reminded us of "the extratheatrical realities we return to—where all the world is *not* a stage" and made those realities "more evidently grey, grim, and sometimes deadly," thereby providing "an enthralling Rorschach test, the provocative effect of which few denied, like it or not" (Clayton, p. 232). Although I saw a later manifestation of the Ciulei than the one here described, I felt at the time that the production provided a dream that still had to be interpreted, as Clayton suggests, and that a "bad dream" is not always a dream *mis*interpreted. The extremity or difficulty presented in a dream is, if Jung is to be believed, an imaging of the radical errors consciousness is making. Brook did not let us forget the explosion that was barely contained in his closure. Ciulei insisted that *we* participate in closure. This version of "closure" is eminently appropriate *to* theater, of course, and had been prepared for, as Hortman suggests: "The many expressions of wonder, bewilderment, and exasperation in this play . . . were now understood as appeals to the common sense of neutral outsiders, as calls for help against the all-encompassing and mind-engulfing deception" (Hortman, p. 217). And we move from the theater, of course, into a "mind-engulfing deception," a fact that was brought home to me as I left the theater in Washington, D.C., as Ronald Reagan ended his residence a few miles away.

Barton used the illustrations of Arthur Rackham as his design principle. We experienced a benevolent world infused with magic, sailing with Wynken, Blyken, and Nod into a sea of dew. As Roger Warren says,

After the return to court [V], some of the trees remained in half-light, as did some of the fairies, "bodying forth / The forms of things unknown" as Theseus spoke of them, and so ironically counteracting his skepticism. The white-clad court lay down to sleep in a circle around the edge of the stage as the fairies blessed them. They later joined in with the blessing rather oddly; and even more oddly they awoke. (Warren, p. 142)

The waking was not odd as I watched it. As Puck said, "Now it is the time of night / That the graves, all gaping wide, / Every one lets forth his sprite / In the churchway paths to glide" (V.1.374–77), the others rose from their dim-semicircle and joined the dance, so that Duke and Amazon, Tinker and Bellows-mender, King and Queen held hands, the mortals *becoming* spirits as the darkness erased their identities. The humans became vague, anonymous, themselves "shadows." It was a powerful ending that went well beyond the rationalism of Theseus, as, obviously, the play does. We as audience were pulled forward into this magnificent closure, participants in a mystery being resolved for us, as opposed to individuals charged with its solution. At the end of the Barton production, as I moved along the Strand, I was still in the theater, re-creating the imagery of incorporation, not figuring out the ways in which fiction and my theoretical "reality" had been distinguished for me.

The Brook and Ciulei versions establish a sexual and physical interpretation which challenges or qualifies the final celebrations. In the case of the Ciulei, we are asked to consider that scripted closure may be the rationalization of "a power struggle that threatens the world with chaos" and that "threatens the order of the supernatural as well as the natural world" (Robert Collins, quoted in Clayton, p. 230). Barton implies an opposite meaning, "of something far more deeply interfused," the sense that spirit is prior to and inherent in all physical things, the "sacramental vision." Both interpretations are possible, but not simultaneously.

Most modern productions do focus on at least some of the darker energies in the script. Of one production, a critic says, "This was a dream which could turn into nightmare at any moment and one was grateful that these slightly menacing fairies chose to be benevolent" (Horobetz, p. 385). It is as if while watching the play we're trying to guess the mood of Richard Crookback at any given moment. The fairies are not always good-hearted. Of a production I will discuss at length later, Elizabeth H. Hageman says, "there were enough signs of fierce tyranny in Oberon and of cruelty in the satyr-like Puck to teach the audience that Shakespeare knew that love and violence are close cousins" (Hageman, p. 190). "For the forest scenes . . . Smoke and sinister shadows filled the stage area and the sounds of a storm were heard. Clearly this was not a benign forest: the fairies were gnomish grotesques, the anger between Oberon and Titania was vicious, and Puck was covered with spiky growths—he looked and acted more like a conventional Caliban than Robin Goodfellow" (Berkowitz, p. 77). "The contrast in the production was less between court and forest than between two kinds of oppressiveness—that of conventional normality and nightmarish affliction" (Habicht, p. 298). "Titania's lust for the ass displayed symptoms of ungovernable nymphomania" (Kennedy, p. 373). [Is nymphomania ever "governable"?] At the beginning of another production, "Many were astonished . . . by cannon fire and the smell of gun-powder, and the black, naked trees of the forest. Athens was at war, and Theseus entered with the Amazonian Queen Hippolyta imprisoned in a net" (Holmin, p. 432). At the beginning of another production, "a trapped Hippolyta was borne off between two spears" (Berry, p. 88). The lovers in the Ciulei production wanted nothing to do with each other as they wandered out of the woods. In another production, "Even the almost foolproof comic scene when Helena thinks they're conspiring against her was played for anger and despair rather than for humor" (Berkowitz, p. 77). And in another: "At the end, battered by experience, she was wary and distrustful of Demetrius, even though dependent on him" (Brissenden, p. 268)—a grim trap for Helena, who mistrusts the drug-induced protestations of the man she has chased through the forest! Titania, in one production, "was powerless to resist the charm but was unconsciously fighting the violation of her being" (Stodder and Wilds, p. 244). Titania does, after all, suggest to Oberon that she is aware that she is trapped in a nightmare (IV.1.47–55), even if a tempting but "False" answer in a "*Dream* guide" that I read recently won't work. It went something like "Titania isn't really affected by the love-juice but pretends to be to make Oberon jealous." Bottom is not necessarily happy to wake up. In one production, he "registered not the usual bafflement, but a turmoil of conflicting emotions. They were acted out in a contest between mind and body: his body stubbornly kicking and stamping to keep the blissful dream from slipping, his mind wonderingly pushing him along toward understanding" (Hortmann, p. 214). In another production, he recognizes "his loss, not just of an altered body, but also of an altered spiritual state and of Titania's attentions; the ineffable loss of something unfathomed in his waking life, something unspeakably beautiful" (Rosen, p. 204). In the Papp production, Bottom's "which was" (V.1. 289) points back to Titania as Pyramus speaks of his own irretrievable past. He has just seen Titania tripping in the shadows in a world beyond stage settings, a world where Bottom's adventure in Borderland has actually matched his heroic pretensions. His dream has been real, a truth that comes to him as he pulls back into the fiction he is enacting. His brief glimpse of Titania enforces the power of chance, randomness, what Hardy calls "hap," of a world where he is left to question the decision to frame lions.

The play turns inside out with time and with the darkness of the twentieth century to inform it and as ontogeny recapitulates phylogeny, as with *Huckleberry Finn,* once a wonderful adventure story, suddenly a grim tale of oppression, death houses, hatred of Walter Scott, and a doomed effort at escape from civilization. The happier version of the play—not necessarily lightweight—does survive, where we are allowed to respond to a benign cosmos and to laugh at our alter egos on the stage—usually Lysander and Helena, I suspect, but possibly even Puck: "just as the human lovers became central, so a redhaired Puck with more than a hint of Huckleberry Finn in his prankishness emerged as most prominent among the forest spirits. Puck appeared almost humanly vulnerable in pursuit of a lithe, elusive fairy dancer" (Wood, p. 340). [I would tend to equate Puck more with Tom Sawyer from the standpoint of "prankishness."] A production can emphasize harmony. "One beautiful tableau [occurred] as Theseus and Hippolyta watched the sleeping lovers [at the end of IV.1] as if recalling . . . the stormy course of their own earlier courtship" (Roberts, p. 207). "The doubling of the mechanicals and the fairies created a charming . . . *Wizard of Oz* effect, with the characters in Bottom's dream becoming magical versions of his real-life friends" (Berkowitz, p. 90). "Bottom's warmth and friendliness drew from [Titania] a tender, intimate response devoid of sensuality" (Warren, p. 88). "At the start of the performance all the children in the audience were invited to choose costumes so that they could dress up and take part in the woodland scene as elves, or animals, or simply be part of the scenery" (Lindblad, p. 461). "Egeus constantly [forgot] his prospective son-in-law's name [it's Demetrius] and had to be prompted" (Goodfellow, p. 231). "Snug . . . was too nervous to be able to roar as a lion, so that the lion's part had indeed to be taken over by Bottom" (Habicht, p. 295). And even that which can seem to threaten, as in a dream, can dissolve into friendly shapes, as in a dream: "Oberon was a limping and grotesque Richard III of the woods, à la *Huon de Bordeaux.* But as he released Titania from her spell, he became suddenly beautiful. That Ovidian transformation gave her 'My Oberon!' a power the script suggests but that I had never before experienced. Hippolyta's aversion to Theseus was resolved when she caught a whiff of Oberon's magic flower and took off after a bemused Theseus with a doggedness worthy of Helena" (Coursen, pp. 97–98).

Much of what can happen on stage depends upon our suspension of disbelief. Film and television usually insist upon a different attitude, one that may make this script difficult to translate or that may insist upon a radical translation. Woody Allen solves part of the problem in his *A Midsummer-Night's Sex Comedy* by introducing a

Theseus figure, Leopold (José Ferrer) who sneers at the supernatural. Reinhardt's 1935 film reaches, of course, for special effects within a field of depth that film affords and a developed tradition that allows film to be surrealistic. He convinces us of the distinction between nature and the supernatural—the Indian Boy, playing with the fairies cannot fly and must pause before a pond over which the spirits waft with ease, and a real donkey bolts at the sight of Bottom's transformation. Black-and-white turns out to be a wonderful medium for *Dream*. It forces us to participate by filling in the colors, by naming the objects that colors otherwise identify for us, or perhaps just by its evocation of a gauzy zone where nature and the supernature touch each other.

The black-and-white BBC version of the 1960s uses a much narrower and shallower scale than the Reinhardt, of course, but succeeds on the basis of its more subtle touches—Benny Hill as Bottom for example, gleefully surrendering to Titania's attention, Miles Malleson's identification of Alfie Bass's Thisbe as "This grisly beast" (the actors having not rehearsed for the Prologue), and other details that make this production deservedly popular with students. The Hall film-for-TV (1970) uses quick cuts and dissolves to suggest a psychic discontinuity within seemingly rational discourse and a dreamlike, even nightmarish quality *within* speeches, where setting and background shift without apparent motivation, even as the speaker continues without pause. As Jack Jorgens says, the camera seems intent on "fracturing naturalistic surfaces" (Jorgens, p. 58) in Hall's effort to escape stage conventions. But *Dream* by Fellini may step over the boundaries of effective *mimesis* and deny us an appropriate distance from the art form. Are we too much *in* the dream? To some extent, Hall's devices are of alienation and anti-alienation. We are told that this is stone by being placed inside the statue. Perhaps my problem with the Hall version is just that it now seems very dated. Reinhardt's does not, because the special effects still work in ways that film can make them work. The 1981 BBC version uses a painterly technique that creates a static picture all too typical of a medium that makes little appeal to our imaginations and that can create no special effects other than the feeble squiggle of a "beam-up."

Most of the film and television versions have been discussed at length.[1] I wish to look at a production that has not been examined in detail and, by inference, to argue the case for the televised live production. The stage may still be the combining metaphor which fuses those unlike things—the modern audience and the Shakespearean script—even on television.

The splendid American Repertory Theatre's (ART) *A Midsum-*

mer-Night's Dream, directed by Alvin Epstein, was televised in live performance at the Wilbur Theater (Boston) in 1981, and directed for television by Richard Heller. The producer, Peter Cook, graciously showed the tape at the Ohio Shakespeare Conference in 1991. This is another example of a live Dream to be compared to the Joseph Papp Delacorte Theater production. In most respects, the ART version is greatly superior. And—it transcends Robert Hapgood's assertion that "It remains . . . simply the record of a stage performance" (Hapgood, p. 276).

Like Papp, the ART version "establishes" itself by showing an audience settling in for an evening of theater. This prelude is particularly appropriate for this script, of course, since it features an on-stage audience watching a play at the end. In the ART production, a gold curtain opens onto a giant tapestry based on Ucello's Battle of San Romano. This background features a titanic clash of cavalry, the phallic thrust of lances, and, beneath, knights and horses lying dead, being killed superfluously by the drive of hooves. Two golden knights enter, mano a mano. Once helmets are doffed, the winner, via a concealed dagger, turns out to be a golden-haired Hippolyta. We infer that this combat is ex post battle, a kind of "foreplay" in which she shows that she is the more clever single soldier, even if Theseus and his legions did overcome the Amazons. She tosses him with a jujitsu move on "Another moon" (I.1.3), setting up his wish for some cessation of combat: "But, O, methinks, how slow this old moon wanes" (I.1.3–4). She signals her acceptance of a truce by rubbing her inner things on "our solemnities" (I.1.11), in an unabashedly sexual production of a script that can also be played very chastely.

Hippolyta sides with her alter ego, Hermia, as Egeus launches his complaint. By this time, Theseus and Hippolyta have donned golden robes. The father, daughter, and two young gentlemen, however, wear costumes of rusty red which pick up the darker tones of the Ucello. For much of the Egeus sequence, the camera looks down upon the dark boards of the stage. This angle permits Egeus's angry finger-waving to dominate a static and befuddled Theseus, who has not been thinking of state affairs, and allows us to witness a splendidly choreographed conflict which reflects some of the destructiveness depicted in the tapestry. Hermia gasps on Theseus's word "death" (I.1.44). We get simultaneous "presentation" and "representation" in this brilliant opening, in which love and war are not just juxtaposed but confused with each other. Hippolyta ignores Theseus's hand, hugs Hermia, and bumps between Egeus and Demetrius for her angry exit.

A controversial aspect of this production is the use of Henry Purcell's *The Fairy Queen* (1692)—via mixed consort, chorus, and solo as interpolation or, a one critic has it, "counterpoint" (Hageman, p. 191). This critic goes on to say that "The majestic music balanced and modified the more violent activities on the stage" (Hageman, p. 191). That is fair, I think, although at times the music accompanies and perhaps reinforces the violence, and I am not sure about the *nature* of the balance or modification. What would the production have been with the orchestra as merely a background or transitional element? Perhaps I have become accustomed to the more legato Mendelssohn as background, à la Reinhardt or Woody Allen, and even the triumphant release of trumpets for the celebrations of act V. When one went to a Paramount flick and the music came up (along with the moon) behind Bing Crosby just about to sing to Dorothy Lamour, one expected the song. The "plot," whatever it may have been, was built to support the moments when Bing sang or when Fred and Ginger danced. But Shakespeare's superbly constructed *play* is another matter.

I have no problems with the music as transition or as a way of distinguishing between the "worlds" of the play. "Musical interludes" are built into this script and into other comedies: *As You Like It* and *Twelfth Night*—where Feste's songs keep pointing at what some of the characters are ignoring—and *The Tempest* features a big "production number" in the Masque. A little segue does no harm to the short *Dream* script.

The transitions in this production are splendid, and worth describing. The first Mechanicals Scene is played on the side of the proscenium. The cream of the arch and the light-gold, umber, and white of the Mechanicals' costumes coordinate in softer tones with the tapestry, which, in turn, makes its own ironic point about Bottom's "mock epic" posturing. They exit to applause. The orchestra strikes up as we watch the tapestry disappear. It is two scrims, as it turns out. The further scrim rises to show a moon, dim behind the battling horsemen, who then rise to the flies, leaving a huge, pockmarked moon looking down upon a ramp. Fairies begin to dart about this silver space, scaring each other. We experience the "illusion" of transition as we are brought through a work of art—a representation for all of its depicted violence—into a nighttime world that is, literally, "beyond art." The Chorus sings the "Echo" song, and another Chorus enters behind four fairies. The "joy" they would bring to this silver-washed space is interrupted as, with a manic screech, Puck slides down the ramp. He traps one fairy who has been late in joining the general retreat. The two spar, testing the power inherent in the

positions of those they serve, a version of the contest between the
retainers of the Montagues and Capulets at the beginning of *Romeo
and Juliet*. The Chorus picks up on this division, becoming Semi-
Choruses, advocates of the King *or* Queen. Titania, on top of the
ramp, removes *her* helmet to ask, "What, jealous Oberon?" (II.1.61).
He wears half-armor. While we are fully in the other world by now,
we are reminded that these two night-figures are the counterparts of
the mortal Theseus and Hippolyta. In watching this sequence, I
realize that Shakespeare's contribution to the concept of light on
stage is as great as that of Vermeer's to painting or Newton's to
science.

Another effective transition occurs before and after the interval,
between III.1 and III.2. Titania and Bottom, with fairies, engage in
an elaborate mating dance, in which she mimes rejection, but finally
slides down the ramp to land between Bottom's spread legs. The
dance neatly echoes the actions of the prim Hermia in pressing Lysander to "Lie further off" (II.2.63), and of horny Helena, eager to
render Demetrius "the rich worth of [her] virginity" (II.1.216). After
the interval, the camera moves out from the moon to encompass the
stage. Invigorating trumpets with tympany usher in the Chorus with
"Hail!" Bottom and Titania lie sweetly entangled, center stage. Oberon's head suddenly appears, down right, with an ironic "I wonder
if Titania be awak'd" (II.2.1). He gets a laugh by insisting that we
share a dissonance that counters the harmonious hopes of the
Chorus.

I have a problem with Helena, who is privileged with two solos
from an alter ego soprano. Why Helena? Why *this* Helena? She
(Cherry Jones) is a fetching blonde who contrasts physically with
Cynthia Darlow's shorter, throaty, and brunette Hermia. Helena's
first encounter with the soloist occurs before her soliloquy at the end
of I.1. "Tearful, my heart" seems superfluous, since the soliloquy is
itself a figuring out of her position and ends with the essential "I
have an idea!" that gets all the lovers into the woods. Why does
"insight" arrive through an intermediary? Perhaps the solo reinforces
Helena's characterization as "dependent" or, since Nedar does not
appear, as without a parent to guide her. The latter thesis won't
work, if Egeus is the model of the Athenian father. The second solo
to Helena, however, is far more effective. Her soliloquy: "O, I am
out of breath. . . ." (II.2.94) is interrupted by a gray ghost who
claims that she will "hide thee from the light of day" and that "he's
gone" and "Thy eyes shall never see him more." Helena tries to avoid
the voice, dancing away while swirling her red skirt in a rebolera,
but returns to listen. Her next lines—"Therefore no marvel, though

Demetrius / Do, as a monster, fly my presence thus"—are cut, so that she picks up with "What wicked and dissembling grace of mine / Made me compare with Hermia's sphery eyne?" (II.2.104–5). She is, then, trapped in a bad dream crafted of her low self-esteem. She realizes that much, interpreting her dream as she has it. She does not realize, of course, that she is soon to be pursued by *both* young men, a swing in circumstances that she will only be able to attribute to an unattractiveness that can attract only a cruel and carefully orchestrated practical joke.

The first solo, then, seems merely interpolated into the script, the second deeply integrated with the script.

The stage movement and choreography (directed by Carmen de Lavallade, who plays Titania)—the physical dimension of this production is worth detailing, even if that element cannot be disengaged from the music, in a production that Hageman calls a "multi-media event" (Hageman, p. 191). The First Fairy becomes a victim of, and an amused actor in, Puck's description of his horseplay, as when the Fairy is propelled onto Puck's back by the latter's right foot, then toppled as Puck slips out from under on "down topples she" (II.1.53). This remarkably smooth sequence makes one wonder how much rehearsal time had gone into its perfecting. The Fairies "sing [Titania] asleep" (II.2.7) while weaving a protective circle around her, and at the same time attempting with their song, to summon the positive forces of the woods up from where they have hidden from daylight. The song begins with swamp noises—gurgles and frogs—whispers "You spotted snakes. . . ." (II.2.9), moves to falsetto on "Philomel. . . ." (II.2.13), and deepens on: "Nor spell nor charm. . . ." (II.2.17). The second half of the lullaby is cut, but the metrical movement of the Fairies combines with the altering levels of their song to seem to communicate with all lurking orders and dominions that might harm her as she reaches sinuously for sleep. All of this elaboration merely enhances what we already know— that she is threatened by her own consort. Her "sentinel" (II.2.33) immediately joins her in sleep, lulled by its own lullaby. Then, to a violin/viola duet, Oberon slides in serpentlike with the love-juice.

Another excellent fusion of music and movement occurs when Bottom enters with his ass's head (III.1.98). His compatriots race back and forth, retrieving props and avoiding him, as Bottom reaches out to them. This "anti-burgomask" is a nightmare prelude to Bottom's "rare vision" (IV.2.203).

As Titania gets to "the moon, the governess of floods" (II.1.103) in her long speech about nature, she holds her hands up, as if cradling the moon. It is a breathtaking vignette, deriving from Art Deco.

After Hermia has rejected Lysander's premature advances in II.2., they sleep. He rolls back toward her. She presses his arm away, but they roll together center-stage and mime lovemaking. Thus do they consummate their relationship in dream. Hermia dreams of a "serpent" (II.2.152), of course, her censor translating her repressed desire into something "cruel" (II.2.156) even as something deeper signals her readiness for the transition from maidenhood to marriage. The ways in which conscious propriety wars with natural propensity are splendidly developed here. Before exiting, Lysander drops his coat on Hermia's face. It is this smothering object that becomes the serpent. She wrestles with it until her hand appears in the sleeve and tells her that this has been a dream. The dream that Bottom and Titania will share is less decorous. His "amiable cheeks" (IV.1.2) are the nether set, and what Bottom thought he "had" (IV.2.207) is not just the physique of a donkey, but Titania.

I find Kenneth Ryan's Oberon sometimes too sing-songy. He keeps hitting all rhymes as "eye," for example, as he applies the juice to Lysander (III.2.41 ff.) and makes absolute caesuras at the end (V.1.396 ff.), coming close to the jiggling rhymes of "Pyramus and Thisbe." Thomas Darrah's Puck, however, exploits his master's voice in the "For I must now to Oberon. . . ." speech (II.2.72–89), hoping off on one foot, in laughter, as if physically impounded by the tetrameter. Ryan and Darrah work well together, becoming a grotesque tree on Oberon's "Stand close" (III.2.41) to overhear Hermia and Demetrius. When Oberon, Titania, and Puck exit in IV.1.101, they make a wonderful six-legged creature suggestive of the plasticity of these deities and akin to Raphael's description of angelic sexuality in *Paradise Lost:* "and obstacle found none / Of membrane, joint, or limb" (VIII. 624–25).

A company that has worked with the script within the energy system created by a live audience learns how to exploit nuances—so dependent on timing—so as to get a response. Of many such instances, I cite only a few. Quince tears up Lion's part behind his back, after hearing Snug's stammer. An effective pause before Oberon asks Titania "How long within this wood intend you stay?" (II.1.138) signals that she has won this round of their quarrel. Oberon's "Fare thee well, nymph" (II.1.245) gets a big laugh. The word glances at Helena's unabased desire for Demetrius. The production borrows from Peter Brook in effecting the exchange of the flower from Puck to Oberon via legerdemain. Titania almost awakes when Oberon says "Wake when some vile things is near" (II.2.40) and he has to exit quickly, lest the vile thing be he. Helena sits on the sleeping Hermia on "Happy be Hermia, where so e'er she lies"

(II.2.96). As Bottom wakes at the end of IV.1 and calls the names of his long-fled companions, their names echo—except for Starveling's, whose shouted name melts into silence. This gets a laugh because it represents what Bergson calls "interference of series," but also because it alludes to Starveling's deafness in this production. He cannot hear to answer.

The interrelationships that this production enforces are best realized, perhaps, in the transition that occurs within IV.1. The Folio says "Exeunt" and "Winde Hornes" after Titania's "on the ground" (IV.1.101), indicating that the Fairies exit as the court characters enter (and suggesting that Shakespeare did not double the roles). Here we get a dance. Oberon and Titania "rock the ground" (IV.1.85) by stepping over Demetrius and Lysander, rolling them as they sleep. Then Oberon and Titania, in silver, and Theseus and Hippolyta, in gold, dance a minuet that marks the reconciliation of the worlds of forest and court and the proper pairing of this set of couples. Earlier combat between the court couple and earlier jealousy between the woodland deities surrender to cooperative rhythms. Two members of the Chorus are on stage to signal a more comprehensive harmony ruling this restoration of order. When Oberon and Titania exit, Theseus, already on stage, can come forward with "Go, one of you, find out the forester" (IV.1.102).

"Pyramus and Thisbe" tends to face the outer audience but occurs between the Ducal audience, seated stage left, and Quince and company, coaching from stage right. This does not, then, attempt to simulate a real stage performance. We observe a kind of cross fire through the performance and thus a nice balance between breakdowns of decorum that occur on both sides of the production. We are not invited to associate with the Ducal audience—particularly given their stage left location—although the camera does, occasionally, observe the play from behind the aristocrats. The attitude is moderated, however, since it shows that audience applauding the Mechanicals' mechanical efforts. At one point, Hippolyta goes on stage to comfort a weeping moon, who parodies Titania's earlier line, "The moon methinks looks with a watery eye" (III.2.193). Here, Hippolyta says "Truly, the moon shines with a good grace" (V.1.264). Our own response is meant, I believe, to be not of superiority but of sympathy. The interplay between Quince and his actors balances that between the actors and their on-stage audience. Quince, for example, signals Wall to make a chink. Wall, however, thinks Quince is signing, "It's going to be great!" Wall returns the gesture enthusiastically, thereby creating a gap in the play by not creating one. This balanced staging opens out to a third point of view, ours, and permits us to mediate between aristocratic sophistication and blue-collar naïveté, and to recognize that both parties are necessary in the shaping of the third set of attitudes, which is that of the outer audience.

This is edited, as one might suspect, toward larger theatrical effects. They translate well to television because we are invited to accept the premises of a live production, even if cameras cannot substitute for being there. Some of the more intimate moments of this script are deleted. Decisions made for the stage, however, are not necessarily valid for TV, or, as I have suggested, for this talented troupe. Gone, for example, are Bottom's interactions with Peaseblossom and the other Fairies (III.2.170–90 and IV.1.5–26), which suggest the splendid obliviousness with which Bottom translates himself into a new "life-style." He does, however, scratch his scalp at the end of III.2, and repeats the action while off-stage as Pyramus, so that the references to having his head scratched in IV.1 are given a visual equivalent. Gone also is Helena's amusingly mawkish description of the "two artificial gods" that she and Hermia had been as schoolgirls (III.2.203–14). Titania's telling description of the artificial pregnancy she experienced through her "vot'ress" (II.1.127–34) is deleted, perhaps because a "maternal instinct" does not suit this sensuous and sinuous Titania. We neither see the Indian boy, nor is he emphasized. Gone also, for some reason, is Titania's revealing couplet: "I am a spirit of no common rate. / The summer still doth tend upon my state" (III.3.148–49).

We probably do not miss Bottom on beards (11.2.80–89), though the disquisition may make some point about "theatricality" versus "nature" (Flute's coming beard and corn rotting "'ere his youth attained a beard": II.1.95), Titania's allusion to "Hiems" (II.2.109), Hermia's reference to Dido (I.1.173–74), or her brief metaphysical poem about "the Antipodes" (III.2.50–55). But Oberon's reference to "the imperial vot'ress" (II.1.163–64) is gone, as is his reference to "the snake's enamel'd skin, / Weed wide enough to wrap a fairy in" (II.2.255–56). The former allusion would reinforce the production's sense of presiding harmonies ruling events on earth. The snake is a symbol of transformation and hints at the ways in which nature and the supernatural relate and cooperate—in contrast to Titania's cruel command to "pluck the wings from painted butterflies / To fan the moonbeams from his sleeping eyes" (III.1.167–68), which is also cut. While Hippolyta gets her hunting story with "Hercules and Cadmus" (IV.1.111), Theseus goes right to "But soft, what nymphs are these" (IV.1.126). His possibly defensive and therefore amusing "My hounds are bred out of the Spartan kind" (IV.1.118) is lost from a production which had informed us already of the competition between the two.

Two major cuts are made—one for the sake of "style," the other to streamline the closure.

Toward the end of IV.1, Egeus and Hermia embrace, and Egeus somewhat reluctantly takes Lysander's hand. He refuses the hand of Demetrius, who shrugs, as if to say, it's not my problem. The lovers' half-awake discussion of their experience (IV.1.186–98) is replaced by a song ("Turn, turn, turn") and a dance in which the lovers redepict the confusions of the night and the fusions beginning at dawn. They are given a solo by a nearby baritone, who blesses all four of them, thus erasing the alienation which the soprano had imposed upon Helena earlier. This is the "harmonious" ending in the Hall-Barton tradition, as opposed to the Brook-Ciulei. At the end of the Barton, at the Aldwych in the late 1970s, as Puck said, "Now it is the time of night. . . ." (V.1.374), all the other characters, their identities erased in the half-light, joined hands in an eerie dance that wove us into the spirit world. In the Ciulei, at the Arena in D.C. in the late 1980s, the lovers returned to Athens still confused and still angry as they recalled the charges and countercharges of the night.

Epstein makes a decision for a stage performance, of course, in modulating his production toward harmony. It is also a decision for television. Television resolves the issues it may raise *within* its illuminated space, which usually shows a room in which Father Knows Best. If *A Midsummer-Night's Dream* is "a civilized equivalent for exorcism," as C. L. Barber says (Barber, p. 139), the exorcism is accomplished within "formal cause" and not as "final cause," on television, with its "fourth-wall" proscenium premises. "The house" (V.1.386) and "this house" (V.1.397) become on television, merely Theseus's palace not, as the words can convey in the theater, the audience out there watching the blessing, being blessed, and soon to be asked to reciprocate. At the same time, however, depending upon the metadramatics of a particular TV production, no reason exists for Oberon *not* to include us with a sweep of eyes and hand, but the energy is centripedal on TV. Prime time is closing up shop. Things are being folded inward until the blankness of the tube reflects our own space as we abandon the station-changer, force ourselves from the lounger, and begin to turn out the lights before our own effort not to "outsleep the coming morn" (V.1.360).*

---

*An exception to what I say about Shakespeare and closure on TV is the Nunn *Othello,* in which McKellen's final neutrality in the face of his evil forces us to

The streamlining has Quince's play certain of performance, if Bottom will only show up, so that Theseus's "call Philostrate (V.1.38) cuts directly to Philostrate's "So please your Grace, the Prologue is addressed" (V.1.106). A lot of interesting material is lost, of course, but the music and dance that the production provides in place of some of the lines more than compensate for what a carping traditionalist like me notices is not there.

At the end, a kinder, gentler Puck than he has been within the frame is afraid that we will call him a "liar" (V.1.431). The sun seems to burnish his right shoulder as he perches on the balustrade stage right. A superimposed shot shows a large Puck and his smaller self juxtaposed against the huge moon. A dissolve (on "Give me your hands. . . .": V. 1.432) moves to the long shot of Puck and the moon. It is one of the few obvious uses of "camera work" in this production, and it works its magic because of its simplicity and because the production has already cast its spell over its audience, both in the theater and on the TV screen.

This is a production that should be made commercially available.

---

conduct our own exorcism, or not. At the end of that production, we are *not* applauding because something has been solved for us or explained to us. I discuss the Nunn *Othello* elsewhere. Nunn notices and emphasizes that that play ends without the rites of passage that close the other tragedies.

Carmen de Lavallade, Titania; Kenneth Ryan, Oberon. American Repertory
Theatre, 1981. Courtesy A.R.T.

Helen Mirren, Titania; Phil Daniels, Puck; Peter McEnery, Oberon. 1981. Courtesy BBC-Television.

"The Rest Is Silence." Richard Chamberlain. 1970. Courtesy Hallmark, Inc.

Kevin Kline. 1990. Photo by Nancy LeVine.

Taping the Ghost, 1980. Courtesy BBC-Television.

"It is I—Hamlet the Dane!" Olivier. Courtesy J. Arthur Rank.

"Alas, Poor Yorick!" Stellen Scarsgaard. 1984. Courtesy WNYC-TV.

"Alas, Poor Yorick!" Maximilian Schell. 1960. Courtesy Kurt Gewissen.

3

"Alas, Poor Yorick!"

A portion of the superb stained glass window in the Reading Room of the Folger Library, part of the engraved glass panel by John Hutton at the Shakepeare Centre in Stratford-on-Avon, the "Shakespeare" card in the "Authors" game depict Hamlet holding the skull of Yorick. Many people who have never read or seen *Hamlet* could quote—or misquote—the line that accompanies the picture. "Alas, poor Yorick," they would say, "I knew him well" (as opposed to what the script tells Hamlet to say, which is "I knew him, Horatio"). Actors playing the role of Hamlet—Kemble, Beerbohm Tree, Forbes Robertson, Bernhardt, Redgrave, Burton, O'Toole, Schell, Kingsley, Williamson, Pennington, Olivier, Wolfit, Guinness, Keach, Day-Lewis, Branagh, Rylance, Chamberlain, Gibson—invariably have their Hamlet picture taken in a two-shot with Yorick.

The moment in the play picks up enormous energy from the drama itself. Hamlet has delivered a brilliant disquisition on the ways in which all pathways beat their way to the grave when he is suddenly confronted by the fleshless face of someone he did know well.* The abstract discussion suddenly becomes personal, as it will continue to do once Hamlet identifies the new occupant of Yorick's grave wending through the deepening tide of tombstones in Elsinore's graveyard.

The moment is also iconographic. It is a picture that captures a concept—man face-to-face with his ultimate physical destiny. Clearly, it is the most powerful icon emerging from Shakespeare, the second being Prince Hal trying on the crown in *II Henry IV* (the young man confronting the power soon to be his). The moment in *Hamlet* showed the late-Elizabethans their own culture, one in which death was a consistent intruder, as shown in the sixteenth-century etchings of Holbein in which, for example, a skeleton embraces a woman selecting clothes from her maid as an hourglass runs out of

---

*Cf. "Alas, poor ghost!"

sand (circa 1530). Both R. M. Frye and Harry Morris have recently shown how ubiquitous was the idea that Shakespeare and his character make so potent in the play.[1]

If Hamlet and Yorick demonstrate and summarize a deep aspect of turn-of-the-seventeenth-century culture, the same moment in a modern production will show us what our culture is *not*, for reasons that Jessica Mitford suggests in her scathing book, *The American Way of Death:*

> Alas, poor Yorick! How surprised he would be to see how his counterpart of today is whisked off to a funeral parlor and is in short order sprayed, sliced, pierced, pickled, trussed, trimmed, creamed, waxed, painted, rouged and neatly dressed—transformed from a common corpse into a Beautiful Memory Picture. This process is known in the trade as embalming and restorative art, and is so universally employed in the United States and Canada that the funeral director does it routinely, without consulting corpse or kin. He regards as eccentric those few who are hardy enough to suggest that it might be dispensed with. Yet no law requires embalming, no religious doctrine commends it, nor is it dictated by considerations of health, sanitation, or even of personal daintiness. In no part of the world but in North America is it widely used. The purpose of embalming is to make the corpse presentable for viewing in a suitably costly container; and here too the funeral director routinely, without first consulting the family, prepares the body for public display.
>
> Untouched by human hand, the coffin and the earth are now united.
>
> It is in the function of directing the participants through this maze of gadgetry that the funeral director has assigned to himself his relatively new role of "grief therapist." He has relieved the family of every detail, he has revamped the corpse to look like a living doll, he has arranged for it to nap for a few days in a slumber room, he has put on a well-oiled performance in which the concept of death has played no part whatsoever—unless it was inconsiderately mentioned by the clergyman who conducted the religious service. He has done everything in his power to make the funeral a real pleasure for everybody concerned. He and his team have given their all to score an upset victory over death. (Mitford, pp. 466–73)*

---

*In a recent review of Twelvetrees Press's *Sleeping Beauty: Memorial Photography in America,* John Updike suggests that "in the course of this lethal century, death has become increasingly abstract. . . . The constant flicker of electronic sounds and images that surround us constitute a mental environment as insulating as the buzzing belief systems of animism, Islam, or medieval Christianity. . . . Open-coffin funerals, the norm in my boyhood, have all but vanished in Protestant middle-class circles. . . . No longer susceptible to the commercial of sex appeal and consumerism, the body becomes trash. Our modern mysticism [is] the worship of disembodied energy." Of the pictures in which dead children are propped up as if alive—sitting

Perhaps needless to say, more versions of the "Yorick!" sequence exist on film and tape than any other moment in the canon. In discussing them, I admit to perpetrating the fallacy described by Martin Wiggins: a 'television' production [is not just] one designed to be watched on a television set . . . the TV set is host to two distinct media . . . broadcast television and the pre-recorded video" (Wiggins, p. 506). The latter, of course, include films made *as* film, films made for TV, broadcast television recorded on cassette, and even a live performance once transmitted as film to theaters around the United States (the 1964 *Hamlet*, directed by Gielgud and starring Richard Burton). My discussion, then, will be of apples, oranges, and lemon peels, but assumes the prerecorded video. Since "Yorick!" tends to be a "close-up" moment, even on stage, the discussion will not do radical violence to the distinction that must be made between the media.

The reasons for zeroing in on a single moment should be obvious. We have a splendid chance to notice variations—what is Hamlet's relationship to Horatio, to the Gravedigger, to Yorick? What does the director include within the frame? How does he edit the scene? And so on. The best way to learn about a script is to observe several of its manifestations. We are at a great disadvantage when we cannot do so. With this play we are fortunate. Not all of the productions I examine are available commercially, but enough are so that the kind of analysis I apply can be made of any moment in the *Hamlet* script, assuming directors have left the script relatively intact. Given its length it usually suffers from an incomplete transmission, particularly and necessarily in film.

The versions I will consider include a snippet from a 1944 production with John Gielgud, the 1948 Olivier film, the 1964 Burton play, as transmitted by Warner Brothers, the Christopher Plummer ver-

---

still for the long process of the mid-nineteenth century daguerreotype—Updike says, "We are disturbed by our own assent to sentimentality's denial of the undeniable." Perhaps. I am appalled by the sentimentality *per se,* which is another version of "memory picture" (Updike, "Facing Death," *American Heritage* (May–June 1992): 98–105. Updike would seem to be suggesting that television insulates its audience from "reality"—perhaps by showing so much "reality." Most audiences of television and film know that the violence therein depicted is simulated. Such violence may reduce a spectator's belief in the value of human life, as pornography is said to do. But coverage of the war in Vietnam and the shootings at Kent State in May 1970, proved television's power as a "realistic" medium. My conclusion is that the effect of television is more complcated than the perceived "simplistic" nature of the medium would suggest. Whatever the nature of the medium's "message," which is usually to sell, often to sell the official line, and sometimes to show some things that cannot be censored out, the message is powerful.

sion filmed at Elsinore in 1964, the 1964 Kozintsev film, the 1969 Tony Williamson film, the 1970 Hallmark television production with Richard Chamberlain, the 1971 television production with Ian McKellan, the 1980 BBC version, the 1984 Swedish film directed by Ragnar Lyth, the 1990 television version with Kevin Kline, the 1991 film with Mel Gibson, and the parody in *L. A. Story* (1991). For a more in-depth treatment of all but the last three productions, see Bernice Kliman's *Hamlet: Film, Television, and Audio Performance*.[2]

The Gielgud is an excerpt from a stage performance, with the action downstage right—the position on stage the audience treats most favorably—Horatio leaning over stage right, the Gravedigger downstage, and Gielgud upstage, sitting on wooden steps, chin in hand. Gielgud laughs as the Gravedigger says "on my head once," pauses as the Gravedigger identifies the skull, and moves his right hand to point on his incredulous "This?" The Gravedigger begins to put the skull down as Gielgud, very curious, says "Let me see." The Gravedigger hands the skull to Gielgud, who turns it to face him. "Alas, poor Yorick!" as if to say, this is all that's left? He turns to Horatio on "I knew him." The next shot is the usual tight two-shot, Hamlet and Yorick. Gielgud, on the left of the frame, is the superior, simultaneously lecturing and commanding a subject. This is a very princely Hamlet with an elegance and precision of diction that might seem a bit old-fashioned these forty-six years later—although the same might be said of many close-ups of stage performances even today. The finest moment in the speech comes when Gielgud asks "Where be your gibes now? your gambols? your songs?" and searches the hollow fragment for these sounds of humanity that once came from it. Where indeed? Gielgud's eyes and expression characterize the intellectual Hamlet, asking real questions as opposed to just being rhetorical. Gielgud's Hamlet is interested in the metaphysics of death. The skull is pristine, a prop designed to elicit the inquiry.

The Olivier version includes a famous moment. The Gravedigger, Stanley Holloway, smiles at Yorick's skull and places it on the side of the grave he is digging. A shadow approaches. The head of the shadow covers the skull and Hamlet's voice asks, "Whose grave is this, sirrah?" It is a filmic metonymy and, in this case, a prediction that the Gravedigger will soon be digging more graves, including Hamlet's. Hamlet's attitude is as John Mills says, "as though he wishes to occupy his mind and considers this conversation as good a way as any to do it" (Mills, p. 247). He is suddenly interested, however, when Holloway identifies Yorick. Holloway pinches the skull's nose on "mad rogue," then hands the skull over for the typical two-shot. Olivier's "let me see" is a reflex of Hamlet's insatiable curiosity, not a command to the Gravedigger. As in the Gielgud version, Olivier is on the left, so that Hamlet is privileged. The skull is the focal point for a speech that is more meditation than inquisition, "more in wonder," as Mills says than in any other emotion (Mills, p. 247). In this case, the two cheekbones, Olivier's and Yorick's, echo each other, so that the effect is like that of a mirror, an effect enhanced by the edges of the gravestones against which the speech to Yorick is set. As Olivier turns the skull—on a "thousand times"—some dirt falls out, a visual equivalent for the earlier line, cut from the film, about "a great buyer of land, . . . his fine pate full of fine dirt." Olivier turns the skull toward the camera on "Now, get you to my lady's chamber," makes a gesture as if applying cosmetics on "to this favour she must come" and whispers "Make her laugh at that" into the side of the skull, where the ear would have been. Like Gielgud's, Olivier's is a princely Hamlet, cast in a favorable mode, probably inevitably by Olivier, who was also the director. It may be that the end of World War II needed fictional heroes, particularly in drab, Socialist Great Britain, and it may also be that the heroic aristocrat seems dated and out-of-place over forty years later. If so, *Hamlet* and Hamlet continue to serve as a barometer of zeitgeist. Franco Zeffirelli's "praise for Olivier's 1948 film of 'Hamlet' is at best grudging" (Jacobs, p. 21). The film, however, does demonstrate how a location shooting brings a kind of morbid specificity to the scene. Olivier also shows us that film is primarily a *visualization* and, for all of the language, not a verbalization.

Schell's is a likable Hamlet in the film made for Austrian TV, and very awkwardly dubbed for English audiences. Here the Gravedigger affects anger at Yorick as he says "mad rogue." Schell, leaning on an elbow at the side of the grave, laughs on "flagon of Rhenish," a Hamlet with a more "common touch" than either Gielgud or Olivier chose to muster. Schell's "Let me see" is a response to the Gravedigger as he sets the skull aside. A few stark crosses rise behind the initial two-shot, which cuts to a tighter frame with Schell's face angled slightly toward the camera as he addresses the skull, on the left of the frame. Here we have the handsome young man in a leather jacket looking at what he will be, for all of his youth and stature. While Michael Cohen claims that "every Hamlet says 'my gorge rises at [Yorick's skull]'" (Cohen, p. 139), Schell does not. "How abhorred in my imagination" is a response to the image of death, not to its physical manifestations. This, then, is a rather antiseptic version of the scene, as we might expect from a studio rather than a location shooting.

The Burton version, recorded before a live audience in the Lunt-Fontaine Theater in New York, is reminiscent of the Gielgud version, as well it might be, since Gielgud directed Burton. Here again, the action is downstage right, with George Rose's Gravedigger imitating work, Burton seated in the center, Horatio sitting on some wooden steps, slightly upstage. Burton is amused by the Gravedigger's information about Hamlet's madness and Hamlet's exile to mad England, and continues to be amused when faced with Yorick. Burton's is ensemble work, even as the camera closes in. He looks at Horatio on "I knew him" and includes the Gravedigger in "excellent fancy" (Rose agrees with a grunt) and "flashes of merriment." With the latter phrase Burton alludes to the Gravedigger's "poured a flagon of Rhenish on my head once." Burton is upstage of the skull he holds in his hand, the skull very white against Burton's black turtleneck. The camera closes up, but Burton does not acknowledge it. The camera may simulate a spectator's concentration but tends to negate Burton's generous ensemble work. We sense a mild collision of genre here. Burton has stood for his apostrophe to Yorick and sweeps his right hand across the skull as he says, "to this favour." It is a cynical jibe at women and their "paintings" that will become intensely ironic in a moment as Ophelia's funeral arrives. Burton's belief that Yorick is funny still will snap back at his Hamlet when he hears the name of a fresher corpse. Burton's Hamlet is more "public," more en rapport with those around him that most Hamlets, but that quality results at least partly from the fact of a stage performance, where working with the other actors is basic to the play's success. Burton is also a Hamlet who shows the Prince flowing into the position empty apparently since Yorick's death—that of court jester. Burton retained that role in the graveyard. As Mills says, "The Clown's irreverence in the midst of mortal decay neither surprised nor saddened him. He even joined in it, juggling with Yorick's skull before returning it. His apostrophe . . . was a report of an emotion once felt but now scarcely comprehensible—simply another of life's vanities" (Mills, p. 260).

The Plummer film is shot, for the most part, from within the grave that Roy Kinnear is digging. We get a feeling for what hard work it is to dig a grave. Kinnear manages to hit an approaching Hamlet with a shovelful of dirt. Plummer's "Let me see" is urgent and his "poor Yorick!" seems to say "too bad." Michael Caine's Horatio remains in the frame (with a tombstone in the background) until Plummer rises on "where be your gibes now?" Plummer's Hamlet rekindles his affection for Yorick as memory reendows the skull with life. This is one of the best skulls we have! On the left of the frame, it seems to be listening intently to Hamlet's instructions to "get you to my lady's chamber. . . ." Plummer laughs at "to this favor she must come," but the camera cuts to Kinnear's chubby face, very serious and listening intently, as if suddenly recognizing that his own profession is linked with his destiny. Plummer puts the skull back on the Gravedigger's shovel and the skull drops back to the dirt at the bottom of Ophelia's grave on "to what base uses we may return."

The Russian version features a slender Hamlet and a beefy peasant of a Gravedigger. As he identifies Yorick's skull, the Gravedigger holds up the rotting jester's cap in which Yorick had been buried, and shakes the bells with a laugh.* Hamlet reaches across the grave for Yorick's skull. Hamlet is in a heavy robe, reminiscent of an itinerant "holy man." He kneels with the skull in both hands, so that the speech resembles a devotional exercise. He traces the flesh that was there with his right hand on "Here hung those lips." Again we have a two-shot, but a broken Celtic cross sits against the sky beyond Hamlet. The right arm of the cross is missing. Hamlet will die, white shirt against the stones of Elsinore, with his left arm stretched out, an echo of the broken icon in the churchyard. Kozontsev provides a wonderful example of how the film becomes a work of art independent of the script on which it is based.[3]

Roger Livesay, the Gravedigger of the Tony Richardson film, was dying of throat cancer as he made the film. His voice has a raspy quality, as if from having worked for so long on and in the damp earth. The film achieves a wonderful moment when Livesay looks at the skull for a long moment, with rheumy eyes, memories of Yorick and of the Gravedigger's association with him taking over. It is a pause that gives *that* relationship a reality and a poignancy just before the Gravedigger hands the skull to Hamlet. We get the usual tight two-shot, very intense. For some reason, Williamson says, "lady's table." He turns the skull toward the camera on "to this favor." In this version, Williamson's left hand, on the left of the frame, toward the camera, is more prominent than in other versions, thus making emphatic the contrast between the living flesh and the dead bone. Williamson's approach, says Mills, is "a disinterested report of yet another casualty by a veteran hardened to casualties" (Mills, p. 278).

Chamberlain is lying beside the grave, languidly running dirt through his hands as he wonders how long a man will lie in the earth before he rots. This is a "romantic" Hamlet, but one who definitely draws the line with his social inferiors. "Nay, I know not!" seems

---

*Edwin Booth also used a jester's cap in this scene. Cf. Mills, p. 148.

to be Hamlet's response to an insult. The frame incorporates Horatio, made up to resemble the young Coleridge. Hamlet shows a slight excitement as he says "This?" and "Let me see!" He cradles the skull, neatly suggesting how Yorick had borne Hamlet on his back. The camera closes up as he looks at it and says, "Here hung those lips. . . ." He whispers his instructions rather coyly to the skull and repeats Olivier's cosmetic gesture on "to this favour." This is an American Hamlet and a typically bland Richard Chamberlain. The scene does, however, suggest a romantic, even a morbid sensibility emerging in a younger generation responding to the rigidity and authority of the end of the eighteenth century.

McKellen plucks the skull from a pile of dirt as the Gravedigger identifies it. Hamlet picks weeds from the skull and seems almost overcome with grief as he utters, "Alas, poor Yorick!" McKellen becomes fascinated with the gristly skull, indeed his gorge does rise. He turns the skull, which still has its lower jaw attached, wipes at it and sniffs his fingers. "My lady" is meant "to laugh" at the stench. The scene seems to equate the smell with woman, as in Lear's "beneath is all the fiends." Horatio (Julian Curry) wants nothing to do with all of this. He tries to keep his own gorge down by watching the Gravediggers. Hamlet, recognizing that Horatio is hardly sharing his fascination with this awful object suddenly thrusts the skull at Horatio, on "of that fashion in the earth." Horatio makes an effort to be polite, but is really anxious to get the hell out of there. McKellen tosses the skull to the second Digger who flips it to the first, who puts it in a bag for the ossuary. They *do* "play at loggats." This is a splendid sequence, animated by McKellen's dry, back-of-throat voice and inward-looking eyes. His questions, as he turns the skull and pokes at it, are directed at the foul physical aspects of death, as opposed to Gielgud, who wonders *where* the human elements, *where* the unique qualities of Yorick have gone, leaving only an empty and neutral shell behind.

In the BBC version, Jacobi borrows from his Old Vic depiction of Hamlet and dons a skull-mask from the Players' prop-chest before the Play Scene. He makes Polonius the butt of his joke about killing a capitol calf—a prediction, of course, of Hamlet's soon-to-come killing of Polonius—and even gets a laugh from Claudius. This is the only production I have ever seen where Claudius responds to Hamlet-as-jester, although the joke is on Polonius. The skull-mask links Hamlet with Yorick, and the Graveyard Scene links up, in a version of retrospective irony, with the Play Scene. Director Rodney Bennett and Jacobi show us that the script, even this vast and complicated web of language, is a sequence of interrelated moments within a single overriding action.

Jacobi is definitely the aristocrat and the Gravedigger, too familiar, provides sniggering, "in-group" jokes about water and its effect on the dead body.* Jacobi looks twice at Horatio, as if to say, come help me here—I can't handle this person! But Horatio stands at parade-rest and lets Hamlet be bested. Horatio does not approach until Jacobi reaches eagerly for the skull the Gravedigger is setting to the side. Suddenly, Hamlet is interested. Suddenly he is personally involved after all the existential, "Waiting for Godot" generalizations. Godot has unexpectedly arrived: "*He* hath borne me on his back. . . ." Jacobi—unlike so many Hamlets—understands the line about the rising of the gorge. He holds the skull sadly to Horatio to verify that Yorick is indeed "quite chopfallen." His injunction to the skull is intentionally ironic, the words summoning up a courtly function totally contradictory to the fact of the skull, the words moving on the cat feet that scarcely conceal the claws of Jacobi's subtext of cynical near-madness. "Make *her* laugh at that." He means a generic lady of the court, of course, but he means Gertrude and the Ophelia whose funeral train approaches. One problem with the BBC production is that the Graveyard Scene occurs on a bare, studio ramp, so that the sense of "graveyardness" is absent and our own relative disbelief tends to become unsuspended. Jacobi, however, is brilliant, a Hamlet who can make us believe in his sense of princeliness while at the same time suggesting that he could have been a splendid jester. This production allows him that role.

The brilliant if uneven Swedish film, shown in this country as a TV program, begins the scene with a nasty rainstorm. A skull is tossed out of the deepening grave and splats into the muck. Hamlet turns it over with a muddy boot and winks at Horatio as the Gravedigger sings on. Hamlet takes Yorick's skull on a stick and plays with it as if it is a Punch and Judy character and then as a puppet of Julius Caesar, dead and turned to clay. This concept and the Hamlet of Stellen Scarsgaard is brilliant and original. The old Gravedigger looks carefully at Hamlet on "here hung those lips," as if to say, I knew Yorick. So did this man. I should know this man. The Gravedigger turns in disgust from Hamlet's animation of the skull. The Gravedigger is old. His bones *do* ache. This young man has time for such games! Horatio calls Hamlet into the present as the latter plays with the skull just as the macabre funeral dances, à

---

*Cf. "The age is grown so picked that the toe of the peasant comes so near the heels of our courtier, he galls his kibe."

la Bergman, over a murky hillside. Horatio knows whose funeral is coming and recognizes that he and Hamlet are trapped. As the cart nears the grave, one of the bearers kicks the skull of Yorick out of the way. This scene is perhaps the strongest in the Lyth film. The location, weather, and the obscene details of the graveyard and of the funeral soon to ensue so shockingly, suggest how potent a filmic version can be, even if it has been scaled-in-advance for presentation on TV. I hope that this film will become commercially available.

The Kline suffers from an awful Gravedigger, obviously an out-of-work actor hired at the last minute, when Kline, the director, suddenly remembered Act V. The Gravedigger pinches the skull's nose on "mad rogue," giggles, and holds the skull up before Hamlet asks for it, like a high school quarterback anxious to get rid of the ball. It is the "I know what happens next" mistake of the amateur actor. Horatio remains in the frame until the camera closes in. Kline reads the speech with no discernible attitude, except perhaps that which says, "This is Shakespeare—very serious stuff!" He does shake the skull on the work "paint," perhaps the only original and certainly the only effective moment in the sequence. The skull itself is pretty well obscured by Kline's hand. The funeral train approaches far off, down the long perspective of the bare boards of this stage set. The set works well in this production but, as in others, we get no "grave-yardness." And how does Hamlet recognize the individual members of the maimed procession? Because the script says he does, it seems. This production has many excellent aspects and moments, but the Graveyard Scene is not, to my way of thinking, one of them.

The Zeffirelli *Hamlet* demonstrates the advantage of a location for the Graveyard Scene. Hamlet and Horatio ride up on horseback, on their way to Elsinore. The graveyard is on a rugged hillside, disorderly and untended, a few gravestones leaning at angles near the pile of dirt and stones that Ophelia's grave has contributed to the wild grass and weeds. Trevor Peacock crosses himself on "But rest her soul, she's dead," surprisingly, the *only* Gravedigger in this survey to do so. The digger tosses the skull to Hamlet, who carries it away from the grave, sharing his "I knew him" with Horatio, as he had shared his amusement at the Gravedigger and as he would share segments of his speech to Yorick (e.g., "Here hung those lips"). Gibson places the skull on a mound of dirt, providing it with a kind of "body"—a set of shoulders at least. He stares across the frame at the skull, and his gorge rises vividly. On "where be your gibes?" we get a radical close-up, the edge of the skull in the left of the frame, Gibson's eyes and mouth dominating the right and center. Hamlet laughs for a moment, almost losing himself in the past. Here is a

Hamlet with a deep humanity and sense of humor. While the emphasis is on Hamlet's fond memories and on his sadness *as* he remembers, Horatio becomes our alter ego, a recipient of Hamlet's remarks. Regardless of the extreme close-up, Gibson does not play the speech as a soliloquy. Again, the treatment of this scene suggests that the film is the medium for the graveyard. The specificity of grass, dirt, and stones takes us there with a vividness typical of Zefferilli. This is a splendid scene which gives us what TV does not—a vividly realized *graveyard*.

In the *L. A. Story* offshoot, Steve Martin leads Victoria Tennant into a cemetery where lie Benny Goodman and Rocky Marciano—and, of course, Shakespeare, who "wrote *Hamlet, Part 8—the Revenge*" in Los Angeles. An earthmover exits a grave, scattering a flock of pigeons and sending Rick Moranis into the hole to do some final touching up. Moranis asks whether they want to know how long it takes a body to rot. "Boy, do we!" Martin responds. "She used to be a woman," he says upon questioning, "but now she's dead." "Finally—a funny grave digger," says Martin. Moranis forces his insights into rotting upon Martin and Tennant, claiming that "some of those Beverly Hills women, they'll last twelve years." "How come?" Martin asks. Their skin is "polished like a bloody shoe," says Moranis, and "them extra parts" are not biodegradable. Moranis tosses up the skull of The Great Blunderman. "Not so great now, is he?" Martin picks it up. "I knew him. A funny guy. He taught me magic." "A fellow of infinite jest," says Tennant. "That's it!" says Moranis, as if hearing something he has long tried to remember. "He hath borne me on his back a thousand times," she continues. "She knows. She's got it!" cries Moranis, as if hearing fragments out of some vestigial ancestral memory—the voice of the archetype. "Where be your gibes now, your flashes of merriment that would put the table on a roar?" she asks. To the sound of *Close Encounters* music, Martin realizes he is in love. An elfin wind brushes across the graveyard. The gravedigger, who is either from Liverpool or learned to talk from listening to Beatles records, looks on. Finally, when it is established that each of the would be lovers is seeing someone else, Moranis asks, "Can I have your friend's head back?" Martin, who didn't realize that he was still holding it, tosses it back. "Come back and see me," says Moranis. "They all do!" Addressing the skull, he says, "Don't they!"

This sequence suggests that the awareness of death is a spur to love. Neither masters nor mistresses can afford to be coy. The lines from *Hamlet*, heritage of the British schoolgirl Tennant had been years before, seem to be recognized on some level by Moranis, who is our alter ego during this brief episode. Martin is merely falling in love, his character—effectively enough—not knowing why. While some amusing moments do occur in the film, this is the only sequence in which it reaches for any sense of depth—of connectedness with the web of meanings beyond the ways of a particular city. For the most part the film is just another warning to stay away from L.A. I wonder what people who do not know of *Hamlet* would have made of the scene. Would it convey the sense of the linkage between love and death as stressed by Shakespeare, Keats, and Rollo May? It may be that the Zeffirelli *Hamlet* gives some film goers a grasp of the takeoff in *L. A. Story*. If so, fine, since it argues that parody is still possible since the work parodied is still alive to be recognized.

A central question for *Hamlet* on television is—how is the Graveyard Scene to be done in a studio? Certainly the available versions are unconvincing. Film, which can go on location, seems to be the medium in which the scene is best realized. The style and scale of TV seldom works out-of-doors and, with this scene, Shakespeare's own stage might have challenged our suspension of disbelief. And here a televised stage production is not necessarily a solution. The scene on stage incorporates the Gravedigger and Horatio. For the camera to close up during a stage performance on a speech which is not a soliloquy can be awkward, as the Burton sequence suggests.

One stage version I would like to see formatted for TV is the sequence featuring Mark Rylance, who probably has more fun with the skull than anyone since Scarsgaard. The Gravedigger and then Rylance spin the skull around on a stick as if it is a child's toy. The skull whispers the joke about being "chap-fallen" to Rylance, who repeats it. The Gravedigger comes up with a lower jaw so that Rylance becomes a puppeteer moving the jaw up and down on "paint an inch thick." Rylance keeps the skull and, just before the duel, turns it face forward so that it can watch. Never have I seen a prop so splendidly animated. Given careful editing that would include Rylance's partner, the Gravedigger, in the frame, the scene would translate well to TV. The RSC version of the production would also have made a splendid version for television. The ART version in Cambridge, Massachusetts, in 1991 would not have fared so well. Rylance was brilliant, but the American cast, including a weak Claudius and a sexless Gertrude, did not support him well, making his performance a tour de force. And, for some reason, the director, Ron Daniels, blurred the anachronistic contrast between the past and present that made the final scene so powerful in the RSC version, when an armored Fortinbras reclaimed Elsinore for the past.

What do we learn from these different versions of the same scene?

We learn that the script is a set of signals to be decoded by actors and directors in radically different ways, some more effective than others, but none necessarily "wrong." We learn that this scene in his long script has been heavily edited for both film and TV (and stage!). One could track the editing decisions easily and ask what is gained and lost by what is cut, by what is retained? We learn that even an effort at objective description of each version leads to an inevitable evaluation. There's nothing wrong with that—it is merely an admission of subjectivity and an acknowledgment that this script, perhaps more than any other, insists upon a personal response. We learn that certain clichés of the scene seem inevitable, including the two-shot as Hamlet says "Alas!" We learn that, in spite of the similarities, each version is very different than every other version. Much of that has to do, of course, with the characterization of Hamlet. But much also has to do with the directors' decisions about whether Horatio remains in the frame and for how long, and about Hamlet's relationship with Horatio, about whether the Gravedigger remains in the frame and for how long, and about Hamlet's relationship to him or attitude toward him about who Hamlet thinks "my lady" is (if anyone). All of these decisions by actors and directors alter our own response to each version. To notice such details is to build the basis for a reaction. For the first time ever we have available the materials and equipment whereby we can study different versions of a minute sequence in a script, and to learn how Shakespeare accommodates to media undreamed of in his dramaturgy.

We can also raise other questions like, Why is Ophelia buried in Yorick's grave? Shakespeare had a reason for that. In one sense, the grave contains Hamlet's happy past—his friend and alter-ego father, Yorick—and it will soon contain the woman Hamlet loved and that Gertrude hoped would be her son's wife—his future. All in general comes to dust. All quite specifically turns to ash. The grave also, as Marilyn Roberts of Waynesburg State University suggests to me, links Yorick and Ophelia. She too has been a "fool," that is, a sayer of truth, some of it seeming to come from beyond a life she only physically inhabits during her madness. We get, then, as at the end of *King Lear*, a conflation of "Fool" and a dead young woman. No doubt other reasons exist. A concentration on a passing moment in a vast play can lead to a sense of that vastness, of the imponderables it contains, and of the fascinating questions that the script continues to ask us.

4

Gertrude's Story

The women's roles in *Hamlet* are perceived as problems, at least by those who see the play as a "written text." "Without Hamlet, Ophelia has no story," says Lee Edwards (Edwards, p. 36), objecting to patriarchy, while not recognizing that patriarchy *is* Ophelia's "story." She escapes only into the ironic liberation of madness. As Anna K. Nardo suggests of the lass in Ophelia's "St. Valentine's" song, "If she refuses his sexual encounter, she will jeopardize [the] marriage proposal; but because she accepts the offer, he withdraws the proposal. Like Ophelia, the lass is simultaneously treated like a whore and told to be a virgin" (Nardo, p. 196). Get thee to a nunnery—convent *and* brothel. That is Ophelia's story. She is torn between "contradictory messages" (Nardo, p.196), "between two worlds, / One dead, the other powerless to be born," in "paralysis between child-like innocence and adult sexual knowledge" (Nardo, p. 196).[1]

One person can claim that "the part of Ophelia [is] underwritten, from the actress's viewpoint" (Fenwick, BBC, p. 26), but the actress playing Ophelia can disagree: "One thinks wouldn't it be nice if there were a scene where Hamlet and Ophelia are happy together. But . . . you don't actually need it. In the end you find it's all there" (Ward, in Fenwick, BBC, p. 26).

The same debate gathers around the role of Gertrude. A director of *Hamlet* once claimed that the part of Gertrude "isn't written." She has, after all, only 128 of the 3,786 lines in the script. It follows that without *Hamlet*, Gertrude has no story. And that is the point. It is a sociological cliché that women define themselves by their relationships. It is also true of Gertrude that "human actors are expressions of a context, rather than its creators" (Zitner, p. 9). Gertrude is defined by the world around her, and it is, let us grant, a power structure composed of males: King Hamlet, King Claudius, Prince Hamlet, Laertes, future-King Fortinbras, Prime Minister Polonius, and even the significant Osric, so toughly delivered by John McEnery in the Zeffirelli film.

Since a production can—and must—provide a "world" within which the words on the page can come to life, Gertrude's role is a function of prior decisions, particularly about the casting of Claudius, Hamlet, and Ghost. The role *is* written but it is written as a response to the world in which a particular Gertrude finds herself. That world will never be the same from production to production. If, however, Gertrude is an "extroverted sensation" type,[2] her characterization involves, primarily, her response to her environment. Her adaptation rests on the premise that all kings look alike in the dark. If *Measure for Measure* "denies [the] free-play of a [feminine] character" (McLuskie, p. 95), the same is true of *Hamlet*. If women in *Measure for Measure* "are seen *vis à vis* men" and are "objects of exchange within [a] system of sexuality" (McLuskie, p. 97), Gertrude accepts that viewpoint and plays to it. She is, perhaps, one of the women described by an unnamed Smith College official, "who made the choice to get their power from identification, from being wives of doctors, lawyers, or whatever" (Mehren, p. 4C). She is no doubt unaware of her behavioral modification, but it is what works for her. She is at least characterized as *sexual,* an energy an actress must bring to the role, regardless of the paucity of spoken lines, and a fact that would make this a seemingly difficult part for the original boy-actor. That is, until we recall the Cleopatra of some six years later.

T. S. Eliot argues that Gertrude is an inadequate "objective correlative" for Hamlet's approach to nihilism: "it is *because* her character is so negative and insigificant that she arouses in Hamlet the feeling that she is incapable of representing" (Eliot, p. 57, his ital.). Indeed, for the introvert, the extrovert who ignores inner determinants is not only inexplicable but often an absolute barrier to communication between persons of opposite orientations. Gertrude can see nothing wrong about a second marriage to her husband-king's king-brother. Hamlet can discern only a cynical "thrift." We have a lot of cold cuts left over—let's have a wedding! It is not just Gertrude, as Eliot contends, who arouses *Weltschmerz* in Hamlet, of course, but she serves as a focal point, an inadequate because too-limited "objective correlative" for Hamlet's reaction to a battalion of problems, an attack launched at least partly from within—that is, if we accept Hamlet's characterization as incorporating a psyche. At the very least, the role demands the psychic participation of the actor playing it.

Gertrude finds her life within the living zone of production, as opposed to that uninhabited area known as "the text." Gertrude can then evoke in us a response that allows us to accept Hamlet's response to her. In the Zeffirelli film, for example, Glenn Close's Gertrude skips down the castle steps to join Claudius for a horseback ride to a favorite picnic spot. Mel Gibson's Hamlet observes, talking of "unweeded gardens," like a would-be playmate kept after school and watching his pals cavort off to their freedom. The moment is reinforced by the opening, in which Gertrude, like the Wife of Bath, catches Claudius's eye across the corpse of King Hamlet, and, later, by Paul Scofield's morose Ghost. He has a right to his melancholy, of course, but one wonders whether he had been a bit like that in life as well. We do know that he had been away from Elsinore a lot of the time.

This is a rare *Hamlet* in which we see the corpse before it becomes a very human Ghost (as scripted), and one in which the genesis of the Gertrude-Claudius relationship seems to come at the interment. The play mixes its metaphors intentionally: funeral-marriage at the outset, and, in the graveyard, a maimed funeral linked to a last hope for marriage. The interment-flirtation fusion seems an excellent cinematic representation of a theme of the play.[3] For Gertrude to be an "objective correlative" for Hamlet's despair, she must be inhabited by flesh-and-blood within a world where her few lines can find their meanings. With Glenn Close as "co-star," the role seems very much "written," even if the film makes it difficult to accept that she could possibly be Hamlet's mother. The "playmate" thesis, however, helps one to suspend disbelief, even to view Hamlet's displacement by Claudius within an Oedipal configuration.

Mise-en-scène can assist in the "writing" of Gertrude. In the Kozintsev film, Gertrude (Eliza Radzin-Szolkonis) gives a quick and satisfied glance at herself in a mirror held by a lady-in-waiting as she remonstrates with Hamlet: "all that lives must die, / Passing through nature to eternity." She utters the cliché even as her action shows that she is oblivious to its application to *her*. In this wonderfully self-referential film, the instant predicts Hamlet's later look into the mirror of Yorick's skull. In the Peter Wood version (NBC, 1970), Richard Johnson's Claudius attempts to pray before an icon of the Virgin and Child. The camera cuts to Margaret Leighton's Gertrude looking into a mirror and fixing her makeup as she and Polonius prepare for Hamlet's arrival. The transition from scene to scene captures the "virgin/whore" dichotomy that tugs at Ophelia and that Hamlet will, in a sense, soon reimpose upon Gertrude. The moment provides a visualization of the play's "cosmetic imagery": "the harlot's cheek," "paintings," and the "inch-thick" application that will not hide the ultimate skull beneath the cosmetic flesh. In each instance, Gertrude is part of a world, and for each Gertrude that world is full of reassuring surfaces behind which other forces are deeply at work.

As opposed to "the text," "the script" is a set of signals meant to be decoded by the players, who then retransmit their "meanings" to an audience. That audience is the "final cause" of drama, and it, like the production, is never the constant that some would make of "the text."[4]

A brief look at three versions of Gertrude—those of Judy Parfitt in Tony Richardson's 1969 film, Mona Malm in the 1984 Ragnar Lyth film, and Close—will suggest that, even within similar conceptions of the role, a wide variety of valid interpretations can occur. If Gertrude is never the creator of her environment, she is invariably a central manifestation of it.

Richardson's long-lashed, ebony-haired Parfitt embodies Elsinore's decadence. Her dissolute nature becomes obvious in the scene where Polonius presents his explanation of Hamlet's madness to the King and Queen (II.ii.). Anthony Hopkins (Claudius) and Parfitt lie in a huge, ornate bed, seemingly oblivious to Polonius's words. They focus on their food and drink, tearing meat from the bone with their teeth like animals devouring their prey. Gertrude's frivolousness emerges as she briefly defines her sense of Hamlet's behavior: "I doubt it is no other but the main, / His father's death and our o'erhasty marriage." She then engages in a long, passionate kiss with Claudius. The marriage seems not to have been hasty enough for her! She enjoys the continuation of her luxurious life-style—this time with a man who shares it with her—and, it seems, her reawakened sexuality.

Ophelia (Marianne Faithfull) acts both as conscience and judge for Gertrude (IV.v.), an agent whereby Gertrude must recognize the depravity below the luxurious surface. Gertrude enters hurriedly, followed by an attendant who urges her to see Ophelia. Irritated, Gertrude shouts, "I will not speak with her!" and roughly pushes her attendant away. She is finally convinced, however, because the distraught Ophelia is strewing strife within the realm. She displays no interest in the plight of the existential Ophelia, who enters, singing and staring directly at the Queen. The camera moves in for a two-shot featuring the intensity of Ophelia's pale face and Gertrude's furtive wish just to get the interview over with. She is offended, and deals with Ophelia as with a troublesome child who is disrupting a pattern designed by and for the grown-ups. The two-shot emphasizes truth and denial, Ophelia's being a voice from be-

yond the grave intruding upon a sybaritic festival. In a production
which provides for no "field of depth"—it was seemingly designed
with television as a model—the confrontation is moving and intense.
Three white candles flicker in the foreground, illuminating the
Queen's face as Ophelia continues to sing:

> How should I your true love know
> From another one?
> By his cockle hat and staff
> And his sandal shoon.
>
> (IV.4.23–26)

Gertrude's question—"Alas, sweet lady, what imports this song?—
is *pro forma*, a mere echo of social necessity. But the song brings an
inner discomfort to Gertrude. She averts her eyes and stares at the
floor, her shame revealed in the flickering light. Finally, her discomfort grows too great and she tries to escape to a dark corner of the
room. The ghostly Ophelia pursues her, however, singing inces-
santly. The emphasis is, effectively, on Gertrude, the unwilling re-
ceiver of Ophelia's message of sanity, mad only in Elsinore. Ophelia
validates R. D. Laing's thesis about the essential lucidity of seeming insanity.
    Ophelia hands Laertes rosemary and pansies as reminders of her
father's death, all the while casting accusatory glances at the King
and Queen. The camera cuts to their faces, their eyes weighted to
the floor with shame and guilt. Their immoral reign is disintegrating.
Ophelia is a harbinger of this demise, a reminder of their appoint-
ment with Death.
    This Gertrude, then, becomes a function of Ophelia's interruption
of a superficially successful career. If the scene in the royal bedroom
"suggests a miniature Eden," featuring "a platter heaped with richly
colored fruit" (Litton, p. 112), Ophelia represents, ironically, the
coming of consciousness to Gertrude. The conflict between the two
women, one mad, the other unsuccessfully resisting awareness, is
brilliantly delineated.
    Moral decadence and luxury also taint the world of Lyth's produc-
tion. Gertrude (Mona Malm) captures the ubiquitous corruption
within the walls of Elsinore, in this case, the abandoned Nobel dyna-
mite factory. The castle is Gertrude's playground, as well as a site
for the perpetuation of her political career. While this Gertrude is
often disgusted by Frej Lindquist's consistently ingratiating Claudius, he *is* King and a partner for the ongoing heyday of her ma-
tronly lust.

The camera pans the outer chamber of the royal bedroom, where stand the attendants to the pair. Their stony faces contrast with the erotic moans coming from the inner room. Suddenly, the Queen emerges, clad only in a sheet. Her lack of modesty embarrasses her servants.

Later, Lyth reminds us of Gertrude's shockingly overtly sexuality. During the Closet Scene (III.iv.), just prior to the Ghost's appearance to Hamlet, young Hamlet (Stellen Scarsgaard) erupts into a violent rage. He is as disgusted with her as she is with Claudius—no one in this Elsinore reflects any vestige of a "good relationship." Appropriately, Hamlet tries to strangle Gertrude with one of the foul sheets from her own bed.

Pernilla Wallgren's Ophelia reinforces the degradation that Gertrude's example has visited upon Elsinore. After Polonius suggests that Hamlet's lunacy may stem from Ophelia's rejection of his advances, Gertrude leads Ophelia off for some friendly chatter. This young woman may be a useful pawn in Gertrude's extemporaneous power-game. After the Nunnery Scene, however, Gertrude simply turns her back on the weeping Ophelia. Nothing to build on there! Time passes. Ophelia is jostled roughly during the tumult attendant upon the breakup of "Gonzago." She wipes vigorously at her mouth, trying to remove the offending "paintings." She awakens in a cell-like room, wearing only a loose cotton shift. Bright, white light enters the cubicle through its only window. It is the light of the world outside Elsinore, a world open to Laertes, but so far denied Ophelia. Her funeral will occur under rain and cloud. Above her cot hang two Holbeinesque portraits of the King and Queen. That of Gertrude catches her eye. The camera cuts to the Queen, stiff and cold, the canvas cracking across her face. The camera cuts back to Ophelia's distraught face. She rises, shouting: "Where is the beauteous majesty of Denmark?" She seeks a lost essence, a splendor gone from her world. She leaves her room and enters a hallway with many closed doors. Behind one door she encounters a priest and servant having sex. She accosts Horatio, who would rather read his book. Still shouting her question, she rushes through the unkempt room of state. Gertrude, elegantly dressed, is enjoying an afternoon garden party on the castle lawn. Warned of Ophelia's approach by a discreet attendant, she says "I will not speak with her," and smiles at her guests. Ophelia breaks through, however, as the Queen smiles and attempts to ignore her. Ophelia grabs the Queen and says "He is dead and gone, lady." Gertrude must now get rid of this disrupter of decorum. She turns her back, again, but Ophelia will not go away, so Gertrude and her servants shove her back into the castle. The dogs that bark behind the crowd remind us of the dangerous conjectures sounding outside the walls of Elsinore, and that Ophelia's status is now that of an offending animal. But she was as the rest of the inhabitants of the castle are now—functioning on instinct only thinly veiled by apparent rationality. So, again, she is an agent of what is to come.

Now in a dark room—the Ophelia medium—Ophelia sings to the King and Queen, only Claudius showing some concern for her plight. "I thank you for your good counsel," Ophelia says, playing at queen but alluding to her abandonment. She exits through two huge doors, bright light streaming in from the outside. She walks slowly into the light. A long shot of her exit creates an ironically ethereal effect. She can find illumination only in death.

Later, she humiliates Gertrude and Claudius as she distributes her flowers. She passes out weeds as she recalls the names she learned when her world seemed to burgeon with edenic possibilities, reminding us, however, that it has become an "unweeded garden," possessed merely by "Things rank and gross." She throws weeds representing fennel and columbines at Gertrude, who flinches. The emphasis would seem to be on the flattery, deceit, and disloyalty Ophelia has suffered at Gertrude's hands. Ophelia confronts Claudius, rubbing his groin and saying, "You must wear your rue with a difference." His sexuality, it seems, has brought him only sorrow. Although Ophelia has been overwhelmed by the corruption surrounding her, her madness gives her a voice for her disillusionment and insists that those responsible know their guilt. She tosses the remaining weeds at Claudius and Gertrude, who cower helplessly, like children suffering a parental castigation, as the weeds shower their faces. Ophelia makes a final exit into the blinding light, singing peacefully. The King and Queen remain in a dark world of their creation.

Glenn Close's overt sexuality is balanced by a girlish naïveté absent in Parfitt and Malm. Close's vulnerability evokes sympathy for the widow, a status stressed in Zeffirelli's film as Gertrude throws herself sobbing at the foot of King Hamlet's bier. But like both Parfitt and Malm, Close finds Elsinore a vast playground. Her activities are more like childish amusements than the shockingly unscrupulous behavior in which Parfitt and Malm indulge. Close runs through the castle giggling, as smiling ladies scurry behind her pretty pastel robes. Along with a degree of innocence, Close displays maternal qualities as Parfitt and Malm do not, although it is with Ophelia and *not* Hamlet that Close acts as a mother. At a banquet, the two women are seated far from each other. Claudius instigates a toast amid the merrymaking and music. Ophelia seems overwhelmed by this great public feast. Gertrude makes eye contact with Helena Bonham-Carter's Ophelia and gives the younger woman a sympathetic smile. Ophelia continues to look at the Queen, as if wondering whether she has found a friend.

Zeffirelli deletes Gertrude's "I will not speak with her" and shows a Gertrude eager to come to the younger woman's aid. In a film where people observe each other from above and below, Gertrude sees Ophelia from a castle tower as Ophelia meanders pathetically along a castle roof. Close puts her hand to her heart in a gesture of distress and concern. As Ophelia massages the codpiece of a stoic guard, Gertrude turns from the window and exclaims

> To my sick soul, as sin's true nature is,
> Each toy seems prologue to some great amiss.
> So full of artless jealousy is guilt,
> It spills itself in fearing to be split.
>
> (IV.5.17–20)

The Queen expresses remorse that Ophelia's madness has evoked and a consequent fatalistic outlook. She has begun to grow up in an atmosphere which, as Ophelia proves, cancels the positive possibilities of maturity.

She descends to meet Ophelia, but is unprepared for Ophelia's fury. Singing "He is dead and gone, lady," Ophelia corners Gertrude, who caresses the medallion of King Hamlet she wears around her neck. She begins to weep as Ophelia exits, stopping to kiss the Queen's hands, still clasping the medallion. "Come, my coach!" Ophelia commands to her subjects as she makes an imagined royal departure. She has symbolically displaced Gertrude as the woman who controls Elsinore. This transition is brilliantly captured. A low angle shot shows a sullen Ophelia, eyes rimmed in black. Behind her, the inner structure of the castle—the keep—circles her head, a huge and oppressive crown for Queen Ophelia of Denmark. Gertrude is left sobbing, while Ophelia wails loudly as she is led away by two ladies who join in this chorus of grief.

Ophelia hands out flowers to the King (Alan Bates), Queen, and Laertes (Nathaniel Parker). Gertrude now wears a large crucifix, signaling her wish for atonement for the sinful past she now recognizes through Ophelia. She accepts "fennel and columbine" which Ophelia gently hands her with merely an averted, guilt-filled gaze, as opposed to the more abrasive encounters between the women in the Richardson and Lyth films.

Each director includes Gertrude's apostrophe to Ophelia:

> Sweets to the sweet! Farewell.
> I hop'd thou shouldst have been my Hamlet's wife.
> I thought thy bride-bed to have deck'd, sweet maid,
> And not have strew'd thy grave.
>
> (V.1.237–240)

In each production, it is Ophelia, as well as Hamlet, who clefts Gertrude's "heart in twain." She experiences a brief and ironic fall into grace—and a grave. The poison—symbolic punishment for excessive appetite—awaits her. It is too late for Gertrude by the time of the Graveyard Scene, but her sincerity in each production is made clear.

The inclusion of Gertrude's "Sweets to the sweet" gives the actress a point toward which to move. That point rephrases the play's concern with oxymoron—the linkage of marriage-funeral that both Claudius and Hamlet made earlier. It also permits Gertrude to express regret as her own divided self looks upon an alter ego, an Ophelia forever cut off from the future for which both women hoped. A director can show Gertrude separating from Claudius via a suddenly available alternate staircase, as in the Olivier film, and a Gertrude delightedly reunited with her son, as in the Zeffirelli film. The script, however, seems to suggest that she remains torn between irreconcilable roles of wife and mother at least until her awareness that the drink is poisoned. Her hope that Ophelia become Hamlet's wife does not necessarily exclude Claudius, the transitional figure through which succession might have been achieved, indeed a King who had named Prince Hamlet his heir early on. By the time of the graveyard, it is too late for Ophelia, almost too late for Hamlet, and too late for Gertrude. Her awareness can be seen perhaps as a mere projection *upon* Ophelia—the "it cannot happen to *me*" pattern— and thus merely a representation of the Gertrude we have known all along. What I think the script suggests, however, is that Gertrude recognizes that her heart and her hopes have been cleft in twain, and that nothing can put them together again. The actress, in other words, points her character ahead to an awareness of irreconcilable divisions cracking through the surfaces that had provided illusory comfort until Gertrude looked into her own grave.

As Lyth's Gertrude attempts at the end to reconcile with Hamlet, he rejects her brutally, as he had Ophelia earlier. This is, clearly, a different ending than Olivier provides. There, Eileen Herlie's Gertrude, suspects the wine and tries to save her son by drinking it.

Gibson clowns at the duel for his delighted mother—"Look, Ma, no hands!" Each ending tells a different story of the relationship between Gertrude and Hamlet, just as each tends toward a similar version of the relationship between Gertrude and Ophelia.

Editing, casting, emphasis, and zeitgeist create different *Hamlets*. The script is primarily "Hamlet's story," although he neither understands it nor gets to finish it. Gertrude's story is subordinate to Hamlet's, but probably more understandable. It is to be understood, however, in different ways within different productions played before different audiences. Even spectators within the same audience, however, are likely to disagree about what they understand as "Gertrude's story."*

---

*This chapter was written in conjunction with Nancy P. Connors of Bowdoin College.

5

Playing Space: The Kline *Hamlet*

I have become convinced that televised Shakespeare works best when cameras show us a live performance. We cannot be part of the live audience, but we can be invited to participate with an approximation of the energy system and asked to suspend our disbelief and participate in the completion of the fiction. That television does not otherwise issue an invitation to our imaginations does not mean that the Shakespearean script must be diminished to the formats of normative TV. Live productions do work on TV, comedies like the Stratford, Canada, *Shrews*, the ACT *Shrew*, the ART *Dream*, the RSC *Comedy of Errors*, and the occasional tragedy, like the Papp-Sherin *King Lear*, with James Earl Jones, and the Sarah Caldwell *Macbeth*. While stage acting is not the microacting that television demands, the "event" of theater, together with the careful placement of cameras and microphones, and granted *good* stage acting, can create a balance between the media.[1]

Given the difficulties involved in televising live stage productions, the next best format is the stage production reformatted for TV. This approach has the advantage of performances that have matured in front of audiences, a production that has tightened over time, often squeezing considerable time from the production without cutting any lines, and a strong sense of what the relationships are in this version of the script. Productions that have worked well in this format are the Miller *Merchant*, and the Nunn *Antony and Cleopatra*, *Macbeth*, and *Othello*. A production that works reasonably well in this model is the Kevin Kline *Hamlet*. Kline claims that "You needn't exclude the big dramatic stuff, because I think the camera can contain that—particularly because with a box that small, I think *you better* get pretty big" (Pall, p. 36). He defies "the conventional wisdom that deems television too 'close-up' a medium to allow for 'grand' theatrical acting" (Pall, p. 36). "But," Kline says, "you . . . can bring the audience to the action and get those private, intimate exchanges" (Pall, p. 36). As I shall suggest, however, I found the television version of this production to be lacking in both "big dramatic stuff," *and* "those private, intimate exchanges."

Kline's television director, Kirk Browning, tempers Kline's enthusiasm. "Shakespeare is so theatrical. It is really so antithetical, in some sense, to television. Kevin's knowledge of 'Hamlet', his feeling for it, this aspect, obviously he knew. Whether he was going to be able to translate that successfully into a technique that took advantage of the medium was the question" (Pall, p. 35). The answer is that Kline is only partly successful—as director and as a Hamlet, who as Frank Rich says, does not express "the soul of a great role" (Pall, p. 35). However an actor does get to the heart of that mystery, I do not sense in Kline's performance the clash of actor with role that creates that third entity known as Hamlet. This is, on TV at least, a "safe" Hamlet, a conventional Hamlet, with the exception of too many tears coursing his cheeks, and a conventionally directed Hamlet, and only occasionally the "passionate, active, thoughtfully ironic young man" that Walter Goodman discerns in Kline's television performance (Goodman, p. 31).

It may be, however, that Kline is as much a victim of format as beneficiary.

Mary Maher describes the adaptation from stage to TV:

> Designer John Arnone took Robin Wagner's stage set, of which the major playing area was a thrust stage about 25 feet by 25 feet, and turned in on its axis in order to create a slightly raised (about three feet) diamond-shaped stage that fit into the television studio. On the frontal sides of the diamond roamed four cameras, shooting at all times, and recording the play from each of their respective angles and points of view. The stage was surrounded by modular set-pieces—columns, red arrases, stair units, a platform stage, runway ramps—which could be arranged and rearranged (or even eliminated) to create different areas within Elsinore. The set was also surrounded on three sides with a painted scrim which was lit to represent time and place. (Maher, "Kline," p. 11)

Kline, meanwhile, found that working with film cameras was not the same thing as working with video cameras: "With one-camera film, you can create infinite permutations of moves. You're free to go wherever you want. But with four cameras, you can't do those wonderful tracking shots, because you're going to bump up against the other cameras" (Pall, p. 36). Certainly the effect of the production is televisual and not filmic. The effect, as in the origins of the production, is much closer to stage, than film.

What that means is that the stage-in-studio with cameras lurking at the edges permits long sequences to be played in the same space as, obviously, they were played on Shakespeare's stage. This seems obvious enough until we compare the "stage" approach to, for example, the Zeffirelli firm, which is "fluid and excitingly paced," as Edward Quinn says (Quinn, p. 1), but in the ways that film is.

Zeffirelli breaks I.2—the Coronation Scene—into three main locations, and an outside the castle and an inside the castle site as well. The potential relationship between Gertrude and Claudius has been established by eye contact over the corpse of King Hamlet in the first scene, which Zeffirelli substitutes for the Parapet Scene. We are not surprised then to find a demure Gertrude crowned and sitting next to Claudius, each enthroned, as he delivers his opening speech and reaches for Gertrude's hand on "taken to wife." They sit in front of giant stone windows which echo with trumpets and applause. Polonius signals that the ceremony is over. The camera cuts to Laertes entering a library room and being asked "What's the news with you?" by Claudius. When Laertes asks to return to France, Claudius rolls his eyes, then shares a smile with Laertes as Polonius gives her permission. Claudius give a jubilant Laertes a kiss on each cheek. The camera cuts to Gertrude running down the castle steps to a waiting Claudius. They kiss at length. Gertrude nods toward a closed door. We'd better do something, she seems to say. They enter a room, Gertrude calling "Hamlet? Hamlet?" Claudius following with a goblet of wine in hand. "Now my cousin, Hamlet, and my son." Hamlet, seated, says "A little more than kin, and less than kind." Gertrude laughs as Hamlet says, "too much in the sun." As Claudius sits down, Hamlet stands up, as if unwilling to accept any equal status with the King. Gertrude has her right arm around a model of a soldier in chain mail—a synecdoche for King Hamlet which she embraces unconsciously. Claudius gives his "courtier, cousin, and our son" speech, holds his arms out as if to say to Gertrude, "There—I have done what I can!" and exits. The dogs outside, waiting to hunt, yammer excitedly. Gertrude continues the plea, personally, almost romantically, looking past Hamlet's shoulder with her own veiled eyes at an irretrievable past. Hamlet's "Seems, madam!" is to her alone—and flattens out a bit without its bite at Claudius ("actions that a man might play"). Hamlet agrees to "obey" Gertrude, and hers is the commendation of his "gentle and unforc'd accord." She runs down a set of inner steps into the palace, is helped into a blue robe by a giggling attendant, and runs out the door again. Hamlet broods in his room about "solid flesh." He looks out the window. "Things rank and gross in nature possess it merely"—Gertrude is running down the outer steps again. "That it should come to this!" Claudius leans from his horse to kiss Gertrude on the word "satyr." She rides gaily off on a white horse, courtiers oohing and ahing, Hamlet still complaining. He shuts his leaded windows. "Frailty, thy name is woman!" Gertrude, Claudius, and party, ride into the deceptive sunlight just outside the castle grounds. Laertes enters a room. "Dear Ophelia!"

The sequence—from "Though yet of Hamlet, our dear brother's death," voiced-over the parapets of Elsinore before we get into the huge room of state, to Laertes finding Ophelia—takes a little more than seven minutes. It slows down—with some violin music—for Gertrude's interview with Hamlet, but picks up the brisk Claudius rhythm, to which Gertrude is delightedly adjusting herself, immediately thereafter. She thinks she has solved her own "transition" problem between son and new husband as she rides out into the sunlit meadows.[2]

One may quarrel with the story Zeffirelli tells, but he tells it brilliantly and economically, establishing relationships and their tensions and using location superbly to signal mood and movement. Field of depth does not necessarily rob the presentation of emotional depth, something that can happen when virtuosity of camera technique becomes the "story." When we come to TV, certainly the opportunity for subtlety and nuance does not necessarily deepen emotional content but often reveals its absence.

Kline gives us a condensed version of the opening scene and even includes the clock striking at the beginning, a sound the subsequent scene calls for but which directors seldom provide. I.2 is an almost eleven-minute sequence carried out within the same space. Gertrude and Claudius kiss beside a column before going "on stage." The court is celebrating with wine and women in 1930ish gowns. Claudius shakes several nearby hands after "for all, our thanks" and then crumples Fortinbras's pestering messages, to laughter and a smile of admiration from Gertrude. Carefully selecting his agenda items, Claudius turns to Laertes, knowing he can deal with this one with the effect of power, magnanimity, and largess. He then turns to Hamlet, seated and looking away, downstage right, with Gertrude in the middle of the frame, looking at Hamlet, and Claudius upstage left. The court, of course, turns toward Hamlet. Thus the camera captures Claudius's application of power. Fortinbras and Laertes have been warm-ups. Gertrude's "Good Hamlet" is private, but she turns on "Look like a friend on Denmark," making it a public request. For some reason, Hamlet's "Seems, Madam!" is delivered via a close-up, as if a soliloquy. Its quality of *indictment* cannot come through. Claudius's "unmanly grief" is privately delivered to a wholly unresponsive Hamlet. Claudius then makes his announcement that Hamlet is the heir. The court applauds. Claudius regrets, as he tells Hamlet that his return to Wittenberg is "most retrograde to our desire." Claudius achieves a good imitation of pressure applied with reluctance. For some reason, a tear comes down Hamlet's cheek at this point.

This is a reasonably effective second scene, dominated by Claudius's dictation of scenario. He is a very plausible King, with a sure sense of timing and a politician's ability to permit his constituents to participate in his sense of good fortune. He signals some insecurity by reaching too often for the wine goblet, but he rationalizes his thirst by dictating this or that cause for celebration. He does not get enough resistance from Hamlet. It is no contest. Claudius is cautious around Hamlet, we infer, because he is Gertrude's son and because, as Crown Prince, he might become a political rival. But Hamlet is certainly passive at the beginning of this new reign and it seems almost as if Claudius makes him Crown Prince to cheer him up.

The strengths and weaknesses of this *Hamlet* as *television* production can be summed up by Kline's treatment of the arrival of Rosencrantz and Guildenstern. After his game with Polonius, which is not very funny, Hamlet falls asleep unconvincingly, his book over his ear. His old school friends awaken him. Rosencrantz is a skinny, bow-tied aristocrat. Guildernstern is a suave black who contrasts splendidly with Peter Francis James's open-faced and honest-eyed black Horatio. Some interesting moments occur between Hamlet and Rosencrantz and Guildenstern. He shakes his hands near his head on "thinking makes it so," suggesting that thought itself is madness. His "No such matter" is enraged, as if he suddenly recognizes that he is stuck with them. He realizes instantly, however, that he is being inhospitable and mitigates his anger to an attempt at "friendship." He says "That *you* must teach *me*," suggesting, against the meaning, I think, that they are some sort of pedagogical mission. He says "I have an eye of you" *to* them, instead of making the line the aside it usually is. He forces them to kneel and holds them close to him as he says that he has "forgone all custom of exercise" and pushes them down to look at the sky for his "foul and pestilent congregation of vapors." They look like schoolboys on a picnic looking up at the sky (in an overhead shot). His "What a piece of work is a man," is also given a close-up, with the effect of a soliloquy, but here, at least Hamlet has something to do with his eyes other than just to avoid the camera. During other soliloquies—particularly Hamlet's "guilty creatures" and Claudius's "My words fly up"—the actor's eyes virtually circle the lens but avoid looking at it directly. Derek Jacobi used the camera extensively in his BBC *Hamlet*—it was the only element with which he could communicate in an Elsinore resistant to his insights about it and humanity in general. His Hamlet was the intellectual in a police state.

Maher discusses the Jacobi technique, its effect and its rationale:

> the fundamental issue here is the issue of *audience*. [The BBC *Hamlet* eschews] the usual theatre tradition of the performance of the tragic soliloquy. . . . The television viewer is only rarely placed in the position of 'overhearing' a character "thinking aloud." . . . The soliloquy still functions dramatically as it should in *Hamlet;* it is still a window to Hamlet's mind, providing plot information, enabling him to make sense out of his feelings as well as comment on the action. But because of the medium, we are taken one step further Hamlet becomes a "narrator." He takes on the role of the viewer's interpreter and commentator—the viewer becomes "dear reader"—and we see all of the events through Hamlet's eyes. . . ." "Media" reasons [exist] for using the one-on-one camera technique. Primarily, camera-lens-contact increases and intensifies the audience's identification with the character. And this objective squares with the stated intention of the Time-Life Video producers: to make these productions a repeatable (and purchasable) repository, widely available for educational use. A direct-address soliloquy is frankly less boring and less likely to lose a potentially inattentive viewer because it is *interactive*. And *interaction*—whether it be between two characters in a scene or between the video-viewer and the on-camera speaker—is what keeps people "tuned in." . . . I maintain that the play is changed—now we see all of the action of Hamlet through his eyes and every 700 lines or so, we check in with him. [This approach] tends to take the dramatic form and to transform it to a more novel-like status . . . the speaker looks into that lens, he/she makes eye contact with each and every one of us *individually* and *en masse*. . . . The subjective camera . . . transforms the television soliloquy into an interpersonal experience, rife with self-disclosure. . . . The actor's autonomy is extended, enlarged, and so is his power over *us*—the viewing audience—to cast *us* into roles as well. (Maher, "Jacobi," pp.16–18)

One of the dangers of the script, and of Hamlet's soliloquies, is that Hamlet is likely to become "our moral interpreter," as Robert Ornstein suggests (Ornstein, p. 235). That danger would be increased were Hamlet given access to us, as Jacobi is. The danger is diminished in the BBC because of Jacobi's frenetic performance— not one with which *we* cautious televiewers wish to associate—and because Jacobi often pulls his insights *into* himself; "Abuses *me*, to damn *me*." The problem could be mitigated (it is not in the BBC production) by giving Claudius some contact with the camera for his "O, my offence is rank" soliloquy—it would be chilling to have him suddenly impale us with "My fault is past" (III.3.51), and perhaps by giving Gertrude the same privilege for her "To my sick soul. . . ." aside (IV.5.17–20). That would at least establish other narrators and suggest that Hamlet is not author of his own masterfiction but rather a "limited point-of-view," like Strether in *The Ambassadors,* vulnerable to having his self-constructed art forms ripped apart by sudden intrusions of "reality." In a sense Hamlet's "Mousetrap" and Strether's Lambinet each trap their creators and expose the games *they* are playing, even if others may be exposed in the process.

If Hamlet does not address the television camera, our role is that of someone watching someone else talk to himself. His thoughts are no doubt interesting, but overhearing someone talking to himself is not very interesting unless the speaker is talking about the eavesdropper. I also think that television can incorporate some of the Brechtian "alienation" technique—that is, the actors reminding us that we are watching a play and not some "fourth-wall" version of "reality." Jacobi did that bitingly, and the Kline production, particularly given its proximity to stage productions, could have done so as well. Maher suggests that Kline's 1986 Hamlet for Ciulei "appealed rather openly to an uncomfortable theater audience in the solo speeches" (Maher, "Kline," p. 11). Kline's television character, however, is "decidedly inward, exploring an interior madness as if it were a canker, an inner sorrow. Consequently, his soliloquies were given to himself, not to an outer audience, and on television that means he never made eye contact with the camera lens" (Maher, "Kline," pp. 11–12). That inwardness, akin to the sorrows of young Werther, is carried over into the *non*soliloquies, making Hamlet more isolated than he is already and falsifying, I think, his position on stage, where he would have to do some ensemble acting and where others would be forced to react to him. The close-up camera capturing that ubiquitous tear simplifies the job of the TV director, perhaps, but it tends to make the production a series of *speeches* without a world around them and without an action fitted to them. Given that tendency and the inclination toward darkness and monochromatic settings and costumes so trendy in the later 1980s and early 1990s, we get the dull production values associated with TV and the dullness too often associated with Shakespeare. The action style as Robert Hapgood says of televised Shakespeare, is "excessively subdued, more restrained than suits the text or indeed would suit plays originally written for television" (Hapgood, pp. 277–78).

The camera moves to a three-shot as Rosencrantz and Guildenstern chuckle at Hamlet's "Man delights not me." The three sit up, then stand as Polonius arrives to announce the coming of the Players.

Kline takes Guildenstern's hands, places them around Hamlet's neck and pretends that Guildenstern is strangling him. It is a wonderful piece of antic business that bewilders Guildenstern, who looks down at his hands then shakes his head at Rosencrantz. It reminded me of the splendidly zany Hamlet of Mark Rylance for RSC in 1989, but was virtually a unique moment here. Later, Hamlet picked Rosencrantz's pockets on "pickers and stealers," but little else seems spontaneous. Maher says that

> the litheness and playfulness of the stage production were lost on the TV screen, partly because each shot had to be tightly rehearsed and planned [and partly because] the live audience inspired Kline's inventiveness and improvisation; Kline's physicalized sense of play and humor provided the wit and the heroic dash in Hamlet's character—that element was underexploited in the television production, partly owing to the medium partly owing to time restrictions. (Maher, "Kline," p. 12)

Maher makes very good arguments for televising the *actual* stage production, where some of that spontaneous energy might get transmitted to the TV audience via the medium of the live audience. The latter, of course, is always in danger of becoming a "laugh track," but that problem is probably more than balanced by the qualities that Maher attributes to Kline's live performance, which, no doubt, would coincide with the experience of many actors enlivened and encouraged by an audience. Jane Howell, indeed, brought people on to the set of her *Henry VI* productions to provide precisely that energy. Howell shows that the studio need not block superb productions and performances, but the Kline production seems to have been diminished by its move from stage to a "stagelike" studio which imposes restrictions and which removes the continuum that an audience provides. My own sense that some of the Kline production is "flat" may also be an unconscious response to my knowledge that, for all of the four cameras at work, they are cameras, and not observing imaginations working with the actors to piece out imperfections by half-perceiving and half-creating.

The play, of course, picks up when the Players arrive, largely because Hamlet himself comes alive and shares his sudden enjoyment with us through our alter egos, these unexpected visitors to Elsinore. And—Hamlet comes up with a plan, at last assuming control of the deceptive surfaces that have been confusing him thus far. The Players appear, shadowy and distant. Hamlet greets them with a ceremonial bow, viewed from a high angle shot behind him. He plucks a dagger from the Player's props, and threaten Polonius on "old grandsire

Priam." Polonius affects fear then laughs, along with the Player who will play the Queen in "Gonzago." It is a deft foreshadowing of what will happen to Polonius as Gertrude looks on, Hamlet gives his "Hecuba" speech on the stage set up for "Gonzago," catches himself overacting—as Kline does several times—then returns to the histrionics. They are no doubt a characteristic of Hamlet, which he tends to despise in himself, but the tendency should not be overdone by the actor, as Hamlet well knows. That such overacting occurs *on stage* here offers a kind of formal excuse for Hamlet and possibly for Kline. But TV as "cool medium" is merciless with overacting and is unkind to Kline on several occasions. As Mark C. Miller says, "passion . . . rarely registers on television, except as something comic or suspect" (Miller, p. 49). As ominous music swells and Hamlet reaches "the play's the thing" and he *might* just break with convention and look at the camera, it cuts from a close-up to a long shot of Hamlet on the stage. The moment is approached than backed away from. Why? Because, it seems, it might really have been exciting. The *reason* for the long shot, of course, is to remind us of the stage in a production that has some sense of the theatrical metaphor that sustains so much of the imaginative activity of the script, but the reasonable approach erases a greater opportunity to make a link between Hamlet and us.

Ciulei's 1978 Arena production created a brilliant moment when the Players bounced out to begin "Gonzago" in gaudy Elizabethan costumes that contrasted with the Prussian gray of the court. Kline's "Gonzago" is impressive, with three candelabra on each side of the stage, and a red curtain as a backdrop (behind which Polonius will be stabbed later) that matches Gertrude's low-cut velvet gown. Ophelia is in a low-cut black gown, startlingly reminding us of the earlier Hamlet, as if she is taking on some of his repressed angst. Hamlet has set chairs on stage for the King and Queen, and leads Gertrude to one of them, Claudius, of course, following. Hamlet then leads Ophelia to a chair to the side of the stage and deals with her brutally, giving a visual equivalent to Lacan's joke about the derivation of her name. Dumb Show and Prologue are cut, so that the Player King enters with "Full thirty times hath Phoebus's cart." The Player King and Queen wear crowns much more ornate than those of their counterparts upstage, although Gertrude sports a magnificent matching tiara and necklace all of diamonds. The Player King wears an ornate, spangled doublet which contrasts with the modern but not specific and, fortunately, not eclectic, costumes of the court.* We do not get the vivid contrast that Ciulei's Players created, however. Kline's Players neatly thread their performance through the court. The Player King and Queen play "if once a widow, ever I be wife" directly in front of Claudius and Gertrude, an economy of camera that allows us to observe the actors and the reactions of their alter egos simultaneously. Hamlet gets between Gertrude and Claudius for the colloquy about the Mousetrap, then introduces Lucianus. Unlike Jacobi, who interrupts his own production by invading the actors' space, Kline withdraws. Lucianus comes down in front of the platform where Gonzago sleeps, pulls a dagger, then opts for poison. He drives the dagger into the boards. Claudius, behind, takes a quick sip of wine as Lucianus pours the poison into Gonzago's ear. On Hamlet's "Gonzago's *wife!*" Claudius, standing, drops his glass goblet with a smash. Polonius says "The King rises," quite formally, a command for others to do the same. Claudius, shaken, says "Give o'er the play. Give me some light. Away!" and stumbles out. The surprised Gonzago gets up and goes off. Hamlet picks up the dagger, gives Ophelia a whirl, and threatens to stab Claudius's chair.

Subsequently, Hamlet practices a thrust with the recorder on Rosencrantz on "make you a wholesome answer." Hamlet, of course, has a prop for "speak daggers." He can barely resist using the dagger on the kneeling Claudius. Here was a good chance to use a voice-over, as in the Olivier film, but Hamlet speaks his lines and even crosses in front of the oblivious Claudius at one point in the soliloquy. Given the theatrical premises of this production, we are willing so suspend our disbelief up to a point. If the director will create some space between Claudius and Hamlet or if *here* we get a shot of Hamlet speaking to himself, without having Claudius in the frame half a foot away, we may believe this sequence. Even on stage, however, as when Roger Rees threatened Brian Blessed from a distance of a few inches in the 1985 RSC production, our credulity can be strained. The positive element in the Kline rendition is his scarcely restrained dagger. It is primed to leap at Polonius without any signal from Hamlet's "conscious intention."

"Ophelia," says Goodman in reviewing this production, "is an annoying case anyway" (p. 31). That may be. Joseph Sommers's

---

* In a panning of the 1986 production, John Simon said "it is surely ill-advised to set the play too close to our own time, and thus intensify an anachronism without achieving contemporaneity. [Since the] costumes can't decide whether they are Victorian, Edwardian, or Georgian, confusion spreads farther" (Simon, p. 95).

Polonius, "a plausible, well-intentioned, self-impressed bureaucrat," as Goodman says (p. 31), arouses a little jealousy in Ophelia by his roughish good-humor as Laertes takes off for Paris, but this Ophelia seems to have induced her own psychic problems. We do not get the chilling Polonius of, for example, Patrick Godfrey in the 1989 RSC *Hamlet*, whose apathy toward his motherless offspring forced them to seek more than normal affection from each other. Diane Venora's Ophelia for Kline is at once lonely and madly in love with an icily indifferent Hamlet.

Ophelia becomes a disaster during her first mad scene (IV.5.20 ff.). I attribute this to the direction and for that no excuse exists since Kline, the director, does not have to direct himself during this scene. Here we get the "wedding dress" Ophelia, although Venora has doffed her gown at the door and plays the scene in a slip. She has worked out every detail of her performance—when to sing; when to croak; when to hop in time to her song; when to amble; when to jig; when to lisp; when to insist that Gertrude become a partner in her dance; how to suggest that Claudius is her illicit, fantasy lover. But all of this is more painful for the audience than for the court because of the scene's exclusive focus on the deranged Ophelia. When the scene works it does so because Ophelia competes against what else is going on, and/or because Ophelia creates ironic levels within her performance—being all *too* sane (cf. R. D. Laing), singing on key and very prettily, for example. Gertrude does not have to be sitting there waiting for Ophelia to show up just because that is what the script says is about to happen. Kline might have learned from Ciulei's 1978 production, where Ophelia broke in upon a state dinner party, so that she represented a breach in decorum and a challenge to the smooth functioning of Claudius's shallow and ceremonial politics. That format created a context against which madness played disturbingly and, in the 1986 Ciulei version, made an ominous comment on "deinstitutionalization." It allowed for a voice-over that could suggest a political not just a personal agenda in Claudius's reaction: "How long hath she been thus?" In the 1990 TV production, the bare stage and the remorseless camera make this a "documentary" on madness and force both court and auditor to respond only to Ophelia. Given this badly directed Ophelia, the process is painful and we who know the script can only wish it over as soon as it can possibly be over.

The camera work is sometimes trite, sometimes interesting. Mannerisms become inevitable in a long studio production. Claudius's soliloquy (III.3.36 ff.) gives us a close-up, semiprofile, then a medium shot that gradually closes up, then a close-up from in front of the face (but without eye contact, of course), then a boom-shot as Claudius seeks a place to kneel. Then the sequence repeats itself. It is all carefully planned and all rigidly patterned. One problem for TV is that if a director does deviate from standard camera techniques the innovation calls attention to itself and away from some necessary question of the play. The predictability and the dullness it induces seem to be built into the medium and can only be contradicted by superb acting.

The camera is used creatively, however, at other times. A dissolve from Ophelia's promise to obey Polonius brings us to a close-up of Hamlet awaiting the Ghost (I.4). Two versions of patriarchal authority are thus linked. Also effective is a close-up of Polonius between the even closer backs of the heads of Claudius and Gertrude—a shot suggesting Polonius's intrusiveness as he presses his own agendas upon the King and Queen. A semioverhead shot of the Ghost as he first appears in I.4 is repeated in III.4. Shots like these—and the depth of field shots when the Players arrive—fulfill the criteria for effective Shakespeare on TV, as outlined by Hardy M. Cook: "a greater continuity of dramatic space and time, a more active relationship between the spectator and the object, more choice about where and how to direct one's attention, and a greater weight given to the spoken word" than in the filmic "montage" technique (Cook, p. 186). In each case, the Ghost appears larger and on a different plane than the onlookers. He is very "natural" otherwise, a bearded face, a military uniform before which he carries a sword, and a conversational voice usually heard from a close-up shot.* Hamlet gives a brief, effective imitation of the victim of a Goya firing squad as he asks "What should we do?" (I.4.57). The later modeling of Hamlet and Gertrude in III.4 repeats the posture of Ophelia and Hamlet during the Play Scene, although the positions are reversed, Hamlet in front of Ophelia and Gertrude in front of Hamlet. We are reminded that each scene deals with "counterfeit presentments." In each scene we look at two kings and, in a sense, experience the appearance of a ghost that only selected eyes can see. On TV—as it would have been on stage—we see both Gertrude *and* the Ghost in III.4, without the "reverse shot" technique that could give Hamlet and Gertrude separate points of view.

One good piece of continuity, more effective I feel than Hamlet's

---

*Frank Ardolino finds the Ghost "an anachronism" (Ardolino, p. 4). Perhaps. In the 1989 RSC production, guards and the Ghost wore armor and thus contrasted with the 1930ish interiors of Elsinore. Hamlet, ambassador to the future, failed—as we learned when an armored Fortinbras took over.

acquisition of a dagger with which to posture and to stab, is Ophelia's letter from Hamlet. She tries to hide it from Laertes, stuffs it away from Polonius, watches Hamlet tear it up, collects the scraps, and distributes them as her flowers in IV.5. It is an effective touch for an otherwise excruciating Ophelia.

The step away from the stage has not always been an advantage here, drying up some of the juices, imposing rigidity on a production that apparently flowed more freely on stage, and exposing as television will do ruthlessly, some of the things that probably did not work well on stage either. Still, the sequential aspects of the script do flow here *as* sequence, showing us something about the way in which the rhythms were designed to work on stage—as opposed to in the radical translation that Zeffirelli, for example, makes from script to film in his quicksilver movements from place to place and from time to time. Montage can create a sense of simultaneity, but that does not necessarily simulate the pressure of the step-by-step sequence that we experience on stage during I.2 of *Hamlet*, for example, and the relationship of the sequence to the character attempting to dictate the scenario or to the character attempting to resist it. For all of his fluidity, Zeffirelli is also fragmented.

The Kline production is competent but unexciting and not quite as good as many critics said it was when it first appeared. It is, as Frank Rich says, "polished, plausibly cast and well spoken" (Pall, p. 35). It is, Ardolino says, an "abstract American rendition . . . in which the lines are delivered slowly and straight forwardly with very little poetry, resembling a Shakespearean *Our Town*" (Ardolino, p. 4).

6

Editing the Script

By "editing," I mean primarily what *words* are retained, as opposed to how the camera shots are designated and juxtaposed against what the other cameras are seeing.

"Visual" editing is conditioned by the medium, as a brief example will suggest. The opening of Olivier's *Henry V* takes us from a model of London to a Globe filling with an audience, backstage as actors prepare, and breathtakingly on-stage with Burbage-Olivier-Henry V for an amusing scene with the bishops. The Branagh film takes us from a modern soundstage, with Derek Jacobi as narrator, to the grubby darkness of a medieval castle. While the movement is back in time, both times are "real." The older time, however, is marginalized, a mere footnote at best. Branagh takes his cue from the final chorus. Olivier's film is meant to inspire, as films once did. Branagh's film seems to have been conditioned by and for the cassette market, making "choices more suggestive of TV than of film," as Bernice Kliman suggests (Kliman, *S on F*, p. 1). It may be, however, that filmic range and depth these days are inevitably conditioned by both the emotional and visual limits of TV, and by a cynicism which TV may promote but for which it is not wholly responsible. The 1979 BBC *Henry V* scales down to the psychic and physical dimensions of TV by depicting the two clergymen discussing politics in whispers as they pretend to pray. Their hypocrisy is vividly revealed through a contrast between word and posture that was not, unfortunately, carried forward as a leitmotiv for the production. Suffice it to say that "visual" editing for television is usually minimal and minimalist, using a three-camera format that sometimes reveals its own ennui by shifting to a reaction shot within an almost invariable close-up format.

Television demands more words than film, but not as much as Shakespeare's stage does. Shakespeare's stage is forever turning the world so that a segment of it, large or small, is facing us at any given moment. It is "The Globe" that is stationary during a production. The language must create that world for us, often repeating images to reinforce them, perhaps with an allegorical interpretation that underscores meteorology with morality. The "pathetic fallacy" suggests to the audience that the characters on stage, at least, believe—or affect to believe, if they are politicians—that they inhabit a world saturated with real but unseen meanings. Richard III can rationalize the "black day" (V.3.280) that "doth frown and lour upon our army" (V.3.283) as he approaches Bosworth Field by saying "the self-same heavens / That frown on me look sadly down [on Richmond]" (V.3.286–87). His energy, however, goes into "Not shine today!" (V.3.285). He cannot see his "shadow" as he passes (I.2.264), his companion and talisman—the hump on his back. Henry V and Hal discuss the weather more confidently as they prepare for Shrewsbury:

> *King.* How bloodily the sun begins to peer
> Above yon bosky hill! The day looks pale
> At his distemp'rature.
> *Hal.*   The southern wind
> Doth play the trumpet to his purposes,
> And by his hollow whistling in the leaves
> Foretells a tempest and a blust'ring day.
> *King.* Then with the losers let us sympathize,
> For nothing can seem foul to those that win.
>
> (V.1.1–8)

The sun, of course, is a symbol of kingship, as it was for Richard II, whose emblem was a sun emerging from or being obscured by clouds, and for princeship, as in Hal's imitation, which permits "base, contageous clouds / To smother up his beauty from the world" (I.2.171–72). By the end of *I Henry IV*, the allegory is merely rhetorical, but it is there: "It pleased your majesty to turn your looks / Of favor from myself and all our house" (V.1.30–31). Worcester goes on at length to describe the development of Henry IV's "dangerous countenance" (V.1.169), now merely the face of power, to which the distempered sun and "the blushing, discontented sun" (*Richard II:* III.3.63) are but distant, metaphoric cousins. Bolingbroke is more accurate when he ascribes anger to political boundaries, as in "the moody frontier of a servant brow" (*I Henry IV:* I.3.19).

Some of the playing with and on words and the sense of magical properties inherent in certain words may be "lost on a modern audience," although some members of that audience may enjoy a world where words retained their lost intrinsicity or echoed with duplicity, as "noble" and "royal" do for Hal (*I Henry IV:* II.4.258–60). But amplified references to the weather are unnecessary on film or TV, and TV—a "realistic" or "naturalistic" medium—cannot contain language which swells with supernatural quality or resonates with the power of nature—except negatively as in the instances of fuel spills, burning oil wells, and problems in reactors, contained and uncontained.

The significance of editing cannot be overestimated, particularly since it usually goes unnoticed in production. Nor can the critic deny that some editing is necessary even in the shorter scripts. Good acting can still convey some Elizabethan jokes, but others—"No die, but an ace. . . ." (*Dream:* V.1.303–6), for example, are best expunged. And even then, one must wonder how Shakespeare intended his audience to understand some of his characters' wordplay. Feste's "there is no true cuckold but calamity" (*12th Night:* I.5.57–58) seems to mean (a) that if a man is married to fortune, he is bound to find that fortune is unfaithful—thus calamity cuckolds him; and (b) that Olivia is married to calamity and cannot even be faithful to it! That seems like a lot of meaning to pick up on the fly.

David Giles's *Richard II* conveys clearly a script that is difficult for any medium. The juxtaposition of Carlisle and York after IV.1.149, as the former is led away under arrest and the latter looks on in stupefied admiration at Carlisle's tirade, is telling. Neither frustrated silence nor eloquent defiance in the face of Bolingbroke's drive to power has any effect. The series of dissolves during Richard's soliloquy (V. 5.1 ff.) shows time passing aimlessly as Richard ponders his self-created paradoxes. The effect could not be simulated on stage with the ease that the camera permits.

One piece of editing to which I object, however, is the deletion of the Gardener's conclusion to III.4:

> Poor Queen, so that thy state might be no worse,
> I would my skill were subject to thy curse.
> Here did she fall a tear; here in this place,
> I'll set a bank of rue, sour herb of grace.
> Rue, even for ruth, here shortly shall be seen,
> In the remembrance of a weeping queen.
>
> (III.4, 102–7)

Instead, the scene ends with Isabel's curse: "for telling me these news of woe, / Pray God the plants thou graft'st may never grow" (III.3.100–101). This ending tends to equate the Queen's personal grief with her political status. While she has the final say here, the scene and the play depict a loss of political power, not just for the royal family, but for the conceptual basis of monarchy itself. The

Gardener's closure suggests an encompassing human sympathy that can ignore another of the play's antiprayers and respond "kindly" (in the Elizabethan sense of the word). He responds not to "body politic," which is a dying, sacramental concept here, as its efforts at negation suggest, but to the ongoing energy of "body natural." His plants *will* grow. The earth will memorialize a woman's tear. His is the prior energy—his is "old Adam's likeness" (III.4.73)—and it continues under the vicissitudes of politics. His is the final word— of ongoing humanity and not of withered roots. But not in this production.

Also missing from this *Richard II* is Carlisle's magnificent closure on Mowbray (IV.1.91–100) and the first rumors of Prince Hal (V.3.1– 12). Carlisle's description shows that Mowbray was exiled to a former time, the time Gaunt describes (II.1.31 ff.), a time or timelessness now lost to England as Bolingbroke's brutal pragmatism takes over. His control begins to echo ironically back at him as an "unthrifty son" hangs like a "plague" (V.3.1–3) over a Bolingbroke, who suddenly remembers that he has not seen his son in "full three months" (V.3.2). Time has opened out for Mowbray in exile to grant him a full chivalric career and a peaceful ending. Time is only the measurement of negation for Bolingbroke. We will learn, of course, that Hal knows exactly what time it is and plans to "redeem . . . time" (*I.Henry IV:* 1.2.190), but it will be a political time capable of "redemption" only during the brief, bright parenthesis of Henry V's career as King.

The plays keep looking ahead and looking back, imitating the fabric of "history" in their dramaturgy. The cutting of lines which convey this tendency permits the production to focus on the story of Richard and Bolingbroke, but it tends to erase the fact that that story is part of a history that Richard and Henry IV tend to ignore until each becomes aware—negatively—of the larger patterns and rhythms that have absorbed the individual wills of those who thought they were shaping those patterns. For the sake of simplifying the script and making it a self-contained work we lose a vital, informing, and basic sense of the context that makes the story of the individuals both meaningful and meaningless.

Almost any production of a Shakespeare script will involve some editing. Production is interpretation, and the interpretation involves what the director chooses to emphasize from the complicated set of signals he inherits. Few productions of Shakespeare are as heavily edited as the Peter Brook/Orson Welles *King Lear* which appeared on Omnibus, 18 October 1953.

Perhaps needless to say, this production was hammered when it

appeared. Alice V. Griffin complains that Peter Brook's "large cast
. . . . did not make the screen seem expansive, but rather accentuated
its limited size" and that "The adaptation by Mr. Brook was unfor-
givably bad; granted that time had to be cut, many precious minutes
were spent on visual effects which contributed little to the play,
while important speeches were omitted or reduced to a line or two"
(Griffin, p. 64). The latter comment suggests radio, which can tolerate only minute segments of silence. Griffin does not account for
even the limited visualization that television affords. In 1981, Robert
Hetherington says,

> given the enormity of the deletions it is surprising the audience could
> follow the story at all. The cutting and reordering of the text does noth-
> ing to clarify the tragedy. The backgrounds are nondescript: the black
> void of a studio where spatial relationships are never clearly contiguous
> and exteriors indistinguishable from interiors. . . . Welles's performance
> struck at least one critic as that of "a man who has been hauled off
> a park bench and hastily pressed into service as Macy's Santa Claus."
> (Hetherington, p. 7)

A positive contemporary review by George Rosen in *Variety* calls
the production "the most definitive Shakespearean TV work" to date,
while also praising Worthington Minor's *Julius Caesar* of March
1949. "Brook's staging," Rosen says,

> did much to push back the walls of the television studio and permitted
> for a natural continuity from scene to scene. . . . The highly creative
> scenic designing transposed the time, place and mood to the TV screen
> with sensitivity and strength. . . . Seldom have the TV cameras contrib-
> uted so flawless an assist to an actor, notably in the closeups.

Rosen notes one problem that time has not solved.

> While it's commendable that the "Omnibus" sponsors waived their usual
> midway commercials for this occasion (settling for fore and aftplugs), it's
> debatable whether "Lear's" mounting dramatic tension shouldn't offer
> the viewer at least one intermission respite. How this could be handled
> without the intrusion of a commercial is something TV still has to resolve.
> (Rosen, p. 1)

The advent of the cassette, of course, is one solution to the question
of interval.

I find the production both coherent and powerful. I believe that
it *does* create relationships within a zone more generalized than film

demands and affords, but within a space that does work for the close-up medium of TV. I also agree with Kenneth Rothwell, speaking of this production and of Welles. "He deserved a better press. . . ." (Rothwell, p. 132).

The Brook/Welles *King Lear* is now available. Not only is it a brilliant reminder of the brief moment when TV was being explored and not exploited, but it is in many ways superior to the two contemporaneous TV *Lears*—the Olivier and the BBC, which have been discussed at length elsewhere.[1]

This version eliminates the subplot of Gloucester and his sons. "Edmund" becomes Oswald, recipient early of Goneril's promises (IV.ii in the conflated *Lear* script) and, later, of Regan's wooing even over the cooling corpse of Cornwall (a translation of IV.v.). "Edgar" becomes Poor Tom only, the denizen of a windmill in the wonderfully orchestrated incoherency of Lear's trial of Goneril and Regan. Gloucester is confronted and blinded right after Lear escapes from the hovel. Lear and Cordelia are captured immediately after IV. vii., which becomes V.iii., the Going-Off-to-Prison Scene. The result is a rapidly placed production that lasts for seventy-three minutes.

This may seem like just a précis of the play, reducing "the script to a scenario," as Hetherington says (Hetherington, p. 7), but Welles creates a Lear that competes with any other. As a King crowned and clothed like an evil ruler in a 1930s serial, with daughters on a literal pedestal who all look very much alike, Welles gives us the "once upon a time, a great king decided to divide his kingdom" version, and it is a powerful allegory. We see the title of the play over a map. The map is suddenly sundered by a sword. Behind the map, of course, is Lear, who hands out rent parchment to his sons-in-law. Cordelia is given her asides (as she was not in Brook's 1962 film), which are a combination of voice-over and her mouthing of the words. Thus her spoken "Nothing, my lord" is remarkably powerful. Kent and Gloucester divide what in the script are Kent's objections, so that these two members of the old order are introduced. The Kent-Gloucester-Edmund prelude has, of course, been cut.

The power of Welles's performance is a function of Lear's effort to understand what is happening to him. His ability to make his eyes look inward—as on his whispered "My wits begin to turn"—shows us a Lear beginning to look at what he has never seen before, the self behind the royal persona. His descent to madness incorporates few pauses. The "I have ta'en too little care of this" speech is cut. As blind Gloucester enters (IV.vi.), Lear mutters "Give me the map there," as if reliving the moments between his first decision and his madness. Other lines crop up in strange places. Welles covers his entrance from hunting (I.iv.) with the much later remark about the fellow who "handles his bow like a crow keeper." At the end, having dragged Cordelia in, Lear slumps to his throne on the second "never" and dies after his fifth. "Look there! Look there!" is *not* there. The camera dollies back. Kent holds Lear in his arms, Albany, on the other side of the throne gets the last lines (à la Q), and Cordelia lies on the steps where she had knelt so long before to be auctioned off to Burgundy or France. Prominent in the expanding frame is the now empty pedestal on which the daughters had stood in the first scene.

Thus, although Peter Brook does not pursue Albany's line and Shakespeare's direction to "Produce the bodies. . . ." (V.iii.234), Brook does echo the first scene with the last. He does so with an anticipation of his concept of "the empty space." His "staging" (the quaint word used in the credits) consists of close-ups, often radical, shots of Lear "upstage" speaking to a foregrounded figure or figures, an excellent triangular shot for Cordelia and France in the foreground, with Lear centered in the background, a shot suggesting a competition between these two kings that culminates when Lear, bearlike, escorts Cordelia to the "kind nursery" of Oswald's prison, a tight two-shot for the splendid Lear-Gloucester meeting (IV.v.). The TV camera structures conflict for us and is not the insane, but powerfully disturbing, camera of Brook's later film. Alan Badel's Fool, inaudible much of the time, receives an effective medium close-up for his, "And I'll go to bed at noon." Badel's Fool, like his master, is trying to figure out what is happening in this world gone beyond the saving balance which it was the Fool's function to provide.

Any fair-minded auditor will notice a few problems. In the Reconciliation Scene (IV.vi.), the Doctor stands over Lear with a cup in hand, looking for all the world as if he is about to conk the old King in the head, either accidentally or on purpose. Lear's "They have some cause, you have none," makes nonsense of Cordelia's "No cause, no cause." In the finale, Regan strangles Goneril and is in turn stabbed by Oswald, who is then dispatched by Albany. It takes about ten seconds to create the heap into which they tumble. Here the problem is not in the removal of bodies but in the making of them.

While I have yet to test this thesis, I believe that this production will serve as an excellent introduction for students to *King Lear*. It is much better than "better than nothing," should lead students back to the script, will lead some of them into the problem *of* the script and others into the issue of editing the conflated script for production. As an example of "streamlined Shakespeare," the Brook/Welles is radical in its cutting, but one of the best examples of accommodation of script to medium extant. As Welles said in 1953: "If we did a full length version [of *King Lear*] it would be too long for television" (Adams, p. 38). Whether Welles is right or not, his version is not "too long for a play."

I wish to conclude this chapter with an examination of the editing of a recent TV production—the Nunn *Othello*—and the effect of the editing on our experience of the script. Nunn seems to want to emphasize human agency, as opposed to any metaphysical possibilities, as motivating the action, and a lack of consideration in Othello, here a character lacking any inner points of reference against which to measure Iago's suggestions. We get a pell-mell rush of events, which does not permit moralizing nor much summing up of what the experience means or has meant. All of these tendencies are inherent in the script, I believe, and are italicized by Nunn's editing. Nunn also edits "amplification," as do many modern editors, finding that the camera can make its own emphatic points.

Recognizing the pressure that Iago exerts within the script, Nunn organizes the "world" of *Othello* on the basis of what Yuri Lotman calls the *syntagmatic* model as opposed to the *symbolic*. The latter, according to Terrence Hawkes, is "a product of the classical-medieval-Renaissance tradition [which guarantees meaning] by metaphor or analogy." The *syntagmatic* model guarantees meaning "by rational causal relationships" (Hawkes, p. 295). The basic insanity of Iago's "rationality" comes through powerfully on this basis, aided as it is by McKellen's powerful performance and a medium which tends to argue from materialistic rather than from imaginative premises— therefore enforces a sense of "cause and effect" rather than a more complicated version of cybernetics or "morphic resonance."

Examples of "amplification" that Nunn cuts, include part of Brabantio's cynical analysis of "labeling" (I.3.233–36, in which the equivocal word "equivocal" appears in its seventeenth-century sense of "equal"). Some of Othello's double epithets are cut: "such accommodation and besort" (I.3.257), "In my defunct and proper satisfation" (I.3.286), and "all indign and base adversities" (I.3.295), for example. Iago's "'Tis to [Cassio's] virtue a just equinox. . . ." (II.3.118–19) is cut, as is Iago's exchange with Montano ("'Tis evermore the prologue to his sleep. . . .": II.3.123–26). Iago's effective discrediting of Cassio has already been established. Part of Cassio's disquisition on drunkenness is gone (II.3.296–97, 309–12), where he emphasizes the descent to bestiality that alcohol induces. These deletions give Iago greater control over the scene and permit him to focus on the politics of reinstatement. Thus we lose some of the foreshadowing of Othello's descent to bestiality as the poison of jealousy invades his sytem. Iago does not need to tell us how Othello's "Unbookish jealousy will conster Cassio's smiles. . . ." (IV.1.117–19). The camera will show us. Lines responding to Othello's slapping of Desdemona (IV.1.292–94, 308–10) are cut to permit our own shock and to emphasize Iago's hint to Lodovico that the "stroke" may not "prove the worst" (IV.1.302). Gratiano's "Thy match was moral to him" (V.2.242) to Desdemona about Brabantio makes "and pure grief / Shore his old thread in twain" (V.2.242–43) unnecessary here, particularly since Clive Swift's Brabantio had been extremely upset in I.3 (even if he did not get lines 60–63 there). A fragment of the Roderigo letter sequence is retained (V.2.357–62), while most is cut (V.2.365–70, 378–83). Usually, all of this is cut, but Nunn gives us enough to show how the "official explanation" tries to rattle on regardless of the deeper activity that cancels any effort at explanation.

Nunn's further editorial principles exclude aspects of the script that (a) complicate character, (b) moralize upon events, and (c) attribute what happens to causes beyond human motivation.

Iago, for example, is "cooler" than the script may suggest, particularly at the outset, when Nunn mitigates his psychopathology by removing a pestilential line like "plague him with flies" (I.1.74–78) and the pyromania of "the fire . . . / spied in populous cities" (I.1.180–82). This is no giggling Bob Hoskins, but a less excitable, more calculating ancient. This Iago does *not* find that "Pleasure and action make the hours seem short" (II.2.381). The assumption here is that Iago always knows what time it is, even controls time, although not as completely as Christopher Plummer did in the 1980 Winter Garden production, where he could caper about in a "freeze frame" that held the other characters immobile. Perhaps to emphasize Iago's control, Nunn cuts his references to "wit's" dependence on "dilatory time" (II.3.374–75).

Brabantio loses his line about his "dream" (I.11.158) which might have signaled a psychic acceptance of Othello's courtship had it not been translated to an obscene nightmare by Iago. Brabantio's external power is also reduced. His lines, "I may command at most" (I.1.199) and "If he do resist, / Subdue him at his peril" (I.2.95–96) are excised.

Othello does not promise to "confess the vices of my blood" (I.3.138). He does not "beseech" the Council (I.3.127) but commands: "Send for the lady" (I.3.129). These small adjustments make Brabantio a victim, not a wielder, of power and reinforce Othello's overconfident belief in his own power.

Cassio's "'Tis my breeding. . . ." (II.1.113–14) can be a put-down of the base Iago, but is cut here, as is Iago's subsequent "you are most apt to play the sir in" (II.1.202–4). The social distinction between the two is clear enough.

One of the deletions from Othello's role has a strange result. He says: "For such things in a false disloyal knave / Are tricks of custom" (III.3.141–42) but does *not* get "but in a man that's just / They are close dilations working from the heart / That passion cannot rule" (III.3.142–44). He has defined Iago *and* articulated his own sense of self. The editing, however, makes Iago defend Cassio from Othello's charge of knavery: "For Michael Cassio, / I dare be sworn I think that he is honest" (III.3.145–46). The effect is that Iago's hyperbole matches Othello's—in spite of the subtle "I think." The technique of overstatement permits the slightest doubt to undercut the totality of previous belief, which is vulnerable precisely because it is so absolute. Iago introduces a qualification ("think") even when he seems to agree ("sworn"). McKellan is superb at picking up and slightly but crucially modifying the speech patterns of the other characters.

Othello loses at least one level of awareness here. His sense of losing control, of his "blood" beginning to rule his "safer guides" (II.3.206–210) surrenders to a "Zwounds!" His later awareness that Desdemona represented "one entire and perfect crysolite" (V.2.171–74) surrenders to the dire drive of Emilia's iteration. His self-serving rationalization that "'tis the plague of great ones" (III.3.308–12) is gone, a deletion that emphasizes the possessiveness of the early part of the soliloquy. The metaphor on "new heraldry" (III.4.50–51) which makes much the same possessive point within the context of male entitlement is also gone. The lines in which Othello compares Desdemona's name to his "begrimed and black . . . face" (III.3.434–36)—where he accepts the racist agenda of Venice—are gone. The line becomes "I'll have some proof. If there be cords, or knives, . . ." making the transition to his contemplation of suicide abrupt, lacking as it does the *self*-hatred that the deleted lines suggest.

Much of what might be taken as "moralizing the spectacle" is also missing from Nunn's shooting script. The deletions no doubt streamline and modernize the production, but as with Othello's enjoyment of piling the modifiers up in front of his nouns, some of the preachments are not mere outcroppings of a medieval tradition but serve characterization. If, for example, Iago's lines to Cassio that "Reputation is an idle and most false imposition; oft got without merit and lost without deserving" (II.3.275–76) are cut, as they are here, then the force of Iago's opposite-but-equal aphorisms to

Othello (III.3.180–86) is muted, as is our sense of Iago's ability to elevate half-truth to all-embracing generalization.

Iago's emphasis in this production is on the terrible *uniqueness* of Othello's position. Iago's references to "credulous fools," "worthy and chaste dames" (IV.1.53–55), "many a beast . . . and civil monster" (IB.1.75–76) are cut. That Othello apparently accepts his singularity is evidenced by his not comparing his plight to that of "great ones" (III.3.308).

Othello's "naked in bed, Iago, and not mean harm?" (IV.1.8) is more emphatic if the next lines, which develop a moral about "hypocrisy against the devil" (IV.1.9–11) are cut, as they are here. The focus is on Othello taking the bait, not thinking about it or pressing it into theological categories. One *could* argue that Othello has picked up the moralizing Iago virus, but this production shows that Othello acquires Iago's interrogative rhythms and forces them upon a helpless Desdemona who is as vulnerable as was the early Othello because she doesn't know where this cross-examination is coming from. Othello's awkward couplet, "Faith of my heart . . . with lust's blood be spotted" (V.1.39–40) is cut, but he loses his aphorism about "woman's tears" proving "a crocodile" (IV.1.268–69), which suggests the insidious "Iago music." Othello also loses his complaint that Desdemona has made him "a fixed finger for the time of scorn" (IV,2,63–66). The latter deletion seems consistent with Othello's inability to generalize as his mistakes rush him toward their results. Gone, for example, is Othello's "O, balmy breath, that dost almost persuade / Justice to break her sword!" (V.2.16–17), and "This sorrow's heavenly. / It strikes where it doth love" (V.2.21–23). Even his later voyage metaphor (V.2.314–15) is gone, perhaps because it merely amplifies his awareness that "Here is my journey's end" (V.2.314). But amplification is, from first to last, one of the devices of Othello's "self-fashioning." This production tends to diminish that tendency even as it suggests little ebb-and-flow in the process of Othello's "cause."

The most obvious cuts involve the "cosmic" dimension—references to the interaction between humanity and the supernatural, and to the interpenetration of religion and human life. Gone, for example, is Iago's "If sanctimony and a frail vow betwixt an erring barbarian and a supersubtle Venetian be not too hard for my wits and all the tribe of hell. . . ." (I.3.377–79), Emilia'a comments about "the serpent's curse" (IV.2.17–18), and Gratiano's reference to Brabantio's "better angel" (V.2.245).

In an effort perhaps to "literalize" the world of *Othello*, Nunn deletes some of what Othello claims for the handkerchief: "A sibyl. . . . In her prophetic fury sewed the work": III.4.79–81; "And it was dyed in mummy . . .": III.4.84–85, as well as Desdemona's "Sure, there's some wonder in the handkerchief" (III.4.114).

The cuts to which I most object are the lines that refer to the cosmos. These deletions tend to scale the play down to a level below the emotion it will sustain, even on TV. "As if some planet had outwitted men" (II.3.184) and "It is the very error of the moon. / She comes nearer earth that she was wont, / And makes men mad" (V.2.131–33) are gone. Nunn is right to let TV do what it can do and not to overreach. His *Macbeth,* for example, uses liturgical music and a praying Duncan to suggest the "holy-supernatural" aspect of the play. It is a simple, ungimicky, and powerful set of images to balance against the potent, darker themes. In *Othello,* however, references to the outer mystery are merely verbal, and not evidence of a set of cosmic coordinates behind or within the world of the play.

While many other plays in the canon show an interaction between the outer mystery and the human world, *Othello* does not. The lines that allude to the planet's manipulation of human will in *Othello* are rationalizations that help us focus on the misadventures of an Othello who has only himself to blame for what he does, regardless of the power that a critic like Harry Morris or a director like Peter Coe grants to Iago. Othello recognizes his guilt with open eyes at last, even if his habits of language continue. In fairness to Nunn's editing, we do get Othello's self-glorifying belief that "It should be now a huge eclipse / Of sun and moon" (V.2.119–21) and his magnificent depiction of his own soon-to-come fall from grace (V.2.320–22). Some of Othello's self-creating rhetoric—the ultimate dimensions he claims for himself and against which he measures himself—comes through. This serves as a context, in this splendid production, for the single heroic action we witness—Othello's execution of an enemy of the state who happens to be himself.

Nunn might have trusted the medium and his actors to let a bit more of the script be heard.

Eileen Herlie and Richard Burton. 1964. Courtesy Alexander H. Cohen.

Claire Bloom and Patrick Stewart. 1980. Courtesy BBC-Television.

"The potent poison quite o'recrows my spirit." Derek Jacobi and Robert Swann. 1980. Courtesy BBC-TV.

John Kani and Joanna Weinberg. 1987. Courtesy Janet Suzman.

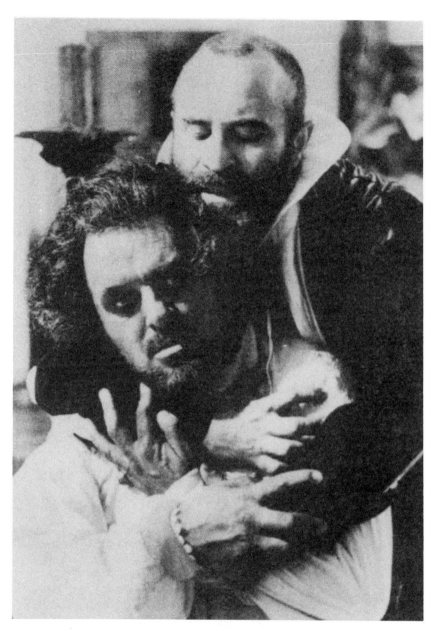

Anthony Hopkins, Bob Hoskins. 1981. Courtesy BBC-TV.

Orson Welles, Suzanne Cloutier. 1952. Courtesy Mogador Films.

Ian McKellen as Iago. 1990. Courtesy Thames Television.

Advertisement. *New York Times,* 1991.

7

Closure in *Hamlet*

The final eighty-three lines of *Hamlet,* from "The point envenom'd too!" (V.2.313), to "Go, bid the soldiers shoot!" (V.2.395), contain a mosaic of events and motives, event competing with event for notice, motive competing with motive for precedence. The ending involves a transfer of power from a King to a Prince—although the Prince must be reminded of the political significance of his own death— through a transitional figure, Horatio—to a foreign prince, soon to be King Fortinbras of Denmark. These final lines contain at least sixteen "beats," in the Stanislavskian sense, perhaps more. Seldom do all of these beats get into production. Hamlet's recognition that the point is envenomed as well as unbated (1) motivates his attack upon Claudius (2). Claudius appeals to his court for support (3) but is forced to drink some of the poisoned wine (4). Laertes asks that Hamlet exchange forgiveness with him (5). Hamlet does so (6), bids farewell to the Queen (7), realizes that he does not have time to tell his story (8) and asks Horatio to do so (9). Horatio claims a non-Christian ethical system for himself that justifies suicide (10), but Hamlet gets the poisoned chalice from him (11) so that Horatio can report Hamlet and his cause accurately. Hamlet asks about the "warlike noise" (V.2.340) and is told that it is Fortinbras greeting the ambassadors returned from England (12). Hamlet gives his voice to Fortinbras and dies (13). Fortinbras enters (14). The Ambassador reports "that Rosencrantz and Guildernstern are dead" (15). Horatio and Fortinbras negotiate a final ceremonial, Horatio suggesting that "these bodies / High on a stage be placed to the view" (V.2.369–70), but Fortinbras ordering only Hamlet to be borne "like a soldier to the stage" (V.2.388). These negotiations represent a sixteenth beat, although they could be broken down further. Needless to say, the lines from "Why does the drum come hither?" (V.2.353) to the end, are seldom heard in their entirety in production.

Of these beats, the unbated point and the stabbing of Claudius are invariably included, as is the exchange of forgiveness with Laertes,

although the lines are often condensed. The forcing of wine on Claudius and the "adieu" (V.2.325) are usually included. Hamlet's address
to the court ("You that look pale. . . .": V.2.326–30) is often cut,
although the lines echo the play's opening by suggesting that the
court is looking at a ghost (cf. Bernardo to Horatio: "How now. . . .
You tremble and look pale": I.1.53). The competition between Hamlet and Horatio for the chalice is sometimes cut. "The rest is silence"
is mandatory, and we usually hear Horatio's eulogy, although "Now
cracks a noble heart" (V.2.351) is often cut. Fortinbras is, of course,
the editor's chief victim and often does not appear at all, as closure
concentrates on Hamlet.

Bernice Kliman suggests that "Papp's *Hamlet* with Sam Waterston
(1975) electrified the audience with its resolute Fortinbras, rushing
in to take over, an interpretation that, in retrospect, changed the
meaning of the whole play" (Kliman, p. 54). "John Gilbert, the
illustrator, in 1864 had depicted just such a Fortinbras, entering
ready to attack, not yet noticing the bodies that make his menace
pointless" (Kliman, p. 54). George Bernard Shaw, Kliman reports,
was so influenced by this illustration that it determined "his own
interpretation of the play." He was shocked and dismayed "to discover Fortinbras cut from contemporary stage productions" (Kliman, p.54).

I would suggest that Fortinbras's "Where is this sight?" (V.2.354)
tells us that he has been told of what has happened in Elsinore's
throne room. That information, however, does not mean that he
might not enter in a defensive posture, his troops sweeping the room
for signs of a possible ambush. Horatio, after all, recognizes the
danger inherent in the moment ("men's minds are wild": V.2.386).
The "strong Fortinbras," however, says Kliman, has not been incorporated into a "moving image production" (Kliman, p. 54). By
"strong," she means a Fortinbras ready to attack, as opposed to
merely asserting his claim to the crown of Denmark.

Closure for *Hamlet* in modern times begins with the 1949 Olivier
film, featuring his famous leap upon Claudius, Claudius's physical
groping for his crown, his dying hand reaching for the crown even
as an instantly alienated palace guard closes in on him, Horatio's
bending to Hamlet—Horatio holding the cross-hilt of a sword to his
head—as Hamlet sits on the throne for an informal coronation, and
the ending funeral march, the camera pausing to look at Hamlet's
empty chair, zooming in briefly on the bed of Gertrude and Claudius, cannons booming, and a sunset dropping behind the tower as
the soldiers carry Hamlet up to the utmost parapet. Fortinbras is
absent, of course, but Horatio gets some of his lines in what is a

fairly standard editorial practice: "Let four captains . . . speak loudly for him": V.2.387–92, and "Go, bid the soldiers shoot": V.2.395). *Then* Horatio gets his more private "Good night, sweet prince . . . to thy rest" (V.2.351–52), and the procession ends the film. The swing is from the public to the private to the public again. This ending, Kliman claims, concentrating on the final retrospective procession, as opposed to Fortinbras's successful ascension, "leaves us with a much more settled feeling than might the text realized on stage" (Kliman, p. 49–50).

The other great *Hamlet* film, Kozintsev's, gives Hamlet a private death, with Horatio alone hearing "The rest is silence" and dropping into a posture of mourning at Hamlet's knees, sans eulogy. Kozintsev, who felt that Olivier neglected the political element of the script does provide a Fortinbras, as Jack Jorgens describes the ending:

> . . . the world has not been transformed by Hamlet's sacrifice. . . . Hamlet dies in the posture of the maimed, one-armed cross so prominent in the graveyard scene. Whether this suggests that his attempt to assert Christian values undermined by Claudius has failed, that his sacrifice falls short of Christ's because he has become a murderer, or perhaps that the insights Hamlet has had are the ones that will ultimately destroy Christianity in the modern world, his posture suggests a Fall—a theme sounded earlier in the ghost's description of the murder and in the tapestry behind Ophelia's broken-doll dance. After Hamlet dies, the camera pans to the weathered layers of ancient rock and holds there for a time until we hear the "music" of Fortinbras: the clank of armor and weapons, the rumble of wheels and boots on the stone. The enigmatic enemy from without, the other revenging son, enters and takes over without a blow. Is he a Claudius-like conqueror, or a worldly savior come to restore health to Denmark? Whatever his arrival portends, it is clear that his triumph is not Hamlet's. Hamlet's knowledge is not transferred to the new king. Fortinbras acts to restore order and to honor the dead hero, Hamlet, yet he also negates what Hamlet stood for. In giving him the rites of a soldier, the new king forces Hamlet into an image of Fortinbras, or perhaps of their warlike chivalric fathers When Hamlet is carried to a "stage" in a long and solemn procession, he becomes a part of the court ceremony, the "show" he had sought to destroy while he was alive. The "seeming" goes on and the world is unredeemed. (Jorgens, pp. 233–34)

I quote Jorgens thus at length because the film remains unavailable on cassette and because Fortinbras's arrival invariably qualifies any ending that focuses on Hamlet and *his* "meanings."

In the 1985 RSC production, Fortinbras had only a mild impact at the end. He realized after his personal sadness and his order for a soldier's funeral that he *was*, after all, King. He raised his arms and forced the survivors of Elsinore to bow to him. A "strong" Fortinbras, to say the least, was that of Ingmar Bergman's 1987–88 production. This Norwegian prince had all the Danes shot down, as if he were the perpetrator of a successful coup d'état. Then, "The bodies of the King and Queen were thrust ignominiously through a trap—after which Fortinbras delivered his own closing speech for the benefit of television cameras" (Trewin, p. 170). The effect for us, now a "studio audience," must have been as ironic as watching Richard Nixon deliver one of his first Watergate chats with a bust of Lincoln placed prominently behind him. In the 1990 RSC production, the armored Fortinbras was a representative of the past, an image of the military fathers, come to claim Denmark from Hamlet, a failed ambassador to the future. The anachronistic conception of the production allowed this profoundly ironic point to be made simply through the costuming (Coursen, p. 29).

My own sense of the Kozintsev ending is that the broken icon in the graveyard is echoed by Hamlet's arm as he dies because neither the principles that Christianity represents, nor Hamlet's manifestation of those ideals, has any power over the ongoing progress of power itself. Those who believe so or try to manifest their belief end up in the posture of broken symbols. Fortinbras, unimpeded by inhibiting generalizations about humanity's participation in matters of spirit, will always march in and take over. But, as Jorgens's description implies, that interpretation does not deny the suggestiveness of the Kozintsev film or the alternative interpretations that Fortinbras invites.

One would think that the inclusion of Fortinbras would be a "filmic" choice, film having the amplitude and inclusive capacity to incorporate this outer circle of political concern in the script. Television, it would seem, would more effectively focus in on the more "personal" story of Prince Hamlet and his failed effort to do whatever he wanted to do—set the time right, revenge, whatever. The breakdown is not as precise between the media, however, as the following survey will show, and is complicated by the recent conflation of film into the cassette intended for the home-video market.

Three well-known versions exclude Fortinbras: the Schell (Austrian TV, 1960), the Williamson (directed by Tony Richardson, 1969), and the Gibson (directed by Franco Zeffirelli, 1990). In each instance, I think the deletion weakens the production, since we are not asked to consider what Fortinbras means in light of what Hamlet may have meant. In a sense, then, we are not asked what *Hamlet* means by these productions.

Schell says "envenom'd"—the spoken text greatly inhibited by the dubbing into English, which is very awkward, particularly in close-ups—"Then, venom (pause), to thy work!" But this very sweet Prince is reluctant. Hans Caninenberg's Claudius, having been blocked from escape, returns to confront Hamlet as ominous music plays. Hamlet closes his eyes, swipes at Claudius, and wounds him. The music stops. Claudius says, "O yet defend me, friends, I am but wounded," but he has no friends, indeed has not had any following throughout the production. Hamlet insists that Claudius drink. Claudius eyes Hamlet contemptuously and accepts the cup. "Drink off this potion!" (Claudius drinks) "Is thy union here? Follow my mother." All of this is done quietly, in a two-shot. The King turns, grasps the throne, and falls to the floor. Laertes says "Exchange forgiveness. . . . Nor thine on me" (V.2.321–23). Hamlet says "Heaven make thee free of it. I follow thee." He closes Laertes's eyes. "I am dead, Horatio." He rises and sits on the throne. The final reference to Gertrude ("Wretched queen, adieu": V.2.325) is cut. Hamlet has held Gertrude in his arms as she warned him about the drink and her "O, my dear Hamlet!" has been their good-bye. His discussion with Horatio is, like his farewell to Gertrude and his dealings with Claudius, private, a two-shot. "Had I but time, as this fell sargeant, Death, / Is strict in his arrest, O, I could tell you—but let it be. Horatio / Thou liv'st; report me and my cause. . . ." Horatio offers to drink some of the poisoned wine: "Never believe it! / Here's yet some liquor left." Hamlet says, "By heaven, let go" and places his hand on top of Horatio's. The latter does not resist. "What a wounded name. / Things standing thus unknown, shall live behind me! / If ever thou dids't hold me in thy heart / In this harsh world draw thy breath in pain, to tell my story. / Horatio, I am dead!" Hamlet rambles into "occurrences of fate," then says, "The rest is silence." Horatio says "Good night . . . to thy rest." Horatio's hand closes Hamlet's eyes and moves the head down to the right. He removes his hand. We get a left-profile close-up. Horatio commands; "Let four captains / Bear Hamlet like a soldier to the stage, / For he was likely had he been put on / To have prov'd most royal." A funeral march begins.

It is hard to say how the editing was affected by the necessity to dub. Suffice it to say that the production suggests that Hamlet, however against his better nature, has concluded his action against the evil Claudius. Horatio's eulogy is accurate here in a production that functions on an intimate level—"up close and personal"—and that takes Hamlet at his own valuation of himself. Thus TV seems to dictate a simple allegory.

The Richardson-Williamson film (1969) looks like a film-for-TV.

"Even the duel never widens out to more than a medium shot," says Kliman: "the intense movements so close up, with the candles between the camera and the man, make an exciting interchange, with every nuance of discovery subtly conveyed" (Kliman, p. 179).

Few Hamlets convey as much hatred for Claudius as Williamson's. The poisoned wine burbles down Antony Hopkins's beard as Williamson furiously attacks him. We hear Claudius digesting what wine he did swallow as he dies. Judy Parfitt's Gertrude dies horribly, but Williamson does not say "Wretched queen, adieu!" (V.2.325). All other lines, except "Treason! Treason!" are included from "The point envenom'd. . . ." (V.2.313) *to* "Wretched queen. . . ". "You that look pale . . . Horatio, I am dead!" (V.2.326–30) is cut—there being very little sense of an audience in or around the straight-on close-ups of this production. Hamlet and Horatio debate about the chalice, and Hamlet drinks what is left to make sure Horatio will stay alive. Hamlet draws a breath before "harsh," his body cuing the adjective. The allusions to Fortinbras and to news from England are cut (V.2.340–44, 346–50). Horatio leans over Hamlet in a lateral two-shot. Hamlet's "The rest is silence!" (V.2.351–52) is a last gasp. Horatio says "Now cracks . . . to thy rest" (V.2.351–52) and closes Hamlet's eyes. The last shot is a close-up of Hamlet, face up, left-profile.

This rapid and violent ending contrasts Hamlet's hatred of Claudius with Horatio's love of Hamlet. It is exciting, as Kliman says, and also intimate, a very personal story about a "nasty, snarling" (Jorgens, p. 20) *and* a complicated Hamlet who can hate passionately and who can attract devotion, but who seems incapable of love himself. The production contains only enough politics to sustain a story of Hamlet the private man. The only relationship the film develops is the incestuous love between Ophelia and Laertes, an inevitable consequence, as Jorgens suggests, of the marriage of Gertrude and Claudius (Jorgens, pp. 20–21).

The Zeffirelli film gives Laertes (Nathaniel Parker) a long confession: "It is here, Hamlet. Hamlet, thou art slain. / No med'cine in the world can do thee good. / The treacherous instrument is in thy hand, / Unbated and envenom'd." (Hamlet looks at the naked point.) "The foul practice hath turn'd itself on me. / Exchange forgiveness with me, noble Hamlet. / Mine and my father's death come not on thee. . . . Nor mine on thee," Hamlet says, apparently intuiting the King's responsibility. Laertes cries, "I can no more!" and falls into Hamlet's arms. Laertes swings his head to the side, spies Claudius, and shouts "The King! The King's to blame!" Claudius laughs nervously and backs away, waving his right arm as if to dismiss the accusation. Hamlet says, "The point envenom'd too." He rises.

Laertes falls to the floor behind him. "Then venom to thy work!" Hamlet rushes toward the dais where the thrones sit and stabs Claudius at the foot of the throne. Some courtiers attempt to defend Claudius while others interfere with the defenders. Claudius cries "O, yet defend me friends, I. . . ." Hamlet forces the goblet on Claudius ("Here thou incestuous . . . follow my mother": V.2.317–19), the wine running down Claudius's beard. The King gives a final burp and dies, rolling down a step. Hamlet looks at his bloody right arm and staggers across to the Queen. "I am dead, Horatio." His "Wretched queen, adieu," is tender. He takes Gertrude's hand, kisses it, and holds it next to his cheek for a moment, staring at nothing with sad, blue eyes.

His final speech is given as he moves toward Horatio and falls in the center of the platform where the duel has occurred. "You that look pale and tremble at this chance, / Had I but time, as this fell sargeant, Death, / Is strict in his arrest, O, I could tell you. . . ." Here, he pauses, as if recognizing that he cannot tell the story. Time is closing in on him. "But let it be. Horatio, I am dead." That awareness motivates his "Horatio, what a wounded name, / Things standing thus unknown, shall live behind me! / If thou didst ever hold me in thy heart, / Absent thee from felicity awhile, / And in this harsh world draw thy breath in pain. . . ." He exhales against his own pain. "To tell my story. / O, I die, Horatio! / The potent poison quite o'er-crows my spirit." His "The rest is silence" is a weary set of syllables emerging from a final exhaustion. A weeping Horatio says "Goodnight, sweet prince . . . to thy rest." Hamlet's eyes remain open in death. An overhead shot shows Hamlet on his back, Horatio kneeling near him, a sword lying nearby, bodies lying in front of the thrones, and the courtiers looking on. The frame widens as the first strains of a requiem begin. The credits begin to roll over the final tableau.

It may be that film can be more "provisional" than TV, more existential and open-ended, and it may also be that a knowledge of the script interferes with a simplified ending like Zeffirelli's. I feel a strong sense of incompleteness at the end of this film, a need for the Fortinbras framing. Strangely, the film as medium seems diminished without this final incorporating rhythm, the drum, the marching feet, the new ruler.

Film, of course, will seek ways to eliminate language, even if Fortinbras's entrance provides opportunities for impressive pageantry. From the point of view of language, it is not surprising, then, that television productions do include some of the Fortinbras material.

These productions include the Chamberlain, the BBC, the Ragnar Lyth Swedish film-for-TV, and the Kline production.

The Chamberlain TV version (Hallmark, 1970) is very active. Chamberlain tosses his sword away after running Claudius through, forces the wine upon Claudius with vigor, and struggles with Horatio over the chalice. Laertes, speaking to the ceiling, emphasizes "noble" in addressing Hamlet, as if at last willing to accept that aspect of Hamlet's persona. Hamlet's "adieu" to Gertrude is tender. He gets most of Hamlet's final speeches, though V.2.326–30 ("You that look pale . . . let it be") and 349–50 ("So tell him . . . solicited") are cut. Chamberlain's "silence" comes after a laugh. The joke is on him.

Fortinbras asks "Where is this sight?" Horatio answers, "What is it you would see? / If aught of woe or wonder, cease your search" (V.2.354–55). Fortinbras then gets the Ambassador's line, "The sight is dismal" (V.2.359). He agrees to hear "How these things came about" (V.2.372) and gets the final lines ("Let four captains. . . . Go, bid the soldiers shoot!": V.2.387–95).

The final overhead shot shows him standing in the midst of the corpses, Queen, Laertes, Hamlet, and the King. In a sense, he stands on what has made *him* King. Kliman suggests that "the four bodies . . . are so symmetrically arranged . . . that they suggest artifice more than violent reality" (Kliman, p. 48). That may be, considering the frantic *activity* but not necessarily the convincing *violence* of the finale, along with the obvious artifice of an overhead shot framing an allegory.

The overhead shot suggests, however, a kind of judgment on both Hamlet and Fortinbras. Hamlet and Horatio are played here as young romantic poets—Horatio made to look like young Coleridge. The "old order" is of the end of the eighteenth century, still contained in and expressed by its heroic couplets, as it were. Hamlet is pulled back by death into a symmetrical world, and Horatio is left to tell a story that cannot be told. For Fortinbras, an apparent symmetry only emphasizes the death that politics inflicts upon its practitioners. He may have escaped it on the battlefield, but he encounters it disturbingly again at Elsinore, regardless of his objections that "such a sight as this" is inappropriate. Politics and war are close cousins, if not identical twins. I am not a Chamberlain fan, but his Hamlet benefits from "concept" and his mild and gentle Prince, given to occasional fits of harmless petulance, is enhanced by the brutality *and* balance of the final tableau.

The BBC version is the most complete of the productions I am considering, only "I'll have it . . . a wounded name" (V.2.335–36) being omitted. Patrick Stewart's Claudius turns to Hamlet after

Laertes's accusation in a smiling effort to placate the Prince. Jacobi's Hamlet, who hates his Claudius as much as Williamson does his, but more pathologically, it seems, runs Claudius through. Claudius complains of "Treason!" and Hamlet pushes him over a table, pours wine down his throat, and dumps him to the floor. Hamlet's "I am dead, Horatio" says don't waste time with me. It is, like so much of the rest of Jacobi's performance, superbly cynical. Hamlet does have to wrestle the cup from Horatio. In a nice touch, some members of the court exit to meet Fortinbras and the returning Ambassadors. Business carries on regardless of the events of the past few moments. Hamlet's "The rest is silence" is laconic, cynical, as if what he has just been saying about his "story" *and* the "election" is meaningless. He is half right, of course. His story, whatever it is, has been told.

We get the complete negotiation between Robert Swann's Horatio, pulling himself away from the death of his friend, and Ian Charleston's tall, armored, crowned Fortinbras, accompanied by soldiers and colors. Horatio is the transitional figure with the delegated authority and specific knowledge that Fortinbras must have. "He never gave commandment for *their* deaths" (V.2.366). He cues Fortinbras to some of the strange "purposes mistook" (V.2.376) represented by the corpse-littered throne room, thus giving Fortinbras the opportunity to express an appropriate "sorrow" (V.2.380) here in Denmark's royal palace. Horatio stands as he tells Fortinbras that the election is swinging his way ("whose voice will draw on more": V.2.384). Fortinbras quietly agrees with Horatio's fears of "more mischance" (V.2.386). It gives him a chance to assert authority and to pursue Horatio's suggestion that some rite of passage is necessary. "To some extent [Fortinbras] is merely doing what he is told" (Cohen, p. 157). Here, he is considering what Horatio says, but agreeing only partly for Horatio's reasons. His final commands to his captain establish his chain of command, make Hamlet "chief elector" by positing the prospect of Hamlet's kingship, translate the scene into a battlefield (however "amiss") by making Hamlet a "soldier" and thus show Fortinbras assuming his "vantage" (V.2.382) as the metaphoric victor here in Elsinore. The script combines with superb acting to express these several reinforcing meanings.

By keeping the script in a time when armor was still worn, the BBC sequence shows that political transition was tricky at any time, regardless of titles and limited "elections." Some can recall their shock when, the day after Kennedy's assassination in 1963, Kendall Merriam, the senior White House correspondent, said, "Good morning, Mr. President." Lyndon Johnson appeared, showing that a constitutional system worked on, regardless of trauma. The BBC production shows a Fortinbras feeling his way and, with Horatio's help from inside the sequence of events, linking his claim to "these things" (V.2.372), shaping order from incoherency and accepting a rhythm whereby he gains the confidence necessary to be the King he is about to be. BBC's intelligent production reveals the intelligence of Shakespeare's script.

An approach that can incorporate Fortinbras into closure without including him is that of Diane Venora in an except from her Hamlet for Joseph Papp (1982). As Hamlet sits on the throne, she hears an offstage cannon and asks about it. She is told, stands to make her announcement, and raises her right arm as she gives Fortinbras her "dying voice." Trumpets and drums accompany Horatio's eulogy. We assume Fortinbras's imminent arrival, but he does not appear. This approach would allow for Hamlet's "How all occasions. . . ." soliloquy (IV.4.32 ff.) without introducing Fortinbras as character in either IV or V. Fortinbras's brief speech at the beginning of IV.4 could be cut or edited to a speech by a captain. The Venora snippet, which comes from a documentary about the production, suggests a condensation and simplification that still allows for a version of political closure without removing the emphasis from Hamlet and his passing. Indeed, this interpretation gives Hamlet a single decisive action as *King*.

In Ragnar Lyth's vivid Swedish film (1984)—again a film designed to translate to TV without reduction—Claudius, covered in blood, smiles and chuckles ingratiatingly. "I am but hurt." A large crow, like those one sees in the garden of the Tower of London, rocks in his cage, and the court cowers against a wall of the dingy Nobel factory where the film was made. The King topples. Hamlet pours the last drops of wine on Claudius, drops the goblet, and looks at the scene as he turns to Horatio. We see Laertes dead on the floor and a pale Gertrude slumped in her chair. "Had I but time. Horatio, I am dead. / Thou Livest. Report me and my cause aright / To the unsatisfied." He hands the King's commission for his death to Horatio and speaks of his wounded name. He touches Horatio's right cheek and leaves a smear of blood there. He hears a loud drum. "What was that?" "I die, Horatio. The rest is silence." He falls to the floor. The camera shifts to a medium shot of Fortinbras, with a large green feather in his helmet. "Where is this sight?" Instead of addressing Fortinbras, Horatio goes to the cowering courtiers, who are now beginning to recognize a new leader. "Let me speak to the yet unknowing world / How these things came about. So shall you hear / Of carnal, bloody, and unnatural acts." The survivors are not

interested. They close their eyes, back away, and fend off Horatio.
He grows desperate: "Of accidental judgements, casual slaughters, /
Deaths put on my cunning, and in the up- / Shot, purposes mistook,
fall'n on / The inventor's heads." The courtiers elbow for a view of
Fortinbras, pushing Horatio aside. "Let us haste to hear it," says
Fortinbras, "And call the noblest to the audience." Osric dances out,
bowing to Fortinbras and to a platoon of Norwegians behind their
Prince. "With sorrow I embrace my fortune," Fortinbras says as a
pro forma prelude to his "I have some rights of old to this kingdom. /
My vantage doth invite my claim. . . ." The courtiers bow, and he
accepts their obeisances. "Of that," he says, absorbing Horatio's
line, "I shall have cause to speak." Horatio says, with marvelous
irrelevance; "Then let it be perform'd, while / Minds are wild, lest
plots all multiply." This is a last effort to gain some attention, but
the courtiers are bowing to Fortinbras. He commands that "Prince
Hamlet" be borne "like a soldier to the stage. Go!" He turns to go
to wherever he wishes his "audience" to be and the others follow
him out. The King, captains, and courtiers depart; Hamlet is carried
out, bouncing unceremoniously on the shoulders of some soldiers.
The crow shakes his cage. Horatio mounts a billiard table and kicks
the cues out of his way. The commission drops from his fingers in
fragments. He hears shots and recognizes gradually that Hamlet's
story will not be told. The Prince is dead. His history is irrelevant.
Long live King Fortinbras. Kliman indicts Horatio's ineffectuality
(Kliman, pp. 222–23), but the emphasis of the ending is on Fortinbras's instant recognition of the political situation and on the ea-
gerness of the Danish courtiers to curry favor with the new regime.
Horatio, who had truly loved Hamlet, is left alone with feelings that
can only be trampled by the march of modern politics. Skarsgaard's
Hamlet is as cynical as Jacobi's without the maturity or the wit and
is no "sweet prince." Nor is Horatio given the eulogy.

The 1990 Kevin Kline TV production, in modern dress, is not a
remake of his 1986 stage version, but it *is* a "staged" *Hamlet*. It
occurs literally on boards and is presented as if to a theater audience.
With the exception of the BBC production, it is the most complete
of the endings—and, like the BBC, effectively so.

Kline slashes Claudius in the neck, then runs him through and
throws the sword away. Claudius's plea for help, however, forces
Hamlet to grab the poisoned chalice and to give Claudius a second
dose of death. Hamlet speaks loudly. Not only is this a "staged"
Hamlet, in a sense overheard by microphones, but Hamlet's is a
public retribution. Laertes gets his full speech (V.2.319–24) and
reaches for Hamlet's hand. Laertes falls to his knees, however, short

of Hamlet's reach. Hamlet slumps near Gertrude, says, "Wretched queen," then grasps her hand on "adieu." His conversation with Horatio is complete but does not seem to address the larger audience that "you" suggests (V.2.326). He forces the wine from Horatio and the goblet clatters away. When Hamlet asks about the "warlike noise" (v.2.341), Osric replies, "Young Fortinbras, with conquest come from Poland, / Gives this warlike volley." Of Hamlet's final speech, then, only "I cannot live to hear the news from England" (V.2.346) is cut, as is the Ambassador's speech (V.2.359–63). Hamlet's "The rest is silence" is delivered via a close-up, Hamlet cradled in Horatio's arms—as if Hamlet is already "there," entering some infinite corridor of silence. He closes his own eyes.

The conversation between Fortinbras and Horatio (V.2.355–59) is complete. As Fortinbras says "cries on havoc" (V.2.356), the camera dollies back to show him standing in a ring of corpses. Horatio says, "Give order . . . these things came about" (V.2.369–72), Fortinbras, in a long brown coat with a captain's four stripes, agrees. "Let us haste to hear it. . . ." (V.2.378–82). He is a little younger, a bit less experienced, a trifle less secure than Charleston's armored prince. When Fortinbras says "claim my vantage" (V.2.382), Horatio looks down at Hamlet. Horatio's response (V.2.383–87) is cut. Fortinbras concludes with the command for Hamlet's funeral and his reinforcement of the inappropriateness of this carnage in a room of state. It will take time for this young Fortinbras to get used to such sights as these. The modern dress of this production suggests that "civilian casualties" will be as frequent as deaths in battle—an insight enforced by Hamlet's "soldier's music and the rite of war" (V.2.391).

Hamlet is carried off, first toward the camera and the assumed audience, then away down the long boards of the stage. Frank Ardolino describes the "image of the dead Hamlet being carried from the stage with his arms theatrically outstretched, straining to touch someone" (Ardolino, p. 5). The procession casts a shadow as it moves away from the static camera, so that the only thing Hamlet's hands touch is the bare floor. Fortinbras is not in the frame, but his presence is felt behind the camera, motivating the removal of his rival from the scene. We sense Fortinbras demonstrating to those remaining that he has learned his first lesson as King.

The Kline production effectively balances the political and the personal aspects of the script within a theatrical production which the camera enhances unobtrusively. While the production lacks the energy of a live audience, it frames the closure for its television audience by trusting the script to know how to end the play.

The problem for *Hamlet* as film is that while the scripted finale may be visually impressive—as it must have been on Shakespeare's stage—the director encounters all that language, and decides to rest his case with Hamlet's silence. In this instance, television shows that it has an advantage over its rival cousin.

8

The Case for a Black Othello

I

Jonathan Goldberg suggests that "ideology is haunted by what it excludes, subverted by what it subordinates" (Goldberg, *Shakespeare Reproduced*, p. 235). In America, at least, we have seen evidence of that haunting and subversion. A television commercial in 1988 showed a powerful and threatening black man coming toward the camera as prison doors clanged behind him. That commercial supported and helped to elect a president. Later, that same president approved a strategy whereby a black nominee would convince the nation that a black and politically conservative woman had somehow allied herself with a white lynch-mob.

I wish to suggest here that the role of Othello should be played by a black actor. While it is true that Shakespeare's Othello, Richard Burbage, was not black, I think it also true that any effort to dodge the racial issue in the script will, indeed, either haunt or subvert the production of the script, either by calling attention to the inevitable and perhaps intentional stereotype that the actor will create (e.g., Olivier) or by creating the vacuum that a white Othello imposes on the script. In the latter instance we have an Anthony Hopkins directed by a Jonathan Miller who claims that the play is not "about colour, but . . . about jealously, which is something we are all vulnerable to" (Wine, p. 78). Miller finds the black Othello a tradition that has built up around the script—if so, only fairly recently, with Robeson (cf. Rosenberg, pp. 180–81)—and tends to pursue the line of the Folger introduction, which though dated is very influential because so often used in schools:

Actors who chose to play Othello as a coal-black man, however, were probably taking Shakespeare's words too literally. Shakespeare was not trying in *Othello* to emphasize any racial differences between the hero and heroine, though the differences in their backgrounds provide Iago with plausible suggestions for Desdemona's alleged disaffection. Othello, as Shakespeare characterizes him, is a soldier of fortune from a foreign country, a hero, who wins Desdemona by his bearing and the romantic recital of his adventures in strange lands. When enemies of Othello want to abuse him, they speak opprobriously of his alien looks and wonder that Desdemona could love so strange a man, but that is part of the reality of the characterization, not a hint on Shakespeare's part of "racism." The unhappy times when men would read some suggestion of racial prejudice into every piece of literature concerned with alien characters lay some centuries ahead. (Wright, xiv)

This 1956 introduction commits the "historicist fallacy" perpetuated by the edition's cover, which depicts an impressive, dark-eyed, dark-bearded white man with an earring in his left ear. This illustration is not identified. Included within the introductory materials, however, is a 1590 "conception of a noble Moor," showing a racially very different face, certainly one that Roderigo could call "thick-lips" (I.1.70).

It is probably impossible for an American of the 1990s to look at this play without racially informed eyes. It is probably wise, then, to befriend subjectivity and argue for race as a central but not exclusive aspect of the script. That, I believe, is what Trevor Nunn does in his recent TV version of the studio production of the play for RSC. Before looking at that production, however, I want to develop a thesis about the play using psychological criticism and, specifically, the insights of Afro-American writers and one, John Howard Griffin, who made himself a black and went into the segregated American South of the late 1950s. The results, I believe, suggest that *Othello* is indeed a profound study of racism and that the racial aspect cannot be replaced by an emphasis on jealousy or evil. Instead, the racial factor *informs* other aspects of the script.

It can be argued, in fact, that a "white" Othello might well result in a "racist" production. It would be haunted by what it tried to repress. In the "real world" we find a David Duke, admirer of Hitler and former KKK member, accommodating himself easily with the "Republican agenda." That Duke's association makes a good man like John Sununu uncomfortable, *might* suggest that good reason for that discomfort does exist. The "white" Othello could be indicted because it pursues the agenda of Samuel Taylor Coleridge, who said "[it is] monstrous to conceive this beautiful Venetian girl falling in love with a veritable Negro" (Hawkes, p. 167), or of Charles Lamb, who spoke of the "unsuitableness of the person [that Desdemona] selected for her lover. . . . This noble lady, with a singularity rather to be wondered at than imitated, had chosen for the object of her affections a Moor, a black. . . ." (Bradley, p. 202, n. 1). These Romantic critics accepted the black Othello, of course, but, in doing so, immediately enlisted under the banner of Iago. To turn Othello into a "suitable person," as Anthony Hopkins so obviously was, is not to resolve the issues the play raises, but to exacerbate them.

While Elliot H. Tokson does not deal with Othello in *The Popular Image of the Black Man in English Drama: 1550–1688*, he does define the kinds of negative stereotyping to which an Othello would have been subjected—and *is* subjected in the play. The basic stereotype that Tokson identifies is the linkage of the black man to the Devil, which Shakespeare in a typical reversal of surface meanings has *Iago* assume for himself. Tokson says that in the period he studied as in racist society today, "the black cannot be allowed to surpass the white" (Tokson, p. 138). Was that true of the sixteenth and seventeenth centuries, or is it, as Estelle W. Taylor says, a "conclusion . . . [that] must be viewed as [a] sweeping generalization . . . made from a twentieth-century perspective"? (Taylor, p. 507). The question is unanswerable, of course. As the scripts move forward in time the times inhabit them. They are structures awaiting the haunting of the spirits of the present and the ghosts of the future. If the scripts do not pick up and reflect our own experience—qualified and conditioned and illuminated by the production—then the works are what most people take them to be: words on a page, capable of being dissected and examined microscopically, but relevant only as fossils are relevant. We must see the plays with the eyes of our culture. We have no choice. Will we see "truth" or "a pebble of quartz"?—"for once then, something." It may help to see the plays, as Jan Kott does, in their *strictly* modern context, in that it shows that Shakespeare was already on to the technique of a Beckett or a Camus. Of course. But to see Shakespeare *only* via the lens of lesser modern dramatists is to discern the pebble of quartz. That is one possible fallacy underlying the present chapter.

Carol Thomas Neely argues that

> the complexities of reading the discourse of madness in Shakespeare and his culture reveal the difficulty and necessity of historicizing: that is, of trying to understand one's own position and that of one's subject(s) in today's culture in relation to the construction of the subject(s) that emerged in early modern culture, of trying to tease out disjunctions and connections. In particular this project reveals that the shape of gender difference cannot be assumed but must always be reformulated in specific cultural and historical contexts. (Neely, p. 338)

It may be possible to historicize the present, in this case to argue the existence of racism as a major if undercover current in American life and therefore to argue its inevitable presence or resonance in a modern production of *Othello* in *any* culture with a white power elite and a black minority or underclass. It is probably impossible to historicize Shakespeare's England, since the evidence is mixed in most cases. It is a fallacy to apply the results of historicization *to* Shakespeare and to restrict his plays to just what his culture may have known. This process rules out his examination and transcendence of commonplaces. He is of an age, no doubt, but, as Ann Thompson says, "In some sense all future readings could be said to be already 'there' in the text, but we have to wait for the historical circumstances which will make them visible" (Thompson, p. 81). The findings of the new historicism are irrelevant to the texts as scripts except where, as Neely shows, we can discern in historical contexts modes of interpreting the plays as potentials for performance (Neely, p. 338). New historicism serves as a kind of brake, in its conservatism, on the more extreme efforts to "modernize" Shakespeare and helps reveal the shallowness of a merely modern analysis, as Kott's tends to be. At its best, as in the Neely essay, it can link up with production. When it does so it becomes immediately and excitingly relevant.

Writing at the beginning of this century, A. C. Bradley said, "*Othello* is a drama of modern life" (Bradley, p. 180). While most of Shakespeare's plays are our contemporaries if our imaginations and sense of our times make an energetic contact with any given script, I want to explore one way in which *Othello* is "modern" in 1993.

My approach will be psychological. I will suggest two conventional psychological treatments—the Freudian and the Jungian—and then develop the area that this play more than any other in the canon invites us—compels us—to examine: perhaps the play's central source of power and mystery, the question of race.

For the Freudian, Othello is a victim of the Oedipal problem that plagues all males. Men unconsciously wish to act out the story that Sophocles dramatized, in which Oedipus killed his father and married his mother. When a man marries, his wife will be imaged emotionally through the filter of the man's unconscious which harbors an incestuous desire for that other woman—his mother.

Desdemona, then, must be perfect. She is being compared to an ideal woman. When Iago delightedly paints a picture in which Desdemona and Cassio look at each other's nakedness, Othello's reaction draws energy—libido—from the primal scene of his mother's sexuality. It is as if Othello is a little boy again, peeking at the forbidden scene of his unclothed mother as half of the beast with two backs.

Othello, who unconsciously wishes to be the other half, merely looks on. "Would you the supervisor," Iago asks, "grossly gape on? / Behold her topped?" (III.3.444–45.) Iago goes on to show Othello the scene Iago says cannot be shown to Othello:

> It were a tedious difficulty, I think,
> To bring them to that prospect. Damn them, then,
> If ever mortal eyes do see them bolster
> More than their own!
>
> (III.3.446–49)

Later, of course, Iago will create an agonizing vicarious experience for Othello by eliciting mocking responses from Cassio about Bianca (IV.1.). Othello, trapped in Iago's cave (IV.1.95), believes that Cassio speaks of Desdemona. Iago manipulates the shadow-shapes of "reality" in front of an Othello whose eyes and ears are now conditioned to accept falseness as truth. Cassio laughs and Othello says, "Now he tells how she plucked him to my chamber" (IV.1.157).

Like anyone who has projected unconscious energy onto another person, Othello has given Desdemona a kind of magical control over him. The mother continues to control her son, particularly in the area of his relationship to women, long after the son has reached a chronological maturity. Even Othello's story can be seen as a kind of "look Ma, no hands!" effort to gain a mother's approval:

> She lov'd me for the dangers I had passed,
> And I lov'd her that she did pity them.
>
> (I.3.166–67)

Here, depending upon an actor's emphasis, the lines can suggest an effort to gain and to respond to approval. I loved her because she loved me! No real exchange has occurred. Othello has moved to no new position. It is only his persona or self-created image that has captured Desdemona, as he sees it. Her love seems to be based on his fictions—his autobiographical narratives which feature himself as solitary warrior and adventurer in realms unseen by other men. The maintenance of this fiction would seem to demand continuing and unqualified support from the mother for whom the boy can do no wrong. It follows that any marriage predicated upon these premises is doomed. Desdemona, facing her father, "perceive[s] a divided duty" (I.3.199). When Othello comes to believe that Desdemona's duty is divided where *he* is concerned, he, the absolutist, will release all his past and present in a great flood of language:

O, now for ever
Farewell the tranquil mind! Farewell content!
Farewell the plumed troop, and the big wars
That make ambition virtue . . .
Farewell! Othello's occupation's gone!

(III.3.392–402)

So great is his unconscious need for his mother's love that when it seems to have been withdrawn by his mother's substitute, Desdemona, Othello feels that the glorious career that has gotten him to this point has itself been erased.

This approach might seem mere speculation were it not that Othello quite specifically gives Desdemona the power over him that—he claims—his mother had over his father. The handkerchief, he tells Desdemona, "Did an Egyptian to my mother give. . . ."

She told her, while she kept it,
'Twould make her amiable and subdue my father
Entirely to her love.

(III.4.63–68)

By this time, of course, Othello himself has reverted to the past—not just that unconscious time-zone dominated by his mother—but to the magic place he had explored before he came to Venice, Christianity, and Desdemona. Desdemona has herself made the handkerchief a fetish—a magic object: "She so loves the token," says Emilia, "That she reserves it evermore about her / To kiss and talk to" (III.3.331–34). Desdemona has assumed part of the role Othello has projected upon her: "he conjured her," says Emilia, "she should ever keep [the handkerchief]" (III.3.332). Desdemona makes a pathetic effort to create a wedding night by bidding Emilia to "lay on my bed my wedding sheets" (IV.2.122). But this attempt at white magic is countered by the handkerchief "spotted with strawberries" (III.3.487). The sheets have become, for Othello, "contaminated" (Iago: IV.1.223) or, as he says, "Thy bed, lust-stained, shall with lust's blood be spotted." The handkerchief—bridge for Othello from the old into the new world—cancels all positive energy within that world and yanks him back into the world he thought he had left behind. The handkerchief and the wedding sheets have become the same stained material, each an emblem for Desdemona's "lust," a parallel often noted. Behind the handkerchief and within its web is the power of woman over man, mother over son. Man must act for other men. He must kill Desdemona, or "else she'll betray more men" (V.2.6). That is "the cause" (V.2.1) of which Othello speaks, unaware of the cause that triggers his action.

If Freud is right, that cause is the unresolved Oedipal conflict within Othello's psyche. Othello claims at the end that the handkerchief was "an antique token / My father gave my mother" (V.2.253–54). But that is not the story he told Desdemona. The later version suggests that Othello and his father have become, in Othello's mind, the same person. One way of getting rid of the father is to become him—in a variation of the Oedipal myth. In each case, that of Othello and his father, the husband would control the wife by giving her a charm that will control *him*. The handkerchief captures the man's awareness that he is controlled by a woman. It was the power Othello's mother held and the power Othello ceded to Desdemona. Othello's linkage of himself with his father makes Othello a version of Brabantio, Desdemona's father. Brabantio reports a possibly "incestuous dream" (Fiedler, p. 146) about Desdemona and claims that only "mixtures o'er the blood, / Or . . . some dram, conjured to this effect" (I.3.116–17) could have won Desdemona from *him*. Othello, we are told, "conjured [Desdemona] that she should ever keep" the handkerchief (III.3.332), so some truth develops around charges that seemed baseless earlier. Othello does not worry about his lack of "sympathy in years" (II.1.261)—that is, that he is considerably older than Desdemona—until Iago begins to work on him. He realizes that he is "declined / Into the vale of years" (III.3.300–301). That Othello may be nearer Brabantio's age than to Desdemona's (cf. Stavropoulos) suggests that Desdemona's elopement is indeed "not unlike [Brabantio's] dream" (I.1.157). If the father's selection of a mate for his daughter—as in the instance of Egeus's preference for Demetrius as Hermia's husband in *A Midsummer Night's Dream*—signals a latent incestuous desire on the father's part, there also exists a hint of the incestuous link between Brabantio and Othello. We notice in this play that Brabantio has no wife and that Desdemona is responsible for "house affairs" (I.3.163) at Brabantio's. Iago draws a parallel between Brabantio and Othello, turning the precedent of the father into Othello's crisis: "She did deceive her father, marrying you" (III.3.233) and echoing Brabantio's warning: "Look to her, Moor, if thou hast eyes to see. / She has deceived her father, and may thee" (I.3.317–18). Iago enforces the parallel by creating a successful suitor for Desdemona—Cassio, a man presumably younger than Othello. Again, as in his saying that his father gave the handkerchief to his mother, Othello takes the father's place and in this instance fulfills the Oedipal pattern of the killing of the father: "pure grief" about the marriage of Desdemona to Othello, breaks Brabantio's "old heart" in two (V.2.242–43). Desdemona, in escaping her father, runs right into a version of Brabantio's revenge against her, conducted on the unconscious level by Othello.

The Jungian approach leads us into the vastness of the script without in any way invalidating the minute distinctions that the Freudian configuration invites. Jung suggests that is dangerous for anyone to believe that the information provided by the senses during consciousness represents reality. Such a state—which denies the superior power of the *un*conscious—is called "inflation," or "*hubris* of consciousness"—*hubris* being excessive pride or overconfidence. We can understand why Othello says what he does when he lands at Cyprus, but we should also understand that his rhetoric predicts and predicates his downfall—the fall that Aristotle attributes to the tragic hero. The tragic hero is not just the victim of accident or chance. He wills his downfall:

> It gives me wonder great as my content
> To see you here before me. O my soul's joy.
> If after every tempest come such calms,
> May the winds blow till they have wakened death!
> And let the laboring bark climb hills of seas
> Olympus-high, and duck again as low
> As hell's from heaven! If it were now to die,
> 'Twere now to be most happy; for I fear
> My soul hath her content so absolute
> That not another comfort like to this
> Succeeds in unknown fate.
>
> (I.2.212–22)

He says too much, claiming a superhuman perfection for himself, his words placing him on top of those Olympus-high hills where the gods live. He ignores the process that is life and thus does awaken death. Having claimed heaven-on-earth he will later describe Desdemona's accusing look as "hurl [ing his] soul from heaven" and down to hell, where "fiends will snatch at it" (V.2.221–22).

Desdemona tries to recall him to human reality:

> The heavens forbid
> But that our loves and comforts should increase
> Even as our days do grow!
>
> (I.2.222–24)

Marriage is culmination in one sense—the aging mercenary is going to settle down at last—but it is also a beginning. Othello makes it an ending, placing himself on top of those "hills whose heads touch heaven" (I.iii.156) of which he spoke earlier. He must fall. He falls not because the gods are angry at his invasion of their space. This play demonstrates no interaction with, or intervention by, forces beyond nature. The point is that if "It doesn't get any better than this," as the guys in the beer commercials say, then any future moment must be less than this and any future movement must be downward. The only thing for Othello to do is to stop everything, but he cannot. What he does do is to turn the control of time over to Iago, who will have no trouble dictating a negative history for Othello from this moment on.

Jung describes Othello's psychology and the importance of an object like the handkerchief to this type, without specifying Othello at all. This is the "introverted sensation type" in Jung's theory of personality:

> Heirlooms are attached to his soul as by invisible threads; any change is upsetting, if not positively dangerous, as it seems to denote a magical animation of the object. His ideal is a lonely island where nothing moves except when he permits it to move. . . . [His] psychic mirror world . . . reflect[s] the existing contents of consciousness not in their known and customary form but . . . as a million-year-old consciousness might see them . . . he lives in a mythological world where men, animals, locomotives, houses, rivers, and mountains appear as either benevolent deities or as malevolent demons. (Coursen, pp. 102–3)

One of Othello's problems in civilized and conventional Venice is that he is "from Wonderland," as Bradley says (Bradley, p. 187). Iago puts him back there, but only where the magic is black magic. We could add that, as Iago goes to work, both handkerchiefs and women turn from benevolence to malevolence, from deities to demons.

Othello—having in a sense denied his humanity by making himself a god—can find no middle ground. In comedy, we recognize our own follies and then see the other person—once the love juice has been dissolved—not as an ideal but as a human being with whom one wants to share the experience of living. And that is what love is. But Othello wants nothing to move, including Desdemona. She must be as Othello's idealized but unconscious concept of his mother is—a virgin adoring her child. If only Desdemona were "one entire perfect chrysolite" (V.2.173)—that is, an exquisite topaz—or "monumental alabaster" (V.2.5)—that is, a statue. But she is neither. She is human, and Othello cannot accept her humanity. She sweats, for example, and Othello finds in her hand "a young and sweating devil here" (III.4.45).

Othello must fall because of who he is and what he does, call it flaw or error in judgment. The Greek word, *hamartia*, means missing the mark, as in archery. Iago dictates the nature of Othello's fall, but he does not cause it:

> O, you are well tuned now!
> But I'll set down the pegs that make this music,
> As honest as I am.
>
> (II.1.231–33)

Othello, as he lands at Cyprus, creates a perfect world for himself and forces Desdemona to join him as a reflective jewel, even over her objections. He basks in the clearing light and in the energy that the fission of his language releases. The enemy has sunk. A few pagan corpses bob in the surf as the storm-rack drops away. It is a great moment, but Othello should kneel and thank God for it, acknowledging the larger powers to which he subscribes as a Christian. But Shakespeare knows what a dull play that would make!

In making Desdemona the beautiful object which completes him, Othello takes her out of time, creating a madonna frozen forever in adoration. This kind of infatuation leads to an opposite valuation. Again—no middle position exists. The conditional, changing, qualified ways in which we understand another person are not available to Othello. And that is his doing, not Iago's. It is all or nothing at all, or, as Othello says, "My life upon her faith!" (I.3.319). Othello's projection of feminine perfection upon his victim may represent the unconscious image of his mother, who remains a virgin in Othello's psyche, even if biologically he knows otherwise. The Freudian and Jungian approaches are not contradictory.

Jung goes further, however, to suggest what happens when the male's feminine qualities are repressed. He projects the image of the mother—all of that unconscious emotional energy—upon another woman. When she turns out not to be perfect, her "dark aspect—the prostitute, the seductress, or the witch is likely to present itself" to the man (Fordham, p. 39). As Othello becomes "the Moor of Venice," as the play's subtitle calls him, Desdemona becomes "that cunning whore of Venice / That married with Othello" (IV.2.104–5). As the potentiality for "hell" is released from its hiding place in Othello's name, Desdemona becomes, for him, the "demon" hidden in her name, the "fair devil" (III.3.536) to which the man blinded by his unconscious translates the woman.

Othello becomes a creature of appetite, a man "whose head . . . grow[s] beneath [his] shoulders" (I.3.161), the "manage[r of] private and domestic quarrel" (II.3.218), soon after cashiering Cassio for similar misdemeanors. He is sold again into slavery (cf. I.3.152–53), perhaps an inevitable part of the black man's background and certainly the inevitable status of Othello's future once Iago hears Othello's fatal music on the shores of Cyprus.

The pattern culminates in Desdemona's murder and Othello's suicide, events made inevitable by Othello, who loads the moment of his landing with more than it can hold, and also by what happens at the end of act III, scene 3. Freud tends to see us as creatures bounded by our own biology. Jung does not dismiss that context but he places it in history and within a cosmos where we can, indeed, choose not to examine our lives. If we do not, however, our lives subject us to rigorous examination.

At the end of the long scene 3 of act III, Othello and Iago kneel and exchange vows. This moment represents an anti-sacrament or, to put it another way, a pagan marriage. Othello speaks to a "marble heaven" (III.3.515), a cold and monumental place like a tomb, containing no Christian deity. Iago calls on "you ever-burning lights above / You elements that clip us round about" (III.3.519–20). Othello is now living in that distant pagan world of stars and their prophetic fury. Later, he will ask, "Who can control his fate?" (V.2.312), claim that Desdemona was an "ill-starred wench" (V.2.319), and speak of "unlucky deeds" (V.2.395), as if what has happened to him and Desdemona had been dictated by the stars.

The end of act III represents a reverse-Epiphany in which the stars, those "ever-burning lights above," lead Othello into the past. The Feast of Epiphany is the celebration of the spreading of the Gospel—the light of Christ—to the Gentiles, or pagans. Its allegory is the coming of the Magi to Christ. These pagan astrologers followed a star out of darkness—the past and its many gods—to a new and single source of illumination. It is a wonderful story of transition, of a shift in paradigms. One of the Magi long before Shakespeare's time was invariably depicted as black (cf. Hunter, pp. 154–55)—Balthasar. This Balthasar, Othello, himself descended from "royal siege" (I.2.24), is reconverted into the old dispensation. Gone are the sanctions and continuities of "his baptism / All seals and symbols of redeemed sin" (II.3.337–38). We see all this clearly and look on in helpless clarity as Othello blindly stumbles among the animated objects of the world he thought he had left behind. Having completed his play and having called it a comedy, Othello finds himself within a play whose scenario is dictated by Iago. And in Iago's play, Othello's great narrative voice is quiet and his heroic stature is shrunk. Othello regains that voice and conception at the end in a speech which talks exotically of tears dropping "as fast as the Arabian trees / Their med'cinable gum." (V.2.346–7). Othello is talking about the shrubs that produce myrrh, a product of Arabia and regions near the Red Sea. The tears may signal Othello's own return to the Christian world he had abandoned. Here they are like myrrh, and it is myrrh which tradition tells us Balthasar the black magus brought as a gift to the newborn Christ.[1]

The Jungian psychologist, Edward Whitmont, says that "The Negro . . . carries the projection of the white man's fear of the dark, the spontaneous, instinctual side of himself which must be exorcised when [the Negro] is met only on this level" (Whitmont, pp. 233–34). This is one explanation of the association of blackness with the Devil. What Iago sees in Othello is Iago's shadow. The shadow, in psychological terms, represents all that Iago has repressed from his own persona, or "image." Othello is imaginative, idealistic, and tends to enlarge any moment to its grandest dimensions. For him, language—his own, at least—has an aesthetic dimension. He uses words to create stories of which he is the hero, not recognizing that his facility is one reason why he becomes a tragic hero in a larger fiction by Shakespeare. Iago is a rationalist who sees the world as tangible: "The wine she drinks is made of grapes" (II.1.282), he says of Desdemona, denying the sacramental possibilities of wine, erasing any sense in which the physical can be consecrated. "Love," for Iago, is merely a subcategory under "lust," which is one of the Seven Deadly Sins (cf. I.3.344–56). He reduces everything to a thing. But, while his point of view is narrow, it is powerful because he has a materialist answer for everything, or, if he does not, a storehouse of commonplaces and aphorisms to fit any occasion. Language for Iago has only a practical dimension. He uses words to manipulate others into his scenarios. If Othello creates his world from the center, Iago stands at the side, a detached observer of the cross-purposes he sets in motion. He shares his creative side—"Knavery's plain face" (II.1.340) only with us.

Iago can be seen as a behaviorist, introducing Othello to a suddenly alien environment, conditioning Othello to the racist agenda of that environment, and reinforcing Othello's reactions to the point where he falls down and foams at the mouth. But for all of Othello's vulnerability, Iago is not quite the unmoved mover he might wish himself to be. Something eats at him:

> I do suspect the lusty Moor
> Hath leaped into my seat; the thought whereof
> Doth, like a poisonous mineral, gnaw my inwards . . .
>
> (II.1.323–25)

Earlier, he had said of the alleged liaison between Othello and Emilia, "I know not if't be true; / Yet I, for mere suspicion in that kind, / Will do as if for surety" (I.3.406–8). Here, of course, is the racist approach. The racist does not worry about the truth. The truth, in fact, would get in the way. If Othello is tortured by Desdemona's physicality because it disturbs his image of feminine perfection—that is, the maternal pattern that controls him—Iago is eaten up by the picture of the black man possessing the white woman. While Iago maintains almost total control over Emilia, he cannot control that dark imagination which Othello suddenly embodies.

The awareness of the black man's alleged sexual potency is not of recent origin. We find it in the Elizabethan England within which Shakespeare was growing up. Travelers to Africa reported black men "furnished with such members as are often a sort of burthen unto them" (Hakluyt: Newman, p. 148). "Early cartographers ornamented maps with representations of black men bearing enormous sexual organs" (Newman, p. 148). This awareness got carried over with interest to the American South. One of the white men who picked up John Howard Griffin—who had changed the color of his skin to black—tells Griffin, "There's plenty white women would like to have a good buck Negro" (Griffin, p. 92). Before he went into Mississippi, Griffin was warned, "If you pass by a picture show, and they've got women on the posters outside, don't look at them. . . ." "Is it that bad?" Griffin asked. "Another man said: 'Somebody's sure to say, "Hey, boy—what are you looking at that white gal like *that* for."'" (Griffin. p. 62). Was it that bad? In August 1955, only a little more than four years before Griffin began his journey, Emmett Till, a fourteen-year-old black from Chicago, allegedly whistled at a white woman in Mississippi. He was kidnapped by the wife's husband, Roy Bryant, and his half-brother, J. W. Milam, who admitted the kidnapping but denied any connection with the bludgeoned body—also shot through the head—that turned up in the Tallahatchie River a few days later. Till's mother identified the body, on which was a ring belonging to Till. The jury acquitted Bryant and Milam—after a struggle of one hour and five minutes. The jury was not convinced that a positive identification had been made. John C. Whitten, the defense counsel, suggested that it might all have been a plot—those agitators from the North sent someone down to stir up all that trouble. Whitten told the all-white jury that he was "sure that every last Anglo-Saxon one of you has the courage to free these men in the face of that pressure" (*New York Times*, 1). The jury swaggered out feeling very courageous.

In September 1962, James Meredith, a young black man, attempted to enroll in The University of Mississippi—"Ole Miss." Riot and death ensued. One psychologist speculated that since "Ole Miss" is the name the slave gave to the wife of the plantation owner, Meredith's setting foot on that sacred soil represented miscegenation—the possession of the white woman by the black man. The term does *not* apply to the white man possessing the black woman, because, as one white man explained to Griffin, "We figure we're doing you people a favor to get some white blood in your kids" (Griffin, p. 109).

The psychological interpretation of the events in Oxford, Mississippi, in September 1962—as Meredith attended classes escorted by U.S. marshalls as the U.S. Army stood guard—may seem farfetched. And it happened a long time ago. More recently, a black rapist, Willie Horton, repeated his crime while on parole from a Massachusetts prison, under a release program approved by Governor Dukakis. The George Bush campaign in 1988 used a commercial showing a menacing black man coming toward us as we sat in the safety of television land. Jail doors shut behind the black man. The beast was out of his cage. The commercial played on racial fears and specifically on fears of black sexual energy run wild. Did the gutless Dukakis campaign fight back against such blatant racism being employed to elect a president of all the people? You bet they didn't. Dukakis was too busy trying to look like a Republican by riding around in a tank.

Iago may appropriate silence unto himself at the end of *Othello*, but what he represents goes on. Coleridge talks of Iago's several soliloquies as "the motive-hunting of motiveless malignity" (Hawkes, p. 171), but Iago the rationalist may be pursuing a unconscious agenda that his own psychology of perception cannot discover or articulate. The rationalist tends to deny the irrational, even in himself. Madness is merely a deviation from the norm. Iago neither knows nor cares whether Emilia and Othello have made love, so it cannot be sexual jealousy that gnaws his inwards "like a poisonous mineral" (II.1.325). It must be that aspect of racism that incorporates and cannot tolerate the black man's sexuality. Iago cannot find the antidote to the poison, so he will "pour this pestilence into [Othello's] ear"—that Desdemona pleads for Cassio for "her body's lust" (II.3.358–59). The "poisons" he administers to Othello, says

Iago, "with a little act upon the blood / Burn like the mines of sulphur" (III.3.368–71).

John Howard Griffin meets an Iago:

> His decent blue eyes turned yellow. I knew that nothing could touch him to have mercy once he decided a Negro should be 'taught a lesson.' . . . it caught him up like a lust now. He entertained it, his voice unctuous with pleasure and cruelty. The highway stretched deserted through the swamp forests. He nodded toward the solid wall of brush flying past our windows. "You can kill a nigger and toss him into that swamp and no one'll ever know what happened to him.' . . . This was . . . the lust to cause pain or fear through self-power. Surely not even his wife or closest friends had ever seen him like this. It was a side he would show no one but his victims. . . . (Griffin, pp. 110–11)

While Iago does not show Othello this side of him, and while he may display some of it to Roderigo, we notice that it is we the audience with whom Iago shares "the lust to cause pain." The play is exploring our own racial attitudes.

Iago's techniques are superb, of course. Notice that he does not merely claim that he saw the sacred handkerchief in Cassio's hand. He says

> such a handkerchief
> (I am sure it was your wife's) did I today
> See Cassio wipe his beard with.
>
> (III.3.488–90)

—as if Cassio has just risen from a greasy meal and finds the handkerchief merely a convenient piece of cloth. Iago employs an apparently innocent simile when Othello forces Iago to say who began the brawl between Cassio and Montano on the night that Othello, it seems, had hoped to consummate his marriage to Desdemona (cf. II.3.9–11). "I do not know," Iago says. "Friends all but now, even now, / In quarter and in terms like bride and groom / Devesting them for bed" (II.iii.181–83). Iago describes what Othello and Desdemona presumably have just been doing. Suddenly the alarm bell summons Othello to duty again. Iago has manufactured an attack on Othello's sexuality and on Othello's ability to make love to Desdemona, and has the audacity to remind Othello of what Othello has just been anticipating.

Iago introduces Othello to Venice and its mores. If Othello is a narcissist as Olivier played him—a man in love with his image and striving at all costs to keep it polished—then he must be placed in a context where his image becomes ugly. Production could suggest, as the script does, that Othello chooses Desdemona because she love *him* and reinforces his love of self. Furthermore, this most beautiful of Venetian women enhances Othello's image: "she had eyes, and chose me" (III.3.216). If he selected Cassio because Cassio was handsome, courtly, and went to the best service academy, Cassio represents another piece in the mosaic of Othello's image-making (cf. Michael Goldman, p. 67). As Nick Carraway says of Gatsby, "He sprang from his platonic conception of himself." Whether we agree with the narcissistic version of Othello—so easy a victim for Iago— we find that Othello is not *of* Venice. He is "an extravagant and wheeling stranger / Of here and everywhere" (I.1.150–51), as Roderigo says, and seems to be a man "from Wonderland" (Bradley, p. 187). To Iago he is "the Moor" and therefore predictable in his inconsistency: "These Moors are changeable in their wills" (I.3.369).

Now Venice *is* a racist society. Not just Iago, but Roderigo, who calls Othello "the thick-lips" (I.1.70), Brabantio, who talks of Othello's "sooty bosom" (I.2.85) and Emilia, who calls Desdemona's marriage "her most filthy bargain" (V.2.189) tell us how Venice reacts to Othello. But he seems impervious to the hatred, and Desdemona is the exception. Iago, however, reduces her *to* the Venetian norm. Stereotypes—or those faceless people who conform to the norm—are easier to manipulate than people. Stereotypes are already programmed to be predictable, even if, as in the case of Iago's assessment of "These Moors," that predictability is *un*predictability. Venice functions on the principle of the go-between. One does not go directly to anyone—one sends an emissary. When people employ the go-between, they empower that person, who can become the equal sign between "x" and "y" and can make either "x" or "y" what he wants it to be. Iago becomes the go-between for Othello and Venetian society. "I know our country disposition well," he says. "In Venice [Venetian wives] let heaven see the pranks / They dare not show their husbands" (III.3.228–30). Iago places Othello back into the environment of his competition for Desdemona against the "wealthy curled darlings of" Venice (I.1.83) and creates a host of phantom suitors:

> Her will, recoiling to her better judgement,
> May fall to match you with her country forms,
> And happily may repent.
>
> (III.3.269–71)

Indeed, her very choice of Othello becomes an action as unnatural as Brabantio said it was earlier. Othello was impervious to the charge earlier, but, in a weakened state, he is vulnerable to its reinforcement by Iago:

> one may smell in [her] a will most rank,
> Foul disproportion, thoughts unnatural. . . .
> Not to affect many proposed matches
> Of her own complexion, and degree,
> Whereto we see in all things nature tends. . . .
>
> (III.3.262–66)

If Desdemona has acted unnaturally, as Iago claims, then Othello is unnatural—as he is in the Venetian mirror Iago holds up to him. Iago can suggest something to Othello for which no evidence exists, that Desdemona "seemed to shake and fear [Othello's] looks" (III.3.234). Othello suddenly begins to consider his race: "I am black / And have not those soft parts of conversation / That chamberers have" (III.3.298–300). And—even more negatively, he equates himself and the seemingly perfect addition to his own perfection: "Her name, that was as fresh / As Dian's visage is now begrimed and black / As mine own face" (III.3.434–36).

Iago has begun to implant in Othello a self-hatred that reflects Venice's racism. The process is vividly exemplified by John Howard Griffin, who changes his skin color from white to black:

> In the flood of light against white tile, the face and shoulders of a stranger—a fierce, bald, very dark Negro—glared at me from the glass. He in no way resembled me. . . . I was imprisoned in the flesh of an utter stranger, an unsympathetic one with whom I felt no kinship. (Griffin, p. 11)

In this example of reverse-narcissism—the recoil in horror *from* the image—Griffin accomplishes the complex feat of being both Iago the racist and Othello the victim of racism. The great black leader, Malcolm X, gives us a powerful analogue to Griffin's experience. Malcolm's mother was born as a result of the rape of her mother by a white man in the West Indies. Malcolm learned to hate the white man in general and specifically, as he tells us, "to hate every drop of that white rapist's blood that is in me" (Malcolm, p. 2). "I hate us," says a black man on a bus to Griffin (p. 60). E. Franklin Frazier, writing of the Negro bourgeoisie, talks of their "self-hatred—which may appear to be directed toward the black masses but which in reality is directed against themselves" (Messner, p. 197). The late black writer, James Baldwin, betrays precisely that bourgeois attitude when he says, "I despised [black people] possibly because they failed to produce a Rembrandt" (Cleaver, p. 100). In one study, developmental psychologists discovered that

> the young [Negro] child acquires value-laden racial labels and fragments of popular stereotypes to describe his own and other racial and ethnic groups. Both Negro and white children learn to associate Negro with "dirty," "bad," and "ugly," and white with "clean," "nice," and "good." For the Negro child, these emotionally charged judgements operate to establish the white group as vastly superior to his own racial group. (Clark and Clark, p. 345)

Othello has never needed to establish an identity with or within his racial group. He has been a singular warrior. Iago fabricates a social setting for Othello predicated on Othello's marriage. It is a social setting, Iago suggests, in which Desdemona will refuse to remain and into which Othello does not fit. The strength of Iago's argument emerges from the truth that Othello fits into Venice only insofar as he is required for military reasons. The racism of black children, say the researchers, results in "rejection of or hostility toward [their] own racial group" (Clark and Clark, p. 347) and is based, as we would suspect, on "existing stereotypes and not in actual experience" (Clark and Clark, p. 347). Obviously, as researchers point out, "The Negro who feels disdain or hatred for his own racial group is expressing—at some level of awareness—disdain or hatred for himself" (Clark and Clark, p. 349). We see in Othello, then, what the researchers call "a mode of adjustment in response to a negative identity" (Clark and Clark, p. 349). All of this comes suddenly to Othello. He does not learn by slow degrees what it is like to be black in a white-supremacist society. Placed in this context, his reactions may seem comprehensible to us, not merely wild or extreme.

Iago, then, gets this magnificent individual, this man who over-insists on his uniqueness—to function as a stereotype, just as Iago manages to reduce the transcendent Desdemona to the level of Bianca, Cassio's call girl. The latter reduction would not have been possible, however, had it not been for Othello's idealization of Desdemona. While William E. Cross has recently attacked as a fallacy the notion that children's perceptions equate to adult notions of self-esteem,[2] it remains significant that, as Paul Winfield, the black actor who played Othello for the Alliance Theater Company in 1978–79, says, the play "is not just about jealousy . . . [Othello] really is an outsider, as far away from his roots as any American black. As his belief in Desdemona crumbles, so does his belief in culture and so-called civilization. He looks back to more savage ways" (Hill, p. 171).

Griffin, in his journey through the deep South, learned how the white man "looked at" the Negro in late 1959:

> As soon as white men or women saw me, they automatically assumed that I possessed a whole set of false characteristics (false not only to me but to all black men). They could not see me or any other black man as a human individual . . . we were irresponsible; we were different in our sexual morals; we were intellectually limited; we had a god-given sense of rhythm; we were lazy and happy-go-lucky; we loved watermelon and fried chicken . . . the white person was not talking with us but with his image of us. (Griffin, p. 180)

Ralph Ellison called the black man "The Invisible Man," because, as Ellison says, "I have been surrounded by mirrors of hard, distorting glass. When they approach me they see only my surroundings, themselves, or figments of their imaginations—indeed everything and anything except me" (Ellison, p. 1). As recently as 12 October 1990, Carl T. Rowan described the racist agenda of David Duke, former Ku Klux Klan Grand Wizard and former candidate for president. People like Duke, Rowan says, "think black people are inherently inferior, allergic to work and bent by nature toward criminal behavior" (Rowan, B–2). When the judge in charge of Malcolm Little—Malcolm X—visited Malcolm's detention home, Malcolm reports that "he would look me up and down, his expression approving, like he was examining a fine colt, or a pedigreed pup . . . it just never dawned upon them . . . that I wasn't a pet" (Malcolm, p. 27).

And here we glimpse perhaps the heart of Iago's plan. Othello is hardly invisible. Iago sees him clearly enough. What Iago must do is "bring this monstrous birth to the world's light" (I.3.422)—that is, to reduce Othello to the level of an animal, to lead Othello, as Iago says, "by the nose / As asses are" (I.3.419–20) or, as Iago says, "to make [Othello] egregiously an ass" (II.1.337). And he will succeed, creating the tragic analogue to the experience of Bottom, the Weaver of Athens.

In reading *Othello* recently, I discovered something I had not understood before. Othello praises Desdemona: "Of so high and plenteous wit and invention! . . . And then, of so gentle a condition" (IV.1.208). "Ay, too gentle," Iago replies (IV.1.209). Eldridge Cleaver in *Soul on Ice* explains what Iago means. Within a construct that Cleaver calls "The Primeval Mitosis," a kind of creation myth,

Cleaver talks of the Ultrafeminine woman—the pampered, per-fumed, elite and elitist white woman, who engages in a constant flight from her body (Cleaver, p. 183). "An appearance of strength in her body is called *ugly*," Cleaver says (Cleaver, p. 184, his ital.). Iago's "gentle" glances at "Gentile," so that the line *can* mean "too gentle for *you*," for you the pagan, you the animal. Iago has created a Desdemona whose very gifts place her—or *should* have placed her—beyond the reach of such a thing as Othello. It is, of course, the position in which Othello has already placed Desdemona. Iago is just agreeing.

At the bottom of the social hierarchy is the Supermasculine Me-nial—the black muscle for the white man's brain (Cleaver, p. 162). Cleaver suggests why Iago hates Othello—Othello can speak, beauti-fully, spellbindingly. "Sonny Liston," says Cleaver, speaking of a late and powerful heavyweight of twenty-five years ago, "is preferred [by white men] over loud-mouthed Cassius Clay [who became Muham-mad Ali], because, after all, it takes at least a bird brain to run a loud mouth, and the white man despises even that much brain in a black man" (Cleaver, p. 164).

The black man provides the muscle and must approve of the sys-tem that oppresses him—the Joe Louis who could stand in the uni-form of a sergeant in front of an American flag and talk glowingly about the country that would make sure he died broke, the black soldier in the Civil War who could not be an officer but who suffered a rate of twenty percent killed in action, the black soldiers in Viet-nam, who, Cleaver says, were "the world's biggest fools for fighting for something they didn't have themselves" (Cleaver, p. 127)—since they were fighting for fascism one could say that they *were* fighting for what they had—the Colin Powell who convinces troops in Saudia Arabia that they are there because Saddam Hussein is the "bad man."

The myth that Iago sells Othello is perfectly captured by Cleaver: "since standards of beauty are set by the elite, the Ultrafeminine personifies the official standard of feminine beauty . . . [but] society has arranged things so that the Supermasculine Menial and the Ultra-feminine are not likely to have access or propinquity to each other conducive to stimulating sexual involvement" (Cleaver, p. 187). While Desdemona is much better than the Ultrafeminine and while Othello is much more like Muhammad Ali than Joe Louis, Iago reduces the marriage to the stereotypical relationship Cleaver de-scribes. "In fact," says Cleaver, "it has not been rare for the Super-masculine Menial and the Ultrafeminine to be severely persecuted, if not put to death, for such sexual contact" (Cleaver, p. 187). Iago is clever enough to manipulate Othello into the position of executioner. Iago doesn't say he hates Othello because he is black. He gets Othello to say so. But Iago can only make an object of Othello—"A fixed figure for the time of scorn / To point his slow and moving finger at!" (IV.2.64–65)—if Othello makes an object of Desdemona.

At the end, of course, Othello kills himself. The flood tide of language returns and he places himself at the center of a narrative surrounded by exotic flora and full of those double adjectives which Othello loads up in front of his nouns. He has been the victim of the syndrome described by Leslie Fiedler: "the man possessed by [the devil] sees him everywhere except where he truly is, in himself" (Fiedler, p. 163). But now Othello finds himself. The Turk which had seemingly sunk in the great storm resurfaced from the Pontic—or Black—Sea of Othello's unconscious. But he regains his government and, in his final act as General of Venice and Commandant of Cyprus, executes the enemy of the state:

> Set you down this;
> And say besides that in Aleppo once,
> Where a malignant and a turbaned Turk
> Beat a Venetian and traduced the state,
> I took by the throat the circumcised dog
> And smote him—thus.
>
> (V.2.405–10)

This is not just suicide. The *self*-controlled tone of the words argues against Harry Morris's suggestion that Othello's "suicide is merely the act of a man in total despair" (Morris, p. 112). Nor is it the action of an Uncle Tom currying favor with the power structure. It is the action of a man who recognizes how low he has fallen and, at the end, reestablishes his identity—or perhaps establishes it for the first time. He has talked of his heroism. Now he shows it to us. He admits at last that he is not complete or absolute, but finite, divided against himself. In acting upon that knowledge, he completes himself.

This is a play about value. Iago can say: "Who steals my purse steals trash. . . . But he that filches from me my good name / Robs me of that which not enriches him / And makes me poor indeed" (III.3.182–86). Desdemona will say that she "had rather lose [her] purse / Full of crusadoes" (III.4.24–25) than the handkerchief. Emilia tells us that she "would make her husband a cuckold to make him a monarch" (IV.3.90). Iago shares his values only with us. He forces us to participate in them. He asks us, then, how we value other

people. And the question demands that we ask how we value ourselves.

II

Trevor Nunn's television version of the 1989–90 RSC Production
makes the racial point brilliantly but subtly. The process of a studio
production in front of a live audience is one that Nunn's brilliant
Macbeth also enjoyed. *Macbeth* became a "domestic tragedy" on
television, but *Othello* is one to begin with. The variations on alienation that all the tragedies explore become particularly intense in this
production as it narrows down to Bradley's "close-shut murderous
room" (Bradley, p. 145).

I saw the Nunn *Othello* at The Other Place in Stratford in 1989
and suggested then that it "was a minimalist production precisely
framed for its limited playing area and for the smaller-than-life space
of television" (Coursen, p. 28). Having now watched the television
version I still believe that Nunn's *Othello* fulfills the criteria that
Peter Brook assigns to the director's role: bringing into contact "a
strong presence of actors and a strong presence of spectators [so as
to] produce a circle of unique intensity in which barriers can be
broken and the invisible become real" (Brook, p. 41). Even on television, this production builds to an almost unbearable tension, as a
good *Othello* must.

Nunn's concept invites, perhaps demands, a response via American history and is, although a British production, remarkably capable
of critique in the terms that Afro-American writers provide. The
context for this way of understanding *Othello* in production has been
available for years, but has not been used, in spite of the presence
of some fine black Othellos, like William Marshall (in the Bard TV
production). While some debate did occur about "setting" and
"time" after the original production,[3] the uniforms were clearly those
of the American Civil War period, suggesting that the time was immediately after the war and possibly after "Reconstruction" failed
and the southern states reverted to a racism as vicious as slavery had
been. This Othello, the great general in the epauletted U.S. Grant
jacket, is sold again to slavery, after his "redemption thence"
(I.3.153). The specificity provides an excellent focus for Othello's
over-emphasis on his "having it made" as he lands on Cyprus. The
debate about setting and time suggests that Nunn's was not an "imposed vision"—*Troilus and Cressida* at Gettysburg, for example—
but one that insisted that the racist agenda pertains, regardless of

laws to the contrary, perhaps because of the rank of the victim. Nunn does not press the issue at us. Iago is no "red neck," no "hysterical small-town segregationist," as Frank Finlay was accused of being in the Olivier production (Wine, p. 60). Instead, a cultural—or perhaps class—racism is implied, as in the look of disapproval that Iago and Emilia exchange as Othello and Desdemona engage in a long kiss early in III.3, after which Othello whispers, "I'll come to thee straight" (III.3.99). Since the Othello *is* black, the moment tests the spectator's own racism. Since Iago and Emilia share very little else in this production, their exchange of disapproving looks is emphasized. Emilia's expression sets up her castigation of Othello later and explains her reserve toward Desdemona, which never quite melts: "She was too fond of her most filthy bargain" (V.2.189). While Othello's elevation may have forced racism underground, its virulence only increases as a result of its suppression.

The medium itself does not insist that a black Othello dictates an emphasis on race. I find little such emphasis in the Bard Production, for example, except where Marshall engages in frenzied ceremonies to a pagan god at the end of III.3. His change in allegiance, however, is as much a function of his foreignness as his race. Nunn's Othello, Willard White, has a powerful baritone voice—he is a singer who has portrayed Porgy, for example—probably deeper than Marshall's and the physique of a light-heavyweight. He is shorter, then, than Robeson, but with a potentially menacing physicality that uncages itself when, for example, he chases and throttles Iago in III.3. Iago is in danger from this monster he is creating and, a moment later, holds a chair between himself and Othello, as animal trainers do. Again, physicality is not necessarily a racial characteristic, but as Iago forces White more and more into the stereotypical "black man's persona," the camera dwells more and more on the agonized face of Othello and emphasizes therefore Othello's racial characteristics. These are never overemphasized as in the Olivier film version where the narcissism of the powerful stage version became a grotesque parody, even while preserving the fact of Olivier's *and* Othello's self-conscious acting for his Venetian audience, an ironic control of levels of meaning that Othello surrenders in both stage and film versions as he lands on Cyprus. Nunn's camera simply notices skin pigmentation without, I believe, ever losing sight of the magnificent "visage" (I.3.274) that Desdemona glimpsed.

White's blackness is set off by Imogen Stubbs's wonderfully spontaneous and ingenuous, very white and blue-eyed and blonde, Desdemona, clothed, of course, in white that contrasts with the dark blue of the uniforms. We really like this Desdemona and really believe that she is in love with this Othello and he, still stunned with his good fortune, with her. A relationship is established, so that Othello's "Desdemona, Desdemona, dead" (V.2.328), in which his face dominates the frame above the wedding bed really works, transcending Mark C. Miller's correct assertion that "passion . . . rarely registers on television, except as something comical or suspect" (Miller, p. 49). The final scene is "earned" here, because it is the function of a relationship built at first on fundamental understanding—on both sides—destroyed by misunderstanding on his side. This "base Indian" has a strong glimpse of the value of what he destroys before he learns of his error. The man is broken and hurt because he *must*, he feels, act out the role Iago has suggested within whatever honorable and Christian formats exist. Our own response issues, I believe, from our awareness of the discrepancy between the shared love we have experienced and the way in which the man whom Desdemona still loves kills her as kindly as he can. The murder is, of course, a perverse coitus, Othello lying on top of Desdemona, both bodies spasming as he strangles her. He then rolls off with a groan. We observe this from an "upstage" angle, one of the very few times that the camera seems to be inside the "playing space." This shift in point of view is meant to disturb us, of course, particularly since it is the "Iago position." We "gape on" and "behold her topp'd" (III.3.444–45).

Suffice it that, as Martin Wine suggests, "In the play Othello *is* black whether played by a white or a black actor. Black actors have not been notably more successful than white ones, and the real test lies in the individual performance—whether it works or not" (Wine, p. 48). It may seem a commonplace that a black actor should play Othello. I cite such white actors as Brewster Mason, Donald Sinden, Olivier, and John Fields as actors who have essayed the role in recent years. I would agree with Wine and amend his statement to read "the real test lies in the individual performance of the *black* actor— whether it works or not." Clearly, black actors can fail in the role, but it is difficult for me to believe that a white actor can succeed, either in the "romantic" or the "realistic" mode. In the former, the magnificent foreigner deceived into the narrow quantitative calculus that Iago promotes, Othello must *be* a magnificent foreigner, not a white man playing at it. In the latter, for which Morocco in *Merchant* is the model, the narcissistic and bombastic self-promoter is little more than Iago says he is at the outset and deserves what Iago dictates later. I doubt that a black actor could play Othello that way, and, while I accept that Othello invites his destruction and is, in some ways his own victim, I would also argue, with Aristotle, that it is the tragic hero's greatness that, since he can never be preeminently good, dooms him. In White's performance Othello's excess of good-will—something he is just beginning to learn from Desdemona—*and* his insistence on trying to get that overabundance into words delivers him to the narrower dimensions of the Iago view. White leans to the "Romantic" Othello, but his Moor is a strong man simply outdone by Iago's virtuosity, not the "pompous, word-spinning arrogant black general" of Dexter's version (Tynan quoting Dexter: Wine, p. 48). Again, a potentially positive trait—curiosity—assists in the fall of White's Othello. He is inexperienced in "peace," as in Venetian ways, and unfortunately accepts Iago's tutelage, the tragic variation on Lucentio and Bianca, Rosalind and Orlando, Viola and Orsino. This Othello is particularly susceptible to Iago's insinuations: "they do let heaven see the pranks. . . ." (III.3.229 ff.), for example. *This* Iago, incidentally, believes what he says about Venetian wives, as I shall suggest.

Nunn's concept is not just of "character"—I don't think any modern production can succeed if based on defining the main character and his relationships—but on culture. That includes the culture that is "final cause"—the television audience. Nunn's modernization is not merely an effort to bring a script "closer" to an audience in the 1990s, although it does accomplish that. One could call the production "Othello and the Military World." By limiting the "worldview" to very precise dimensions, Nunn accommodates a limited medium. All of the play's official business is carried out in a military manner: salutes—more American style than British—about-facing, standing to attention, and marching—with arms swinging in the British not the American way—are the order of the day. Iago is a master at mimicking the junior officer, even as he corrodes with the poison of being overaged in grade and passed-over. We are not permitted to dismiss the initial motive, even if it seems inadequate to what it finally engenders. This is not the fallen aristocrat (Ron Moody in the Bard Production) whose relationship with Roderigo is of social equals, nor the psychopathic sergeant (Bob Hoskins in the BBC Production) who is more of an outsider than Othello (Anthony Hopkins), nor is this the hard-core NCO (Finlay) who understandably hates the dandified Cassio (Derek Jacobi), who has clearly been selected as a function of Othello's self-image. McKellen's Iago *is* an officer, but a graduate of OCS, not West Point or Sandhurst.

Sean Baker's Cassio is handsome, likeable, but inexperienced, as his wanting to *be* liked shows. This Cassio's inexperience leads to prudery and, by this declension, to hypocrisy. He can laugh with the help of alcohol at the homosexual games of the BOQ, but he draws a suddenly sober line when it comes to him. "I hold him unworthy of his place that does those things" he says (II.3.96–97), as his drinking buddies move in to depants *him*. Like any inexperienced officer, Cassio *must* have a loyal and knowledgeable subordinate. He gets an absolutely convincing model of military correctness—Iago.

The "military metaphor" also provides a role for the civilians. They are a minority here and are granted the restricted status of visitors on a military base. As Othello and Desdemona pass by the BOQ at the beginning of II.3, she enters, curious, and even tests the comfort level of a cot—Iago's. The moment alludes to her yet-untested wedding bed and, in her interest in the soldier's life of which she has often heard her husband speak, mirrors Othello's curiosity about Venice. The cashiered Cassio in his white planter's outfit, with straw fedora and string tie, suddenly resembles Roderigo, who is now wearing Union blue. That each is a "reflector" of the other, in a Jamesian sense, is nicely suggested by their change, exchange of outfits. When Cassio approaches some noncoms in III.1 and identifies himself as "one Cassio," they recognize their former superior and exchange a glance. The Soldier (Clown in F1) says, "She is stirring—sir," the final word a sneer. Cassio's "Do, good my friend" is a cynical insight into his own fallen status. A moment that would otherwise show merely how Cassio and Desdemona get together for Iago's telling "I like not that" (III.3.38), becomes energized and captures, for an instant, the mechanics of Venice's "go-between" culture (cf. Long).

Bugles sound their four notes to divide day and night into precise military segments, serving as a kind of auditory grid against which to chart the disorder that is taking over Cyprus. A bugle sounds, for example, as Othello says, "And yet, how nature erring from itself. . . ." (II.3.260). Othello's "wild justice" plays out against the form and pressure of a context whose definition keeps getting reasserted in increasingly ironic ways. This rhythm is inverted by a braying bugle that accompanies the male horseplay in the barracks. The military frame provides a precise and powerful focus for Othello, as he regains command at the end. He executes an enemy of the state—a "Turk" (V.2.407) who happens to be himself. Iago has conditioned Othello to become a stereotype. At the end he returns to soldiership and command and tries and executes the black offender. His final moments show Othello transcending his racial stereotype, as he had believed he had done earlier.

With its eye for detail and quick movements from viewpoint to viewpoint, television is an Iago medium. McKellen's performance is brilliant. He uses *things* far more than he was allowed to do in the austere, closed-in, and almost propless (but powerful) *Macbeth*. Left alone after the smoke-filled midnight council at the end of I, Iago filches some of the Duke's cigars as he says "That think men honest. . . ." (I.3.418). With an experienced hand he adjusts Roderigo's shoulder strap, the latter being unused to uniforms. He explores Cassio's head carefully for wounds on "Marry, God forbid!" (II.3.268). He can parody Othello ("'Certes,' says he . . .": I.1.7, and "all seals and symbols of redeemed sin . . .": II.3.346) *and* Desdemona, providing her sympathetic tremor to "She for him pleads strongly to the Moor" (II.3.357). He binds up Roderigo's wounds expertly and gives Emilia an angry warning glance and downward look at Desdemona, whom he cradles, when Emilia mentions the "squire [that] made you to suspect me with the Moor" (IV.2.169–71). He savors his role as racist bully as he holds a lamp to a black "Bianca" (Marsha Hunt) and sneers, "What, look you pale?" (V.1.122). In an effective aside, he turns to the camera and whispers of the "little web" with which he will "ensnare as great a fly as Cassio" (II.1.197–98). It is as if he is whispering in the ranks—to us!—and thus are we implicated in his plot. In the stage version, McKellen had paused occasionally, looking at the audience, as if seeking there and finding the cuing of his next idea. Othello's soliloquies, although sometimes to the camera, neither issue the invitation nor create a sense of relationship. They cannot do so, of course, since they are predicated upon untruths from which we distance ourselves—even as we are pulled into Iago's fabrication of them.

Not the least of McKellen's skills is his timing. He matches Iago's sure control of rhythm—understatement to force someone else to make a point, pressure when he must force a point, and hyperbole when he utters a pious maxim or homily. He tempts Cassio toward a concupiscent sense of Desdemona at the beginning of II.3, "warming up" for his manipulation of Othello, particularly in III.3 and IV.1, where he pulls the Moor back and forth as a psychic puppeteer. Othello repeats this rhythm in his brutal cross-examination of Desdemona in IV.2. Iago makes a puppet of Othello and discovers an ironic point much later when Emilia fills in the dying Desdemona's last speech.

McKellen's superb Iago does not overpower the production, as did Christopher Plummer's in the 1980 Winter Garden version. James Earl Jones's Othello was so understated and Plummer so spritely that it seemed to me at the time to be more *A Trick to Catch the Old One* than *Othello*. Plummer convinced Robert Brustein, at least, that "Iago is the true author of Othello's play" (Wine, p. 64). McKellen's Iago was much more than Leavis's "mechanism necessary

for precipitating dramatic action in a tragedy" (Leavis, p. 141). While
Othello does make the tragic error that delivers him to Iago, the
latter's extemporaneous skills convey a sense of improvisation that
enlivens the long denouement signaled by Iago's "as honest as I am"
(II.1.233). One of Iago's strengths is that he knows he is best when
forced to be spontaneous, as in battle, as on darkened streets where
he can see and pretends he cannot ("Signior Lodovico?": V.1.79,
"Signior Gratiano?": V.1.108). Iago is not quite quick enough to stab
Cassio during the confused scene "in the dark" (V.1.75), but is himself unconfused and able to dictate the actions and responses of the
others who stumble around within Iago's allegory. At the end of
V.1, McKellen drops Cassio's coat on Roderigo's face and holds his
lamp toward us as he says, "or fordoes me quite" (V.1.151). As
almost everyone in the play takes his cue from Iago, so does this
production. At the end, McKellen gazes on the deathbed, expression-
less, pondering his own absence. The vacuum he creates forces us
to ponder our involvement with this evil man and with his evil. Iago
does not dominate the production but he informs almost its every
moment and leaves us to contemplate the silence he promises with
his last line (V.2.354). Onto that silence we must inscribe our own
evil. Depending upon one's own orientation, the sense of evil may
constellate around an attitude toward race. Let this example suffice:
as Othello and Desdemona embrace after the storm, Iago smiles
benevolently upon the reconciliation. On the week I watched this
production a picture appeared in the newspaper. It showed a "sworn-
in" Clarence Thomas kissing his wife while President Bush smiled
in the background. I saw Iago again.

The Nunn production uses "economy of scale" superbly, as any
television version of Shakespeare must. The Bard production uses a
pseudo-Elizabethan theater that implies an audience without providing one. We are much more aware of the empty and unresponsive
space beyond the timber and stucco facade than we are of the lack
of an audience in the Nunn version. The Bard uses close-ups and
foreground exclusively and creates some good moments, as when
Marshall embraces Cassio on "a friend that loved her" (I.3.180), and
Moody's sparing but chilling eye contact (e.g., "is never seen 'till
used": II.1.340). The Bard, however, wants us to suspend our disbelief—in the Quay Scene, for example—in ways inappropriate to the
"realistic" medium. Nunn convinces us of his fiction by using a set
that is a stage, but is also a flexible *set*, as is Jane Howell's "playground" in the BBC *Henry VI—Richard III* sequence. While Howell explores her space—and gets very good at it in Part II, as
Shakespeare was getting good at it in the 1590s—Nunn exploits a

zone that can be many things as the script makes its shifts from place
to place, inside to outside, day to night, street to bedchamber. The
set features a colonnade that can be hallway or sidewalk with windows above, heavily shuttered. Perhaps because of my need to place
the production in the South of Reconstruction, I find the set to
resemble the French Quarter in New Orleans. The outer structure
could contain a lamplit council chamber or a sun-drenched court-
yard, a barracks, a quay-side dominated by a giant, brass telescope,
or a midnight city square. The locations are defined by the props
and lighting, the dialogue and characters present, and by the careful
framing of the camera. The windows above the grillwork become
Brabantio's house in Venice and the site of Othello's eavesdropping
in IV.1.119 ff. I find the latter scene—partially observed from behind
Othello—a bit awkward since it is one of the few times that the
camera is placed upstage. It is a notoriously difficult scene, of course,
but it represents a kind of "perspective of knowing," in which an
upstage and upstaged Othello is "encave[d]" (IV.1.95), a victim of
the shadow-shapes that Iago creates for him. The cameras do, however, what Nunn's original stage version could not do, that is, provide "the gap between what Othello sees (and does not hear) and the
truth the playgoer sees *and* hears," as Alan Dessen says (letter, 2
September 1989). And, in a world with electricity, we lose the
"flaming minister" for Othello to "quench" (V.2.8). In the Bard
production, Marshall squashes out a candle flame with the palm of
his hand in an utterly convincing visual equivalent of his words. In
two instances Nunn allows time to pass by having a character take
a siesta. Iago nods off to awaken with "How now, Roderigo!"
(II.3.365), and Cassio naps to be roused by Bianca's "Save you,
friend Cassio!" (III.4.186). The technique maintains "unity of time
and place."

The set, then, can accommodate the play's few large scenes—council, quay, and bedchamber (the latter often very awkward on stage)
and concentrate on the intense one-on-one confrontations that characterize *Othello*. The camera is splendidly cued to the dimensions
of each scene. It may be, of course, that the play's scale is better
suited to TV than, say, *Hamlet* or *King Lear*. That possibility, however, in no way diminishes the brilliance of Nunn's direction, as
evidenced earlier in what must be one of the most difficult plays to
translate to TV, *Antony and Cleopatra*. I still do not understand why
BBC did not "go to school" on that production when BBC produced
the canon in the late 70s and early 80s.

A moment that works on TV, although I had said it would not
when I saw the stage production, is the long pause in II.1 after line

195, as everyone awaits Othello's arrival. What makes the pause work is not its imitation of the aimlessness of daytime TV, but the pressure of a script awaiting a moment that cannot be rushed. Emilia whistles tunelessly and the others try to "kill time," once Iago has run out of sexist comments. No Hamlet is present to play games with cloud-shapes, and no one comments on the *nature* of absence, as in *Godot*. There is nothing to say. This parenthesis underscores the flood of Othello's language as he sees his "soul's joy" (II.1.213) and steps forward along the fatal fabric of his own rhetoric after the estrangement of the storm. "Will she love him still for prating?" (I.2.256) Iago will ask Roderigo, as the former begins to set down the pegs of the "Othello music."

A critic's attention to detail is likely to falsify the *flow* of performance, the movement so essential to the overall aesthetic and emotional experience, a factor so crucial to the presentation of this script. Nunn's attention to detail, however, greatly diminishes the notorious problem of Othello's characterization—when he chooses to "peak," how the actor meshes the earlier nobility with the later savagery, for example. Marshall deals with the issue by having Othello ebb and flow, from credulity to doubt and finally to a certainty clothed in the format of Christian propriety. I did not notice a problem in White's performance, primarily, I think, because it is so woven into the contexts Nunn creates, as opposed to becoming isolated from the many minute details we are asked to observe and consider. Michael Gradage's Roderigo *is* in love with Desdemona—who could blame him?—and is upset at Iago's obscene comments in front of Brabantio's house in I.1. Roderigo is a conventional young man who recognizes almost right away that he is getting in over his head. It is too late for him, right away, to set limits *within* the social norms and goals of community consensus. He is a racist appalled by Iago's obscene version of the same disease. In IV.2, line 198, Iago surprises Roderigo, who is searching Desdemona's dressing table for the jewels he has supposedly given to Desdemona via Iago. Roderigo refuses to shake Iago's hand, and the latter recognizes that even this fool has become dangerous. On Desdemona's dressing table is a daguerreotype of Brabantio, a pathetic reminder of the father she has loved and lost and an echo of the scene at the end of the Council when she had tried to trap him into reconciliation around the round council table. Both Othello and Desdemona have left a life behind to marry, but Othello's marriage is a result of, and a sequel to, his war stories. Hers is a poignant divorce from her past. The dressing table also functions in the wonderful Willow Scene. At the beginning of III.3, Cassio brings a box of candy to Desdemona, a polite way of thanking her for her intercession, and something that may remind her of the life she had lived among the "curled darlings" (I.2.83) of Venice. Later, she remembers the candy and brings it delightedly from the drawer of the dressing table to share with Emilia. It is a schoolgirl's guilty secret, only to be shared after "lights out." This is the kind of repeated detail we expect of a good novel. Here it is an emblem of her innocence and of the terrible loneliness her marriage has brought her. I felt that Stubb's "subtext" here is the agony of homesickness which she tries to cover with a pathetic gaiety. This plays powerfully against Zoe Wanamaker's superbly balanced disapproval of the marriage and sympathy for its victim.

Nunn's brilliant casting of a black "Bianca" permits the script to make a point it has never made before. The Cassio-Bianca liaison mirrors, of course, the marriage of Desdemona and Othello. The gender-reversal, however, allows Cassio to suggest that, while of course he will use the black woman for his purposes, he will never *marry* her. Iago's suggestion draws roguish laughter from Cassio (V.1.133–35). Cassio's earlier "fair Bianca" (III.4.189) can only be racist cruelty, as is Iago's later reiterated "Look you pale?" Bianca becomes, literally, a "monkey" (IV.1.145), a dark plaything to be cast back to her poverty once the white lover becomes bored. Cassio knows what the world of the play knows—one does not *marry* a Bianca, or an Othello. Othello and Desdemona, then, are entangled in a problem that goes beyond the merely personal but emerges from the basic and unexamined assumptions of the society they would at once join and defy.[4]

The racial aspect emerges strongly in the end. Desdemona makes a futile dash to the locked door. She kneels in an attempt to buy some time by praying. Then, in a terrible moment that suggests the cooperation between the executioner and his victim, permits Othello to help her up. Her struggle, however, moves beyond any vision of "black Othello embracing in death white Desdemona" (Wine, p. 75). This is a rape, after which Othello rolls from Desdemona with a groan. We observe the murder from in front of the bed, but many of Othello's speeches are observed through the metal bars of the bedstead. (There is no curtain.) We hear "O ill-star'd wench" and the rest of the "compt" speech (V.2.319 ff.) through the bars. The face behind the bars suggests, of course, the jail of Othello's "misprision," from which he will free himself even as he simultaneously admits his fitness for punishment. For an American audience the allusion is inevitable. It is to Willie Horton, the rapist coming toward us as the prison gate shuts behind him.

The centrality of the racial element in this production does not obliterate an even deeper issue. If Iago's motive were merely that of the racist, the "answer" would be as easy as Harry Morris's assertion that Iago is the Devil. Underlying the racist agenda is the chilling self-hatred that John Howard Griffin discovered in the white man who picked him up on a Louisiana highway. Somewhere in that syndrome, which can justify the killing of other human beings, lies the mystery of human iniquity, the evil that calls into question the value of life itself. Iago raises the question with his ironic brilliance, and McKellen's Iago ponders the mystery, the meaning, and meaninglessness of life, as he stares without expression at the dead couple on their error-stained wedding bed.

III

> When a black actor [plays Othello], it offsets the play, puts it out of balance . . . it makes it a play about blackness, which it is not. . . . The trouble is, the play was hijacked for political purposes.[3]
>
> —Jonathan Miller

While in London recently, I was fortunate enough to see Janet Suzman's 1988 *Othello,* as reformatted for television. The production occurred in the Market Theatre in Johannesburg under the ominous shadow cast by the John Foster Square Police Station.

In her introductory remarks for the television production, Suzman says that the Market is "a completely non-racial theatre, completely without government subsidy." She finds in *Othello* "a metaphor for the present." It seems, she says, "the least overtly political of Shakespeare's plays—except to South Africans like me." She compares Iago's "cramped world-view" to that of Eugene Terré Blanche, Führer of the Afrikaner Resistance Movement. She feels "no need to update" Shakespeare's script.

"It is a foreigner that Shakespeare requires" as Othello, she says. Here, of course, she is supported by none other than David Garrick, whose argument is hardly free of racial stereotype: Shakespeare "had shown us white men jealous in other pieces, but that their jealousy had its limits, and was not so terrible. . . . In Othello he had wished to paint that passion in all its violence, and that is why he chose an African in whose being circulated fire instead of blood, and whose true or imaginary character could excuse all boldness of expression and all exaggeration of passion" (Barnet, p. 272). Paul Robeson is even more supportive of Suzman's decision, haply because he is black: "The problem [of *Othello*] is the problem of my own people.

It is a tragedy of racial conflict, a tragedy of honor, rather than of jealousy" (Barnet, p. 280).

Suzman's selection for the part is John Kani, a black South African whose native tongue is not English and who had no prior experience with verse speaking. The choice is brilliant.

Kani's Othello finds his way carefully through the language. It is not so much a version of "self-fashioning," but a rhythm of discovery that fascinates Othello. Kani underplays Othello and therefore avoids the histrionics of which Garrick (and others) have been accused as they played stereotypical "Africans." Othello's language, as Kani deals with it, is, for Venice, unfashionable, artificial, and *acquired*, somewhat as Mary Shelley's Frankenstein's monster teaches himself a ponderous Miltonic syntax.

While Kani's Othello touches his new language with wonder, not arrogance, it is an epic language, not a subtle and understated system of sounds that completes their meanings in a tortured psyche. For Othello, words project great deeds upon the imaginative screen of admiring listeners. When Iago says, "men should be what they seem" (III.3 126), Othello repeats the words as if the aphorism is a sudden, new, and alien concept—who would claim otherwise? Othello is being introduced to "second meanings" and "hidden agendas," the semiotics of duplicity that Iago controls. Kani is a superb "story-teller," as if he acquired the skill around a tribal fire. His narratives— to the Senate, to Desdemona about the handkerchief, and his final speech—are spellbinding. The "personality" of the teller is projected *into* the story, so that the narrative is depersonalized, a crafted entity that resides between teller and audience. But this self-effacement is dangerous for the teller, because it permits other narratives—or "discourses"—to be introduced. Othello's "beginning, middle and end" is superseded by Iago's more powerful behavioral conditioning.

Othello's personal vulnerability lies not in his belief in his words but in his belief that other men are as virtuous as he. He *is* "of a constant, loving, noble nature" (II.1.289) and *does* "think . . . men honest that but seem to be so" (I.3.391). He never understands why Iago should have thus ensnared him. Men should, after all, be as they seem. Othello, at the end, touches Iago's foot to find his cloven hoof.

Because Othello is "a foreigner," Iago can introduce him to a language where the same words emerge from a different premise, one that "colors" the words, shades them, darkens them. It is Venice's premise, the "cramped vision" of racism that Othello accepts. Kani's Othello is also "foreign" to Desdemona's response to him. This is the first counter-response to who he is and knows himself to be. Clearly, it transcends the issue of skin pigmentation. But it is a dangerous transcendence in this—or any—society. She saw his "visage in his mind" (I.2.247), glimpsed his "perfect soul" (I.2.30) but saw what no one else sees—including Othello, as Iago works on him. Othello's story drew "pity" (I.3.167) from her. An actor can suggest, of course, that these grand narratives merely circle back to him, the central heroic figure and locus of response. Kani's Othello, however, feels Desdemona's compassion. It opens a passage for his return of love. This is, for a moment, "unreflecting love," to borrow Keats's phrase, neither narcissistic nor requiring thought.

The problem, of course, is that such a love must develop a dynamic stronger than Aristotle's time, which is a medium for decay. In the production, Othello's landing at Cyprus is the climax. Desdemona holds Cassio's sword up to Othello as he descends a gangplank from ship to quay ("O my fair warrior!": II.1.179). Then, in one of the production's few unconventional camera angles, we see her, having returned the sword to Cassio, gliding up the steps. They meet— halfway between sea and land in a zone of their own where "comfort" and "content" are "absolute" (II.1.189–90). Suspended in time, or out of time for the moment, they must descend to the island, where Iago is eager to twist the pegs of the instrument that "makes the music" (II.1.198). As Othello and Desdemona exit, the camera catches the shadows of the steps on which they have experienced their dreamlike reunion. A dream casts no shadows, but this one does.

Othello's subjugation by Iago is clearly charted. Othello enters the world of Iago's experience when the latter reminds Othello that Desdemona deceived her father in marrying Othello. "And so she did" (II.3.208). Kani makes this a discovery for Othello. He realizes that human beings—even one *he* loves—can be deceptive—even to ones *they* love. Iago camouflages his own deception by forcing Othello to concentrate on Desdemona. This virtuoso Iago explains his "illusion" only to us.

Kani translates his love into grieving, powerfully understated, so that the scenes with Desdemona from III.3 onward, tend to be perverse love scenes (as IV.2. 24–93 certainly is) emerging from their inability to communicate when it had seemed so natural, so effortless before. Again, the concept of "foreignness" is significant. Othello struggles with Iago's Venetian concepts, even as the inner nature— "the tranquil mind" (III.3.345)—that the intuitive Desdemona loves grows darker. Desdemona's initial "error" is explained by Brabantio who can indicate the ugly Roderigo as a "wealthy curled darling" (I.2.67)—the latter giving an arrogant and affirmative nod. Thus Othello begins to become a subject in the Iago "story," in which

Othello is a despised foreigner, not just a stranger. He tries to tell Desdemona what's wrong, but cannot, partly because of his inexperience with gender issues, partly because he begins to consider his race, and partly because—even as they continue to love each other—they have entered a zone in which no language exists, particularly since she *has* been faithful. They grope blindly past each other, until it is, indeed, "too late" (V.2.83). Jealousy, of course, is a unique and powerful emotion—a singular category, a terrible caring. Desdemona continues to love Othello in *her* way, of course, and television, with its tight focus on restrained acting, delivers this version of the story powerfully. Kani's Othello never stops loving Joanna Weinberg's very white, blonde Desdemona, but her "defection" does show that "Chaos is come again" (III.3.92). She is the locus of all his faith. As Paul Winfield says, "As [Othello's] belief in Desdemona crumbles, so does his belief in culture and so-called civilization. He looks back to more savage ways" (Hill, p. 171). Kani's Othello tends not to look back but to drift in the great sea of sadness that his loss of faith has released in him. In the Murder Scene, he performs a self-dictated ceremony in an effort to place his savagery within his acquired Christian format. Even Othello as Kani creates him, seems aware of the terrible discrepancies that fissure his "sacrifice" (V.2.65). The candle he has dowsed and "plucked" (V.1.13) smokes on behind him as he bestrides Desdemona to strangle her. A superb moment occurs when, in a radical close-up, Kani says "the affrighted globe / Should yawn at alteration" (V.2.99–100). His agony is the more convincing for the fact that no one is listening to his dictation of a cosmic response. He has become empty words, Iago's creature.

The love story, quietly and movingly depicted, benefits from the violent world swirling around it. Bianca is dragged off, for example, not by arresting officers but by rapists. We see Brabantio, crushed by Desdemona's elopement, dying before our eyes. Iago stands on top of the ducal throne like a figure in Fludd's cartography. The world surrounding the lovers has little respect for culture or civilization. Those who challenge these negative assumptions must be dealt with. This production wonders whether the relationship between Othello and Desdemona isn't doomed automatically, whether Iago is there or not.

Richard Haddon Haines plays Iago with dazzling skill and Roderigo is a considerable figure—as often "on stage" and never "in the text"—as nastily depicted by Franz Dobrowsky. The raucous scenes between Iago and Roderigo contrast vividly with the muted Desdemona-Othello sequences.

Haines moves easily through his black-and-white world. Iago, after all, can see in the dark. "Colour" is not introduced until Othello enters (I.2) sniffing a rose à la Olivier, but this one, we assume, a gift from Desdemona—not just an emblem of self-indulgence—and wearing an elegant cream-colored doublet with rose-colored straps. This is a man who has "made it," but who is calm and conscious of the effect of his dignity. Haines's Iago, by contrast, is frenzied, amplifying his words with gestures. He raises his arm obscenely, sticks his fingers in his nose to imitate a monkey, mimes a description of sexual prowess ("asses": I.3.393), kneads his fingers on "Soliciting" (I.3.387), and outlines pregnancy on "monstrous birth" (I.3.395). His remarks are often directed to the audience (camera). "I did say so" (III.3.326), for example, is a response to Othello's entrance and equates to "for example." "I am your own forever" (III.3.476) is not to Othello, but to the audience, meaning you have me (racism) always with you.

And that is the problem with this Iago. It is not just the overplaying that could work on stage, but is more than the cool medium can absorb. Haines is far more of a racist than Olivier's Frank Finlay, who emerged prominently on film from a virtual background position on stage against Olivier's tour de force Moor. Haines ignores the advice of Edwin Booth, a great nineteenth-century Iago: "Don't *act* the villain, don't *look* it, or *speak* it (by scowling or growling, I mean), but *think* it all the time. Be genial, sometimes jovial, always gentlemanly" (Barnet, p. 277). Haines's Iago does convince us of his own sexual jealousy, but I doubt that we believe that such a manic, obsessed, "beside himself" Iago could be so cool in planning, so smooth in execution, or detached enough to recognize that his own strength lies in improvisation. The contrast between private and public Iagos is too great, too Hyde and Jekyllish. While a psychoanalytic theory no doubt exists to bridge the gap between these two Iagos and while the performance probably negotiated these extremes on stage, it overpowers the small screen. It makes this production too much about race and proves that "PC" can distort performance. Race resonates within the script, regardless of the demurrals of Jonathan Miller. I can hear white spectators saying, "At least I am not as bad as *that*!" rather than sensing their own racism through a more plausible but just as evil Iago.

I have just seen Ian McKellen in the part, and I have no idea how the Haines's Iago would have played in Johannesburg. As I write—in February 1992—Terré Blanche's neo-Nazi movement grows in South Africa. His followers march, singing "This land is for the Boers. Shoot the Kaffirs. Shoot!" Militia leaders like Servaas de Wat and Marty Markow claim that they are ready for war and indeed that they "will open up the gates of hell on Mandela and F. W. de Klerk" (Ottaway, p. 3). In the United States the rhetoric is sometimes more subtle (cf. Edsall, pp. 7–11, and Rosenthal, p. 7).

We need more aesthetic distance from this Iago; perhaps the problem lies in the formatting of the stage production for TV. To begin in black and white, when both Iago and Roderigo independently observe Desdemona's elopement via gondola is to begin in a "filmic" way without establishing the *stage* as the locus of all activity, inside and outside, from soliloquy to brawl. Thus the production tends to prove Elijah Moshinsky's thesis:

> One of the strengths of television is the constant present, which is also its weakness if you are trying to build up a narrative structure. In a theatre, the space stays the same when different actors enter and leave the stage, and so a sense of continuity develops through the fixed relationships between the audience and stage. But on television, it's just a constant present. (Elsom, p. 124)

Suzman's production tends to stay in the "constant present" when it could establish precisely "the relationship between the audience and stage" that Moshinsky says cannot occur on television. Televised versions of live stage productions prove otherwise, as does Jane Howell's versatile unit set for the BBC *First Henriad*. Late in the Suzman production, the Lodovico scenes (IV.1 and 3) provide a full view of the stage and of the possibilities for "narrative continuity" that the production has failed to exploit until then. We tend here to observe a kind of political soap opera which Iago's extremism emphasizes. Part of the problem is that this television production is unwilling to reveal and take advantage of its basic medium, the stage.

No performance of a Shakespearean script is free of the zeitgeist is which it appears, even if it tries to be. Suzman's production does *not* try to be. It would succeed more if it were more "its own metaphor." While I admire the production's committed position, such a blatant racist as this Iago dictates our response rather than permitting us to formulate it. We believe in Othello's foreignness and in his love for Desdemona and hers for him. We might find Iago more frightening if we believed him to be sane.

This powerful production is commercially available and can be compared and contrasted with the Trevor Nunn version, which also emerges from a stage production and which also, in Willard White, features a black actor in the title role.

9

"'Tis Nudity": Peter Greenaway's
Prospero's Books

To say that the film is tasteless is to ignore Shaw's qualification of the golden rule. It does not take the risks that Polanski takes—with an occasional brilliant success like the infinite progress of mirrors that issues from Banquo, and the eerie procession observed by Macbeth's severed head. It lacks the dazzling visual qualities of Zeffirelli's Shakespeare films. It does not give us, as Fellini does in *Juliet of the Spirits*, a sense of interhabitation of consciousness and the unconscious. It does not do as Bergman does—force us to *think* about images until we recognize for ourselves that imagery is the stuff of the imagination, not the intellect. Yet all of this will be claimed; some of it has been claimed for *Prospero's Books*.

It is a film in which two "contents"—Shakespeare's script and the books that Peter Greenaway invents for Prospero—compete with each other. The effect is not "irony," but incoherence. The books themselves are potentially interesting, though introduced randomly, as they were randomly dumped, it would seem, into Prospero's boat. Shakespeare's script is delivered with all the fire and originality of a late Victorian proscenium production in Liverpool. Indeed, it can be said that the title cards are more interesting than the film they would explicate.

Since the film is likely to attract considerable and considered response, it is worth including here, particularly since it represents an importation of television *into* the film, both technically and thematically and therefore suggests the pervasive and contaminating influence of TV on our "culture." This is not a matter of putting Shakespeare on the television, but one of putting television *into* a film that is not just "based on" Shakespeare, but that stays close to the words of the script, indeed privileges those words by having Prospero's handwrite many of them in front of our eyes.

The problems here are not merely attendant upon the "promotion" of television to film—as opposed to the reduction of film to a "made for TV" format. Nor are the problems merely those of the "scale" of TV, which Peter Greenaway finds "frustrating" (Rodman, p. 37). This film could probably accommodate itself on the outsize TV screen depicted on the cover of the 22 July 1991 issue of *Sports Illustrated*, where a fan simultaneously reaches for popcorn and roots for the Seminoles, as his dog stares at his master's choice. The problems result, then, only partly from a self-defeating merger of media.

Greenaway seems incapable of making decisions, like the decision for technicolor that *Oz* makes, or the decision to sacrifice the Prospero figure, as in *Forbidden Planet*, where Dr. Moribus realizes that his own repression of psychic energy has resulted in pressures that finally crack the tectonic plates of his planet. Even an inability to make a decision can work, as in *Casablanca*, where neither Bergman nor Bogart knew how the ending had been scripted and thus gave that scene above Rick's Place a potent tentativeness. But here we return to the script and recognize that all of this activity has been at the service of a new arrangement of blocs and—regardless of the newfound voices of Prospero's enemies—has been merely an inscription of his will. The latter point is signified when Prospero dons the black and white of his ducal outfit. It is merely another embodiment of the black and white of his pen upon parchment. He can now afford to dump his books into his pool.

One can ignore the "discourse on colonialism," but in doing so, Greenaway ignores that version of "intertextuality" whereby zeitgeist can inform a work of art, as opposed to being an alienated opponent to it. Greenaway praises Bergman's *The Seventh Seal* for having "not only a strong narrative, but a great sense of metaphor and metaphysics. It was very happy to play with mythology, with concepts of received history, with grandiose ideas" (Koehler, F-7). Greenaway imports a mass of such material into his film, superimposes it upon Shakespeare's play, which does incorporate a lot of "presentation," and makes a film designed to alienate, not to educate, those who come to see it.

The "focus" of the film is diffused among the story being told, the narrator, and the interruptions—"insets"—of the books. The latter add nothing beyond their own ingenuity. Prospero may have used some of them at some point, but they are not the stuff of the story he is telling in the film. The "Book of Utopias" is from the script, but has little to do with his "narrative of revenge" and, even if a point of balance between optimism and cynicism, is an ironic inset in Shakespeare's play. Gielgud as narrator displays more vocal virtuosity than most writers at work, but he is otherwise as uninteresting as a writer at work. And the story he tells is dull, its characters indeed puppets, neither individualized (with the exception of Caliban, a naked dancer with a grotesque deformity) nor differentiated. To "tell" *The Tempest* as if it were a Henry James novel may be valid in theory. But the film has neither the brilliant characterization of those external to James's limited-point-of-view technique, nor the piercing epiphanies of Isabel Archer or Lambert Strether by fire or riverside.

It is difficult to know what assumptions the practitioners of the media make about their audiences in the 1990s. Empirical—some would call in anecdotal—evidence suggsets that today's college student has read less than his contemporary of twenty-five years ago. Once upon a time, "survey courses" insured a knowledge of a "corpus" that might have included some Chaucer, a couple of plays of Shakespeare, *Paradise Lost,* some Romantic poets, and a couple of Victorian novels. Such courses were "traditional," focused on male writers, and tended not to examine the assumptions and hidden agendas of the literature itself. The texts were seen as independent entities, not as texts that are unintelligible "except in their differential relations with other texts" (Barker and Hulme, p. 192). Students read more literature years ago, even if that reading amounted to a brainwashing, and even if the reading was a prelude to an unexamined, suburban, Republican "life-style." Recently, a major English department admitted that it gives its undergraduate majors a copy of the Norton Anthology at the end of their college careers so that they can "catch up" on some of the things they may have missed while they learned *how* to read texts.

While one can blame Ronald Reagan and his successor for launching an attack on American higher education that is making it accessible only to the upper middle class (public universities) and the upper class (private colleges and universities), one cannot blame Reagan for the mugwump mentality of the nation he led for eight years. While an uneducated and racist president hardly creates a positive "role model," the status of education at the end of the millennium merely signals an erasure of the hope that "education" was somehow the panacea for all social ills. With the exception of the G.I. Bill, which benefited mostly males, the effort to offer educational opportunity to other than the middle-to-upper classes was never made in the United States. The promising start of the Great Society surrendered almost immediately to the insanity of the war in Vietnam and then to the calculated flow of drugs into American cities as directed by Donald Gregg and his agent, Manuel Noriega.

Mass audiences are invariably ignorant. Today's mass ignorance is only partly a function of a zeitgeist that incorporates drugs, television, and Ronald Reagan. As Martin Esslin suggests, "the rational culture of the Gutenberg Galaxy never extended beyond the very narrow confines of an educated minority elite . . . the vast majority of mankind, even in the developed countries, and even after the production of universal education and literacy, remained on a fairly primitive level of intellectual development" (Esslin, p. 106). Those who dispense mass media know as much. As Ethan Mordden says of an allusion to Nabokov in Sting's "Don't Stand so Close to Me," "rock's audience doesn't know anything" (Mordden, p. 112). Zeffirelli makes the same assumption about his audience:

> Nobody knows anything about *Hamlet*, about Shakespeare. They don't know anything. They go there in a dark room and they see something on the screen and want to know what the story is, and you have to tell them the story from scratch, from the beginning, in a convincing way, using a language that will make clear and accessible every single word of William Shakespeare. (HBO Promo Tape)

Greenaway, it would seem, expects an *educated* audience. The range of his allusiveness is vast, and only the most erudite could pick up the distinction between Botticelli and Veronese as the montage technique replaces the long sequences of the tracking shots. Two things are crucial, however: we are not *learning* anything. Our ignorance is being exposed, no doubt, but that darkness is not being lightened by Greenaway's display of what *he* knows. And, second, perhaps even more crucially, the allusions do not serve the purposes of film, or of *this* film. If it will not instruct us, it might at least entertain us. Bergman makes the occasional mistake of making film an intellectual event. It is not. Nor is Shakespeare. Greenaway's film is self-indulgence masked as "intellectual." The film's apparent wish for an educated audience is itself an illusion.

The outmoded "modernist" approach to literature argued for unity, for a single coherent theme that pulled seemingly disparate elements of a work into a formula like the Aristotelian infinitive phrase that Francis Fergusson championed, or the binary oppositional approach that Richard Levin demolished over a decade ago. In 1967, I was arguing, convincingly I thought, for "the unity of *The Spanish Tragedy*." We are not told in such criticism to seek that which subverts the text—the undercutting pattern beneath the manifest content—or the "discourse" of which the text is context. Shakespeare's better critics and directors have been doing that sort of "deconstruction" for a long time, often with exciting results in the theater, at least, and without the jargon that conceals the usually very conventional readings that tend to emerge from the newer critical modes. For all of Greenaway's post-modernist posturing, his "vision" of *The Tempest* is crushingly conventional.

Adding to central artistic confusion is a mishmash of styles, an eclecticism that argues an inability to make a decision. As Greenaway says, "The division between fact and fiction becomes indistinguishable" (Greenaway, p. 1). Prospero sits "in his study, imagining himself bathing" (Miramax, p. 1). But the pool is *realistic* and the ship model on which Ariel pisses at length is a real model. We get *sur*realism when pages fly up from their books like frightened birds, and when Caliban and his confederates are chased through their self-inflicted nightmare. We get a painterly style, as when a little blonde girl—Miranda, we assume—runs out of a dark frame, as if from Captain Cocq and Company. "My great advantage over Veronese is that I can make the people move," says Greenaway (Fuller). Well, other differences exist as well. We also get a "stagy" style—Prospero sitting within a portable proscenium stage, sometimes with a couple of naked girls playing chess in front, and curtains that open to reveal singers hitting a pitch just below that of the dog-whistle. We also discover "straight" television and a version of MTV. The film's greatest weakness, among many candidates, is its insistence on using televisual techniques—an aspect I shall discuss later.

The styles do not blend. The variations are intended as Brechtian alienation devices, as Greenaway explains:

> I always tend to feel the most sympathy for those works of art which do have that sort of self-knowledge, that say, basically, "I am an artifice." I very much like the idea that when somebody sits in the cinema and watches a film of mine, it's *not* a slice of life, it's *not* a window on the world. It's a constant concern of mine to bring the audience back to this realization. (Rodman, p. 38, Greenaway's ital.)

No danger exists that this film will be taken for a "slice of life." The constant and unrelenting artifice calls attention to its irrelevance, to its effort to mask purposelessness, and *not* to the relationship between art and our participation in its illusion.

We get, for example, two brief allusions to film itself in *Prospero's Books*, both interesting, each irrelevant.

During Prospero's tirade about premarital chastity, two of his books are suddenly introduced: "The Ninety-Two Conceits of the Minotaur," and "The Autobiographies of Pasiphae and Semiramis."

In one, we see a monstrous bird-man perform a sequence of jumps borrowed from Eadweard Muybridge's experiments with the Morey wheel—a perforated disk rotating behind a camera lens. Greenaway animates an 1884 version of "moving picture." In another, we see a boxer aim a right to the body of a naked woman. The allusion is to Ruby Robert Fitzsimmons (1862–1917), the lean Cornishman who defeated Jim Corbett with a left to the body—the solar plexis punch—in the fourteenth round in Carson City on 17 March 1897. This was the first heavyweight championship fight ever filmed— although the nitrate began to disintegrate as the kayo occurred. Again, Greenaway glances at the beginnings of his own art which, he claims, "hasn't even reached its cubist phase" (Koehler, F–6). But what do these glimpses signify?

Prospero's books predict the future of the image. It will be made to move in imitation of the way the eye sees natural movement. Are we to assume that Prospero is creating that illusion for his enemies on the island? No—the spirits that they see are "unprojected" and human enough, with the exception of satyrlike horns for some of the boys. Are his enemies *subjects* of "motion pictures"? No—they don't rewind, fast-forward, or wipe, and are subject neither to slow motion nor stop action. Are we to assume that some competition exists between Prospero's calligraphy and the images in his books? In some illuminated manuscripts, lascivious monkeys cavorted in the margins of sacred texts. We could, after all, have a combat between a priggish narrator, which this Prospero certainly is for all of the nakedness of his kingdom's inhabitants, and the concupiscent proclivities of his creations. We could have an allegorical struggle between Protestant print and Catholic iconography. We could have something interesting here, and even intellectually challenging. But we don't. The books themselves are, for the most part, curiosities and have little if anything to do with *The Tempest,* whether it be Shakespeare's play or, as here, Prospero's. Prospero dumps all his books in the drink at the end and Caliban—why Caliban?—saves the books, including Shakespeare's plays and the play of which he is a character, *The Tempest.* Is this Caliban seeking "for grace"?—a line he is denied here, even after gaining his own voice. Suffice it to say that Greenaway raises enticing possibilities, but pursues none of them.

On the level of mythology, none of the myths themselves seem relevant. The "Book of Mythologies" looks like a faded high school yearbook. We may get a trace of the Minotaur myth, in that Ferdinand wanders through an apparent maze of wheat (as opposed to maize) to stumble onto Prospero's porch. Miranda, bookworm that Prospero has made her, is reluctant to leave her herbal, but does so and, like Ariadne on seeing Theseus, falls in love. Here, the maze precedes the falling in love, but one of the cunning qualities of a maze is that it seems to lead easily toward the center until a final hedge or wall blocks entrance. Then must the maze-trodder circle all the way back, almost to the beginning, as the goal becomes increasingly distant. So Ferdinand is denied "too light winning," even as his father and party stagger around in their "maze trod indeed," as Gonzalo calls it. But I am probably pursuing here an allusive pattern the film does not create—my own self-crafted maze.

I don't find any Semiramis allusions in the film. She was Queen of Babylon when Pyramus and Thisbe lived there. Shakespeare translates the myth into *Romeo and Juliet* and, a play later, burlesques the story in *A Midsummer Night's Dream*. But the treatment of "Pyramus and Thisbe" obscures the nature of their world, one of blind chance or mere accident, not a purposive cosmos. In Ovid, the lion arrives because it wants to slake its thirst. Shakespeare does not even give it that motivation (cf. Walter Herbert). The borders of that world—where Poseidon could punish Pasiphae by making her fall in love with a bull, or worse, where death can occur on the basis of a wrong conclusion—like the suicides of Aegeus and Pyramus (and Romeo)—are touched in the film but not entered.

Another skein of reference surprisingly unpursued is Sebastian's reference to "one tree, the phoenix' throne; one phoenix / At this hour reigning there" (Anglo-Saxon "Phoenix"). The phoenix should have been eminently adaptable to Greenaway's layering process from celluloid to high definition television tape, and back to light sensitive material, and, beyond the process, the symbol of renewal and transformation, both of cyclic rhythm and teleological vectors. It would seem to have coincided with the film's themes. But unless I was nodding, I believe the line was cut.

The phoenix emerges from the ancient Egyptian cult of sun-worship—Ra, the sun-god—something that this Prospero would have known about since he builds pyramids. When the phoenix requires renewal, according to the Anglo-Saxon Christianized version of the myth, it goes to "the loveliest of lands, a goodly island," bathes in *fons vitae*, moves into a nest woven of the sweetest of herbs, and is born again out of its own ashes, symbol not of the sun but of the Son. Milton uses the myth at the end of *Samson Agonistes* to suggest that Samson is a "type of Christ."

The rebirth of the phoenix coincides, of course, with the vernal equinox. If Greenaway refers to the mythology at all, it is in the trite seasonal tableau at the end of the film, where Ferdinand and Miranda represent "Spring." But that obvious pattern seems to derive as much from Spenser or *The Winter's Tale* as it does from the phoenix myth. The latter, with its allusion to the distinction between the earthly and terresrial in I Corinthians, might have created a few rich moments here. At the end of the film, Prospero's books are consumed by both fire and water. Perhaps *that* is where the phoenix myth is located. The phoenix survived the ancient time when "the sea floods covered the compass of earth" and "shall flourish til the fire of judgement." But since the line about the phoenix was, I think, cut, I find myself rationalizing irrelevant and unconnected images.

The film does have the virtue of forcing its auditor into a compulsive wish to redesign it. One book I expected was the Cabala—how did Gonzalo forget a work that can be said to blur the distinction between white and black magic ("graves at my command. . . ."), that links up with astrology ("A most auspicious star. . . ."), that at times approximates pantheism, that merges the tradition of the Creator-God with a sense of His inner life, that comes to emphasize the "intelligible lights" of Islamic and Jewish new-platonism, that puts forward a mystical theory of history, argues a separate realm of demonic emanations, suggests a "lost Shekhina," introduces a "feminine principle," and describes a "celestial garment"? But then, that could have been Prospero's *Book*. As it is, his books do not "illuminate" the script. Or, they derive directly from it, like the "Book of Utopias," introduced without even the irony the script provides, since we are given the authority of Gielgud-Prospero-Shakespeare's literal inscription of the idea which overrides any undercutting of it. We get no sense of intertextuality, of course, but instead an "effort of ideological containment, an attempt to harness the unruly energies of the text to a stable order of significance" (Norris, p. 66) and, thus, a "persistent allegory of errors" (Norris, p. 66). "Finally, says Greenaway, "there would need to be books to encourage revenge" (Greenaway, p. 2). No such book *is* listed among Prospero's books (although there is a "Book of Love.") Furthermore, the argument that Prospero must overcome his desire for revenge is antique and undercut by his early reassurances to Miranda. And why, given what has been done to him, would he need a *book* to spur him on? He does need, says Greenaway, a book on "how to colonize an island, farm it, subjugate its inhabitants" (Greenaway, p. 2). Behind the film lie assumptions that Conrad explored and exposed a hundred years ago.

Perhaps needless to say, Greenaway backs away from the issue of Caliban. He represents the kind of incoherency "nurtured" by colonialism, a force that lurks in the shadows behind the harmonized spaces of *A Midsummer Night's Dream*, *The Tempest*, or the middle-class suburb. Here, Caliban is a dancer who twists on every other line and, unlike a serpent, loses direction and makes himself vulnerable as he pursues his sinewy thread. Furthermore, he is seen as a function of Prospero, who does more actual *writing* of Caliban's part than of the other parts—"I know how to curse" and "All the infections that the sun sucks up. . . ." for example. Gielgud seems to be contemplating the negative shadings of language during these cut-throat moments, like T. S. Eliot considering the Anglo-Saxon four-letter words. This Prospero does not wrestle with a "thing of darkness" that he must admit is "his own" in the sense of the Jungian shadow. Ariel is his superego (Nevo), but we get little if any underpsyche from Gielgud. Caliban is, then, neither an external nor an internal threat, but merely a whim of Prospero's mildly Tolkienesque imagination.

With a meaningless Caliban, we "are not particularly moved" (Fuller, p.37) by Prospero. The conflation of Gielgud-Prospero-Shakespeare means that Prospero is virtually an unmoved mover, that we get the sentimental "autobiographical" reading of the role, and that we are given no stance from which to make an independent assessment of the character and his actions. "In the film," says Greenaway, "it is intended that there should be much deliberate cross-identification between Prospero, Shakespeare and Gielgud. At times, they are indivisibly one person" (Greenaway, p. 1). This is just poor old Shakespeare thinking of his "first best bed"—his grave—under the chancel in the church at Stratford. Gielgud's is an austere Prospero who does not weep—the lines about "fellowly drops" are cut. Would Arthur's butler weep on his deathbed? Gielgud refused to play a neurotic Prospero for Peter Hall in 1974 (Hall, Bravo interview) or perhaps could not. For all of the nakedness to which Prospero pays no attention, Gielgud's filmic Prospero does not share Hall's belief that "There is running through Prospero an absolutely paranoid distrust of sexuality and sensuality" (Hall, Bravo interview). As Gielgud renounced his magic in the 1974 production, he closed his book angrily on "here abjure," mimed the breaking of his staff, and exited stage left, leaving a huge and chilly moon above the empty stage. Prospero seemed the loneliest man on the face of the earth. As Robert Speaight says of the 1974 *Tempest*, "reunciation, like forgiveness, came hard to [Prospero]. Nor did he join the others in the return to Milan" (Speaight, p. 394). That was a powerful performance. By granting all power to Prospero, the film robs the character of any power but that of a puppeteer who finally joins his own show as a reverse Pinocchio.

"He creates their lines," Greenaway says of his Prospero, "and if he creates them, he might as well say them, too" (Ebert, E–3). Feminist critics, particularly, will object to the blatant version of patriarchy whereby Prospero voices over Miranda's lines and whereby the other characters are permitted to speak at the end "with their own voices, brought to a full life by his act of compassion" (Greenaway, p. 1). Prospero is their "mouthpiece," says Greenaway, "for as long as *The Tempest* is guided by the traditions of the revenge tragedy" (Greenaway, p. 1). Greenaway isolates the "reversal" as Ariel's admonishment "for the ferocity of the revengeful humiliation [Prospero] forces" on his enemies (Greenaway, p. 1). While Prospero claims that "virtue" is an action "rarer" than "revenge," he has promised early on not to harm any of the creatures on the vessel and is certainly working out a relationship between the king's son and his own daughter as the play goes along. What happens is that Prospero's emotions fall into the trap his intellect has set up for others. The same thing happens to Hamlet at the Mousetrap, but there with negative results. Proof of Prospero's descent back to humanity, are the tears he sheds in response to Gonzalo's model of compassion. Miranda, Ferdinand, Ariel, Gonzalo—and finally Prospero, respond to the suffering of others. Here, Greenaway's theory is close to being accurate, as Helen Gardner suggested years ago (Gardner, pp. 25–51). But you can't play a concept or, if you can, no emotional gradations escape through this cacophony of images. Since Prospero has his team of Ariels draw a huge blue circle which becomes the charmed circle into which his enemies wander, we get no indication that he has surrendered his control in light of Ariel's admonition. The other characters speak only after their lines have been pretty well dictated in advance anyway, and Prospero's only show of emotion is of residual rage at Antonio.

Had the film introduced "media" to suggest that competition for their control is a key to power, then the Caliban sequences might have been interesting. Here we would have seen Caliban's effort to "possess [Prospero's] books" as a way of dictating the moving images. Then, like the modern politician, Caliban would shape the narrative of his power by means of his own moving images. As it is, the text remains at the service of "the juridicao-political contracts that it guarantees," as Jacques Derrida would have it (Derrida, p. 95). The possibility that the conspiracy might be dramatic is glimpsed in that three of Caliban's imaginings are created for us on the film's superimposed television set—Prospero lies amid the torn parchment of his library, his throat cut with his own quill, Miranda endures Stephano's lovemaking, and Stephano sits on the throne playing juggler's tricks as Miranda sits sullenly beside him. But since Caliban is solidly subject to Prospero's narrative control, we must attribute Caliban's imaginings to Prospero's encompassing imagination—a case of a character growing a trifle independent of his creator's will. Greenaway makes sure that Caliban's conspiracy is not to be dreaded by having Caliban accompanied by one of the Ariels. One wonders why Greenaway bothered to include Caliban, Stephano, and Trinculo—a burlesque of the colonial narrative—since he does not allow it to make its commentary on Prospero or to parody the script's other conspiracies.

The way Greenaway introduces television destroys the ways that film works. Greenaway shot the film in Holland, went to Japan to add the special effects and optical superimpositions, then transferred the high-definition tape back to celluloid. Greenaway's aimless tracking shots alternate with the superimposition of a television screen upon the background. The screen is past and present—and future, insofar as it predicts the future of the image—but its foreground position blocks the movie screen from developing any field of depth. The only instance where a relatively deep field works effectively is when Prospero enters purposefully to interrupt his wedding masque. In other words, the possibilities of film are traded for the disadvantages of television.

The masque itself features a twelve-minute interlude of "minimalist music" by Michael Nyman in which the words are inaudible. Cupid is played by one of the Ariels, another erasure of tension, since Cupid in the masque mirrors the threat that Caliban represents in the outer play. The troupe of spirits marches by to present gifts to Ferdinand and Miranda. The spirits are rigidly choreographed— nothing "erotic" here, no matter what *Playboy* claims in the ad for the film. In fact, this is what Leni Reifenstahl would have left on the cutting room floor had she done something called *Naked at Nuremberg!* This is a rigid, pointless, and seemingly endless twelve minutes. I doubt that many will share Roger Ebert's belief that "This is a film that really cries out for the stop-frame capacity of a laser disc machine so that every shot can be examined as if it were a printed page" (Ebert, E–3). The gifts that the happy couple receive are superimposed on the procession by means of a smaller screen. We get something akin to the display of wonderful things that used to be given away on game shows or some version of home shopping network, all to the tunelessness of MTV. "Technique" shallows out the aesthetic response and hollows out any intellectual response.

Given the "close-up" proliferation of images, it is no wonder that a film-goer might feel overwhelmed. Greenaway can make his figures move, true, but his "canvas" has no design, no arrangement in space.

This is like staring at a canvas from too close-in and discovering that is makes no sense when we back up and try to glimpse the gestalt. The individual shots are disorganized and, for all of the film's emphasis on "geometry," lack perspective. Assuming that Greenaway alludes to Thomas Eakins in the Muybridge sequence, in the obsession with nakedness, and the emphasis on anatomy, Greenaway might have learned something from, for example, "William Rush Carving His Allegorical Figure." Eakins makes the sculptor almost invisible, the sculpture a mere wash, and illuminates the haphazardly tossed clothes of the model, which are front and center. The model's left side—flesh not stone—and the left arm and face of the chaperone are also lighted. While the painting can be called "a still life suggesting the act of disrobing" (Adams, p. 56), the painting is a study of the way light from the left plays randomly but naturally across the grouping, selecting what the painter must then depict. The painting shows how much Eakins was learning from photography in the 1870s and how much he still has to teach photographers—and filmmakers. If the painting is "about" anything, it is about the superiority of painting over sculpture—at least over allegorical sculpture—and about the cooperation of "nature"—a source of light—and the artist's eye. Eakins's genius invariably results from his willingness to let the painting *come from* the subject, so that he half perceives and half creates. He could, for example, be powerfullly "Freudian" without the benefit of Freud, as in "Miss Van Buren." Greenaway imposes *on* his subject. In describing his work with high-definition television in Tokyo, he says, "I can be a painter and a collager. Using a computerized stylus—which can be programmed as a paintbrush, a pen, or charcoal—I make marks on an electronically sensitive pad, and the images appear on the screen. It allows up to 17 million different color hues" (Koehler, p. F–7). This process serves the unwelcome reverese migration of television *to* film. If Prospero's books are "the metaphor for the whole enterprise" (Rodman, p. 38), the books compete with whatever Shakespeare's metaphors may be (calm and storm, dream and wakefulness, control and chaos, nature and nurture, language—elements that old-fashioned thematists used to explore), and the entire effort is smothered by the superimposition of television and *its* value system of acquisition upon the celluloid thesis of colonialism ("how to . . . subjugate its inhabitants"). Here, technique subjugates content. We get no sense that Greenaway and the script communicate with each other as partners.

At the end, Prospero asks for forgiveness by means of a close-up on that superimposed screen. The screen grows smaller and closes in on Prospero. We are meant to assume that *we* control him from our position in the lounger, our fingers summoning the titanic effort to eclipse him with a thumb. Perhaps the receding image makes *less* difference than that. Yet will this film be taken at "face value."

We the audience are really meant to implicate ourselves in the contract of guilt which is the basis of Christianity and in the equally suspect covenants of colonialism. The Epilogue represents "Prospero's last attempt to appropriate responses" (Goldberg, p. 133). But here, film which might have moved us, is canceled by television which cannot move us—even assuming some modicum of compassion for the old actor for whom the film is "obituary" (Greenaway, quoted in Koehler, F–7).

In 1939, I and many others went to the New York World's Fair in Flushing Meadows and waited in long lines to ride around in huge chairs within a Perisphere through a wondrous model world in which alabaster cities gleamed, surrounded by the perfect windrows of fields open to the sun as monorails sped and posted over land and lake. The only problem for a little fellow was that he could not lean back and listen to the descriptive voice in the cushion and lean forward to look down upon this brave, new world. Most of us, I would guess, chose to lean forward. When we emerged into the murky light of the "real world," we were given a pin that said, "I have seen the future." Writing of *The Tempest* in 1939, Mark van Doren said, "Any set of symbols, moved close to this play, lights up as in an electric field. Its meaning, in other words, is precisely as rich as the human mind. . . ." (van Doren, quoted in Eastman and Harrison, p. 306). One would have to say, in light of Greenaway's film, that the experience of the play is a function of the richness of the mind of the person who chooses to interpret it for us. But Greenaway chooses *not* to interpret the play for us, chooses *not* to permit two visions to cooperate and produce a third, a synthesis in which the original work is reshaped into something rich and strange. Greenaway's symbols obscure the play, casting it into some subordinate position from which it can say nothing, or, if it says anything, the *wrong* thing.

It may be that Greenaway is correct to proclaim "a new Guttenberg revolution, marrying television and computers. I really do think we're on the cusp here of something very exciting—and not just for cinema, but for television, and probably for book production, and certainly for photography, and, who knows, maybe painting. All over the world now these new technologies are being ripened, and HDTV is only one of them" (Greenaway, quoted in Ebert, p. E–3). Perhaps the fusion of light sensitive and magnetic imaging systems will produce something beyond the bizarre. And Greenaway may be right, as opposed to merely self-serving, when he says, "even if we have created something unsatisfactory [in *Prospero's Books*], I shan't cry copious tears over it, because I can now see the potential" (Greenaway, quoted in Rodman, p. 39). There may be potential in marrying film and a television technique which has a film-style aspect ratio and far greater resolution than standard TV. But that marriage will not work if the final result is something that looks like standard TV superimposed on chaos. If the film does represent the future, it does so only as epitaph. Greenaway has held the inherited script up only to the blinding light of his own ego. He needs to do much more, as Fuller says, "unless he is to be marooned on an island of artistic obscurity" (Fuller, p. 37). Those of us who believe that the energy system known as "Shakespeare" has a future, will be happy to leave Greenaway on his island in search of his private Friday the thirteenth.

10

Epilogue: The Stage in the Global Village

We are in the midst of a technological revolution that is changing the way Shakespeare comes at us. The tension between visual image and spoken word continues, even as the former grows more complex on film and larger on TV and the latter dwindles toward cliché and incomprehensibility. "Presentation" modes—Prospero's narratives in I.2 and the Choruses in *Henry V*—may still work for an educated ear as voice-overs for film, even as film seeks for the visual equivalents of Shakespeare's language. Assuming that television learns to use the depth-field that larger screens afford, it too will be able to accommodate voice-overs, special effects, location shooting, and rapidly shifting montages. Whether it will or not is questionable. Its own techniques, conventions, practitioners, and audience expectations have been confirming themselves—atrophying—for decades, and its overtly commercial premises make it an even more conservative medium than film, both in content and technique. And television may yet fall under the domination of political control or subjective determinants, in which, for example, a nation can watch with (almost) unanimous assent, as an administration employs a mercenary army primarily to showcase weaponry in the Middle East, or when a person can see the face of Christ in a forkful of spaghetti. As Paul Kurtz says, "A TV-saturated culture in which dramatic visuals overwhelm critical analysis invites such subjective perceptions" (Jacobson, p. 2). To some extent, we have become "the camera," overwhelming what is presented with our own inner imagery in some radical version of paranoia, or accepting what is presented uncritically as an elected government lobotomizes us.

The Shakespearean "text" is indeterminate, problematized, incomplete, and subject to an "infinite deferral of the signified," not just because deconstructionist critics say so, but because the text's "radical openness to interpretation . . . is intrinsic, not willed by the interpreter" (Dunbar, p. 1). The openness is willed by the maker of the script, who devised a set of signals to be interpreted by actors and, as theatrical history has evolved, by directors and designers. As Gary Waller says, the "Shakespearean script [is] a mode of producing, not merely *reproducing* meanings . . . as it is loosed into the world as production, within changing signifying systems and historical formulations" (Waller, *SQ*, p. 103, his ital.). The script, Waller argues, is not a set of "fixed textual meanings waiting to be read atemporally . . . by the attentive critic armed with appropriate . . . terminonogy" (Waller, *SQ*, p. 102). Such a viewpoint conflicts, of course, with that of textual critics who claim that "performance limits the 'true nature' of the text, concealing its verbal constructs and the connotative, metaphorical, and psychologically associative connections they potentially induce in readers" (Hodgdon, p. 57). But, as Barbara Hodgdon suggests, both "critics [and] performers fill in an elliptical text [therefore rewriting] the play's intentionally puzzling narrative rhythms" (Hodgdon, p. 63). A text, she says, will naturally "be disturbed by time" (Hodgdon, p. 65), all platonist wishes to the contrary. Performance *is* that disturbance.[1]

Ironically, the cassette becomes the "text"—immutable, ascertained, recoverable. And it, like any critical interpretation, is subject to its zeitgeist. One cannot help but notice that Eileen Herlie's high-piled hairdo as Gertrude in Olivier's 1948 *Hamlet* is the same as Vivian Leigh's as Scarlett in the 1939 *Gone With the Wind*. Production gets trapped in the sign-systems of its decade. The historical moment and its cultural and ideological constructs determine what is possible in a production of a Shakespeare script, just as the production signals the possibilities and limitations of the historical moment, as in the contrasting examples of the Olivier and the Branagh versions of *Henry V*. That oxymoron known as "popular culture" constantly reappropriates the Shakespearean script and sends it forward into history and into the debate that is partly what history is.

"Large scripts"—those filled with political struggle, manipulation of image and word for the purposes of deceit, and issues of dynasty and empire—can work on television through an accretion of carefully selected details that add up to a metonymy for the encompassing frame of the Shakespearean stage and for language that could flash the imagination across green Neptune's arching back and return it back again in an instant. The challenge to the modern imagination and its media, issues from a stage that was apparently more flexible in 1600 than any area we can muster today, and from a moment in time in which the sacred and the secular balanced in a poise that was at once competitive and cooperative. The old formulae, transferred from the sanctuary to the stage, could still invite the energies of conscience and compassion into the dramatic continuum. In a world where people are intentionally torn from their cultural heritage—because it represents an imprisoning patriarchy—the continuum, assuming it can be created by mechanical media, must be new-created with each event. We are the rock audience that knows nothing. But the production can educate us to its issues if it gives us great acting within the range of ensemble work involving a few actors down to the close-up. Again, productions as different as Nunn's diaphanous *Antony and Cleopatra* and Jane Howell's splintery-board *II Henry VI* show how it can be done, with Janet Suzman and Richard Johnson, Julia Foster and Bernard Hill providing some of the details and the articulation that recreate for us a sense of the excitement of the scripts, even as the actors explain what the scripts also explain—the events behind the characters and the characters behind the events. Acting becomes the primary source of the mosaic that ultimately creates the final effect, which can be as somberly impressive and calculated as Suzman's Cleopatra, lying in profile like a newly minted sarcophagus, or as apparently spontaneous as a cloth dropping down in front of a fence announcing "Henry the Sixth, Part Two" in crudely painted letters. The best of Shakespeare on television can focus the middle ground of jostling motives that Zitner describes (Zitner, p. 38), which can include intricate ensemble acting, like that of Nunn's opening scene of *Antony and Cleopatra,* and Gloucester's defense in Howell's *II Henry VI.*

As I have argued, some of the good moments of Shakespeare on television and often the only ones that give us a sense of the enclosing or framing element of Shakespeare's stage are television translations of actual stage productions. For all of the elaboration and projection that a large auditorium demands, such productions can be translated effectively to television and still retain a trace of the experience of live theater. Such a process may result in the bringing into contact of "a strong presence of actors and a strong presence of spectators [so as to] produce a circle of unique intensity in which barriers can be broken and the invisible become real," as Peter Brook says (Brook, p. 41). Without that intensity, the experience of Shakespeare becomes as irrelevant as *Prospero's Books.* We do not have enough Shakespeare on tape—and certainly not enough live Shakespeare. I think, for example, of how well Peter Hall's *Merchant,* with Dustin Hoffman, would have translated to television, of John Retallac's 1990 *Measure for Measure* at Oxford, of Ron Daniel's RSC *Hamlet,* etc.[2]

I am convinced that the future of Shakespeare on television lies entreasured in the beginnings of Shakespeare, that is, on the stage.

The "interface" with the future is, as always, at hand. Larry Friedlander's "Shakespeare Project" at Stanford, incorporated a videodisc with scenes from two versions each of *Hamlet, Lear,* and *Macbeth,* which "allowed the user to switch between versions and observe the same 'beat' as directed, for instance, by Welles and Polanski [and] also allowed students and teachers to add notes to the scenes, to select excerpts from the scenes, and to compare the performance text with the original[s]" (Donaldson, p. 8).

Friedlander and Peter Donaldson are now collaborating on The Shakespeare Interactive Archive, which

> will be an easy to use, multimedia environment in which scholars can examine multiple performances of Shakespeare's plays [which] will offer indexing capabilities which will allow the researcher to compare literary, filmic, and performance elements formerly too elusive to capture . . . with enough precision to contrast divergent readings of the same line of text; or identify aspects of film style such as the use of specific camera angles or visual motifs as they appear in different scenes of the same film. (Donaldson, p. 1)

In addition to ready access to available texts and a virtually instant command of filmic and televisual manifestations of the play-text, the scholar will have the use of an "Interactive Lexicon of Performance Terms" and an "Interactive Lexicon of Film Style and Terminology." These lexicons will be a great help to those of us who grew up with conventional literary vocabularies and who tread very gingerly among the words and grammars of the camera, too often a foreign language which practitioners of Shakespeare have avoided.

The claim here—one that this book certainly supports—is that "Central to the new developments in the study of Shakespeare film and performance is the view that these studies are not merely sub-specialties within Shakespeare scholarship, but rather that the plays themselves are best understood in terms of the performance issues they raise and the performance options they afford" (Donaldson, p. 5). Certainly the taped or filmed performance represents a "text" within the field of "intertextuality," that is, if we assume that such a cross-referencing continues in time and is not merely a function of "historicity," which is restricted to *a* time, and an increasingly past time at that. The Interactive Archive seeks to foster the

> cross-fertilization [between the insights of film and performance special-ists and the insights of literary critics] [by presenting] these two bodies of criticism in a common medium—not the visually restricted medium of print, but the visually rich world of multimedia, where filmic and performance insights can be illustrated and made concrete, and where literary scholars can enrich their analysis by observing the ways in which

the text has been interpreted in different media and moments of cultural history. (Donaldson, p. 5)

The problems for those who argue *script* over *text*, have issued from the transitory nature of production. Those who would use available productions on cassette or film are "thwarted by the difficulty of accessing, manipulating, and citing such materials" (Donaldson, p. 3), difficulties which this book makes clear enough. "Similarly, the debate in American criticism over whether text or performance has priority has been limited by . . . the lack of a standardized terminology for discussing [specific performance moments]" (Donaldson, p. 4).

The ability "to view a performance, consult glossaries, textual notes, and background materials, see a single performance from multiple perspectives or a single moment in various productions, take notes and write multimedia essays—all in the same workplace" (Donaldson, pp. 6–7) should lead to an increase in "performance criticism," particularly with a generation of scholars who are "literate" in the modes that have replaced the superheterodyne and the Royal Standard in what seems to me to be a brief instant of time. The Interactive Archive will "prepare the way for such an archive to exploit advanced interactive technology to the fullest extent possible" (Donaldson, p. 7). It "is a step toward shaping the computer medium [for] the kinds of tasks that humanists engage in" (Donaldson, p. 8).

It will be its own multimedia event and should combine the visual and the written texts with more coherence and more satisfying results than, say, *Prospero's Books*.

The implications for teaching are obvious. It is likely, in fact, "to foster a new kind of Shakespeare teaching. . . . The Archive would serve as an inspiration for more sophisticated, segmented, comparative uses of video material in Shakespeare classes, and modified or scaled-down versions of the archive could be installed as workstations for use in electronic classrooms and language laboratory settings" (Donaldson, p. 8).

We now have—for the first time in "the history of Shakespeare"—a means of comparing different versions of the same production and ways of exploring the text as "troue"—that is "fill of holes which need to be filled by another kind of text, performance" (Anne Ubersfeld, paraphrased in Donaldson, p. 4). And we soon will have a quicker, more accurate, and more complete way of evaluating performance and our response to it.

And now that we are on the threshold of yet another breakthrough, we need more performances to serve and to inform the new techniques. Philip McGuire offers this possibility:

> The Archive also holds out the prospect of another level of integration. The Royal Shakespeare Company and the Stratford (Ontario) Festival have for some time now recorded their productions on videotape. It is conceivable that . . . the Archive could include . . . those videotapes, thus making it possible to analyze side-by-side and with greater precision than is now possible both productions for the stage and for the mass media. (quoted in Donaldson, Addenda, p. 8)

Some of those productions, of course—the RSC *Comedy of Errours* and the Stratford (Canada) *Taming of the Shrew*—were televised *as* television. Even those productions that were merely recorded by a single fixed camera would be an invaluable addition to the production canon available to scholars working in this expanding field of energies.

Notes

Chapter 1. Some Problems, Some Responses

1. Cf. William Blakenburg and David G. Clark, *You and Media* (New York: Harper, 1973); Norman Corwin, *Trivializing America* (Secaucus, N.J.: Lyle Stuart, 1983); Todd Gitlin, *Inside Prime Time* (New York: Pantheon, 1983); S. L. Harrison, "Prime Time Pablum—How Politics and Corporate Influence Keep Public TV Harmless," *Washington Monthly* (January 1986): 3; Frank Mankiewicz and Joel Swerdlow, *Remote Control* (New York: Times Books, 1978); Ron Powers, *The Newscasters* (New York: St. Martin's, 1977); and Marie Winn, *The Plug-In Drug* (New York: Viking, 1985).

2. Cf. David Marc, "Understanding Television," *The Atlantic* (August 1984): 33–44.

3. Cf. Alvin Kernan, "This Goodly Frame, The Stage," *Shakespeare Quarterly*, 25 (Winter 1974): 1–5; and *The Playwright as Magician* (New Haven: Yale University Press, 1979), 129–35.

4. Cf. Paul Robinson, "TV Can't Educate," *The New Republic* (August 1978): 13–15: "Television is superbly fit to amuse . . . and it gives us a sense of union with humanity, if only in its foibles. Herbert Marcuse might even contend that it keeps alive the image of an unrepressed existence. . . . But it can't educate. . . . The only way to learn is by reading." I would add that writing is also, potentially, a mode of learning.

5. Cf. essays by James Bulman et al., in *Shakespeare on Television*, ed. James Bulman and H. R. Coursen (Hanover, N.H.: University Press of New England, 1988).

6. The case for text *as* text is presented by Harry Berger, *Imaginary Auditions* (Berkeley: University of California Press, 1990).

7. Cf. Dennis Bingham, "Jane Howell's First Tetralogy: Brechtian Break-Out or Just Good Television?" *Shakespeare on Television*, 221–29; and Coursen, *Shakespearean Performance as Interpretation* (Newark: University of Delaware Press, 1991), 153–59. For contemporary reviews, see Michael Manheim, "The Shakespeare Plays on TV," *Shakespeare on Film Newsletter*, 8, no. 2 (April 1984): 3–4; John J. O'Connor, "Shakespeare's Challenge Brilliantly Met," *New York Times* (10 April 1983); and G. M. Pierce, *Cahiers Elisabethains* 24 (October 1983): 28.

8. For discussions that deal with the differences between the experience of live and televised sporting events, discussions that deal with the behavior modification induced by television, see William Oscar Johnson, "Sports in the Year 2001," *Sports Illustrated*, 75, no. 4 (July 1991): 40–48; Ron Fimrite, "What If They Held a Sporting Event and Nobody Came?" *Sports Illustrated*, 75, no. 4 (July 1991):49–52; and John Bush, "Watching the Road Games at Home," *New York Giants Newsletter* (23 September 1991): 13.

Chapter 2. Style in *Dream:* The ART Version

1. See, for example, John Russell Brown, "Free Shakespeare," in *Shakespeare Survey*, 24, edited by Kenneth Muir (Cambridge: Cambridge University Press,

1971); Thomas Clayton, "Shakespeare at the Guthrie," *Shakespeare Quarterly*, 37, no. 2 (Summer 1986): 229–35; Samuel Crowl, "Babes in the Woods: or, The Lost Boys," *Literature/Film Quarterly*, 21, no. 3 (1983): 135–39; Anthony B. Dawson, *Watching Shakespeare* (London: MacMillan, 1988), 12–25; Henry Fenwick, "The Production," *A Midsummer Night's Dream* (London: BBC Books, 1981), 18–25; R. A. Foakes, *A Midsummer Night's Dream* (Cambridge: Cambridge Univesrsity Press, 1984), 12–25; Anthony W. Price, *A Midsummer Night's Dream* (London: MacMillan, 1983), 189–98; David Selborne, *The Making of 'A Midsummer Night's Dream'* (London: Methuen, 1982); J. C. Trewin, *Going to Shakespeare* (London: George Allen & Unwin, 1978), 98–106; Peter Thompson, "A Necessary Theatre," in *Shakespeare Survey*, 24; edited by Kenneth Muir; and Roger Warren, *'A Midsummer Night's Dream': Text and Performance* (London: MacMillan, 1983).

Chapter 3. "Alas, Poor Yorick!"

I am indebted to Prof. William Watterson's Honors Seminar at Bowdoin College in October 1991, for adding some excellent insights to this discussion, particularly to Eileen Hunt for pointing out some aspects of the Chamberlain performance that I had neglected, and to Curt Perrin for noticing the Ophelia-Cordelia-Fool equation.

1. Ronald M. Frye, *The Renaissance 'Hamlet'* (Princeton: Princeton University Press, 1984); and Harry Morris, *Last Things in Shakespeare* (Gainesville: University of Florida Press, 1987).

2. Bernice W. Kliman, *Hamlet: Film, Television and Audio Performance* (Madison, N.J.: Fairleigh Dickinson University Presses, 1988).

3. See Jack Jorgen's cogent discussion, to which I am indebted. *Shakespeare on Film* (Bloomington: Indiana University Press, 1977), 218–34.

Chapter 4. Gertrude's Story

1. For a detailed analysis of several Ophelias in production, see H. R. Coursen, *Shakespearean Performance as Interpretation* (Newark: University of Delaware Press, 1992), 85–102.

2. See Coursen, *A Jungian Approach to Shakespeare* (Washington: University Press of America, 1986), 79–80.

3. On Denmark's inability to contact the "supernature" via ritual, see Coursen, *Christian Ritual and the World of Shakespeare's Tragedies* (Lewisburg: Bucknell University Press, 1976), 89–176.

4. For a development of the thesis that the audience is an essential part of "drama," see J. L. Styan, "Psychology in the Study of Drama," *College Literature*, 5 (1978): 77–93.

Chapter 5. Playing Space: The Kline *Hamlet*

1. On televised versions of live stage productions, see Barbara Millard, "Husbanded with Modesty: Shakespeare on TV," *Shakespeare Bulletin*, 4, no. 3 (1986), to which I am indebted here and elsewhere.

2. On the use of light in Zeffirelli's *Hamlet*, see David Impastato, "Sunlight Makes Meaning," *Shakespeare on Film Newsletter*, 16, no. 1 (December 1991): 1–2.

Chapter 6. Editing the Script

1. See the recent excellent book length treatment of these productions by James Lusardi and June Schlueter, *Reading Shakespeare in Performance: King Lear* (Cranbury, N.J.: Associated University Presses, 1991).

Chapter 8. The Case for a Black Othello

1. Cf. Bede, *Collected Works*, v. 541: "Tertius . . . Balthasar nomine . . . per myrrham filiam." On Myrrh, see Pliny, *Naturalis Historia*, 12: 14–15.
2. William E. Cross, *Shades of Black* (Philadelphia: Temple University Press, 1991).
3. On this and other issues, see Stanley Wells's superb review of the stage production: *Shakespeare Survey* 43 (1990): 191–94, and my *Shakespearean Performance as Interpretation* (Newark: University of Delaware Press, 1992), 216–19.
4. On the sexual stereotyping of the black *woman*, see Estelle B. Freeman, "The Manipulation of History at the Clarence Thomas Hearings," *Chronicle of Higher Education* 38, no. 18 (14 January 1992): 32–33: "Gender-specific racial myths placed Professor Hill in the tradition of the promiscuous lascivious black woman" (B–3). I have learned that Flora Robson played a "black" Bianca in the 1930s.
5. Quoted in Sylvan Barnet, "*Othello* on Stage and Screen," *Othello* (New York: Signet, 1987), 285.

Chapter 10. Epilogue: The Stage in the Global Village

1. See my argument on this point in *Performance as Interpretation* (Newark: University of Delaware Press, 1992), 23–48.
2. For other suggestions see Elijah Moshinsky's commentary in John Elsom, *Is Shakespeare Still Our Contemporary?* (London: Routledge, 1989). Among other things, Moshinsky says, "If in the future, television gets round to Shakespeare again, the plays should be done on film, not on video tape, and independently from a large bureaucracy and more time should be given to the work of each production so that such problems don't pre-empt the artistic judgments" (Elsom, 122). He is, of course, referring to the BBC series of the late 70s and early 80s.

Works Cited:

Ackroyd, Peter. Review of the BBC-TV *I Henry VI*. *The Times,* January 1983.

Adams, Henry. "Thomas Eakins: The Troubled Life of an Artist Who Became an Outcast." *The Smithsonian* 22, no. 8 (November 1991): 52–67.

Adams, Val. "Random Notes on a Shakespearean Rehearsal." *New York Times,* 18 October 1953.

Ardolino, Frank. "Three Reviews." *Marlowe Society of America Newsletter* 11, no. 1 (Spring 1991): 5–6.

Barker, Francis, and Peter Hulme. "Nymphs and Reapers Heavily Vanish: The Discursive Con-texts of *The Tempest*." In *Alternative Shakespeares.* Edited by John Drakakis. London: Methuen, 1985.

Barber, C. L. *Shakespeare's Festive Comedy.* Princeton: Princeton University Press, 1959.

Barnet, Sylvan. "*Othello* on Stage and Screen." *Othello.* New York: Signet, 1987.

Berger, Thomas. Review of *Shakespeare on Television. Shakespeare Quarterly* 40 (1990): 237–39.

Berkowitz, Gerald M. "Shakespeare in Edinburgh." *Shakespeare Quarterly* 34 (1983): 90.

———. "Shakespeare at the 1988 Edinburgh Festival." *Shakespeare Quarterly* 40 (1989): 77–78.

Berry, Ralph. "Stratford Festival: Canada." *Shakespeare Quarterly* 29 (1978): 225.

Bradley, A. C. *Shakespearean Tragedy.* London: MacMillan, 1904.

Brissenden, Alan. "Shakespeare in Adelaide." *Shakespeare Quarterly* 30 (1979): 225.

Brook, Peter. *The Shifting Point.* New York: Harper & Row, Publishers, 1987.

Bulman, James, and H.R. Coursen, ed. *Shakespeare on Television.* Hanover, N.H.: University Press of New England, 1988.

Clark, K. B. and M. "Emotional Factors in Racial Identification and Preference in Negro Children." *Journal of Negro Education* 19 (1950): 73–87.

Clayton, Thomas. "Shakespeare at the Guthrie." *Shakespeare Quarterly* 37 (1986): 229–36.

Cleaver, Eldridge. *Soul on Ice.* New York: Dell, 1968.

Cohen, Michael. *Hamlet: In My Mind's Eye.* Athens: University of Georgia Press, 1989.

Cook, Hardy M. "Two *Lears* for Television: An Exploration of Televisual Strategies." *Literature/Film Quarterly* 14. no. 4 (1986): 179–86.

Coursen, H. R. *The Compensatory Psyche: A Jungian Approach to Shakespeare.* Washington: University Press of America, 1986.

———. "The Decisions a Director Makes." *Shakespeare Bulletin* 7, no. 6 (1989): 26–29.

———. "Shakespeare in Maine." *Shakespeare Quarterly* 34 (1983): 97–98.

———. *Shakespearean Performance as Interpretation.* Newark: University of Delaware Press, 1992.

Cross, William E. *Shades of Black.* Philadelphia: Temple University Press, 1991.

de Laurentis, Teresa. *Alice Doesn't: Feminism, Semiotics, Cinema.* Bloomington: Indiana University Press, 1984.

De Lillo, Don. *White Noise.* New York: Penguin, 1986.

"Defendants Freed in Mississippi Trial," *New York Times,* 24 September 1955.

Derrida, Jacques. "Living on: Border Lines." In *Deconstruction and Criticism.* Edited by Harold Bloom. London: Routledge and Kegan Paul, 1979.

Dessen, Alan. Letter to author. 2 September 1989.

———. "Shakespeare and the Supernatural on Television." *Shakespeare on Film Newsletter* (December 1986): 1 and 8.

Donaldson, Peter. *Shakespeare Demonstration Interactive Archive Project.* Cambridge: MIT Press, 1991.

Dunbar, Mary Judith. "The Playtext." Paper sumitted to the "Performance as Interpretation" Seminar, Shakespeare Association of America, 1992.

Eastman, A.B. and Q.B. Harrison. Editors, *Shakespeare's Critics.* Ann Arbor: University of Michigan Press, 1964.

Ebert, Roger. "Director Works 'Magick' with Bard in 'Books'." *Chicago Sun-Times,* 24 November 1991.

Edsall, Thomas Byrne. "Willie Horton's Message." *New York Review,* 13 February 1992.

Edwards, Lee. "The Labours of Psyche." *Critical Inquiry* 6 (1979): 32–44.

Eliot, T. S. "Hamlet and His Problems." In *Hamlet: Enter Critic.* Edited by Claire Sachs and Edgar Whan. New York: Appleton-Century-Crofts, 1960: 53–58.

Ellison, Ralph. *The Invisible Man.* New York: Random House, 1947.

Elsom, John. *Is Shakespeare Still Our Comtemporary?.* London: Routledge, 1989.

Esslin, Martin. "Aristotle and the Advertisers: The Television Commercial Considered as a form of Drama." *Kenyon Review* 1, no. 4 (Fall 1979): 96–108.

Fenwick, Henry. "The Production." In *Hamlet.* London: BBC Books, 1982: pp. 17–29.

———. "The Production." In *Richard II.* London: BBC Books, 1978: pp. 19–26.

Fiedler, Leslie. *The Stranger in Shakespeare.* New York: Stein & Day, Publishers, 1972.

Fordham, Frieda. *An Introduction to Jung's Psychology.* London: Penguin, 1953.

French, William M. "Lime Kiln Festival." *Shakespeare Bulletin* 6, no. 2 (1988): 16.

Frye, Roland M. *The Renaissance HAMLET.* Princeton: Princeton University Press, 1984.

Fuller, Graham. "Shots in the Dark." *Interview,* November 1991.

Gardner, Helen. *The Business of Criticism.* Oxford: Oxford University Press, 1963.

Goldberg, Jonathan. "Shakespeare Inscriptions: The Voicing of Power." In *Shakespeare and the Question of Theory.* Edited by Patricia Parker and Geoffrey Hartman. London: Metheun, 1985.

———. "*Macbeth* and Its Source." In *Shakespeare Reproduced.* Edited by Jean Howard and Marion O'Connor. London: Metheun, 1987.

Goldman, Michael. *Acting and Action in Shakespearean Tragedy.* Princeton: Princeton University Press, 1985.

Goodfellow, William S. "Utah Shakespeare Festival." *Shakespeare Quarterly* 30 (1979): 230.

Goodman, Walter. "In Kevin Kline's 'Hamlet', A Less-than-Melancholy Dane." *New York Times,* 2 November 1990.

Greenaway, Peter. "Introduction to 'Prospero's Books.'" Miramax Films, 1991.

Griffin, Alice V. "Shakespeare Through the Camera's Eye." *Shakespeare Quarterly* 6 (1955): 63–72.

Griffin, John Howard. *Black Like Me.* New York: Houghton Mifflin Company, 1960.

Habicht, Werner. "Shakespeare in West Germany." *Shakespeare Quarterly* 31 (1981): 298–99.

Hageman, Elizabeth. "Shakespeare in Boston and Cambridge." *Shakespeare Quarterly* 32 (1981): 190–91.

Hapgood, Robert. "Shakespeare on Film and Television." In *The Cambridge Companion to Shakespeare Studies.* Edited by Stanley Wells. Cambridge: Cambridge University Press, 1986.

Hawkes, Terrence. *Coleridge's Writings on Shakespeare.* New York: Capricorn, 1959.

———. "Shakespeare and the New Critical Approaches." In *The Cambridge Companion to Shakespeare Studies.* Edited by Stanley Wells. Cambridge: Cambridge University Press, 1986.

Hearst, Stephen. "It Ain't Necessarily So." *The New Review* (Summer 1978): 3–13.

Herbert, T. Walter. *Oberon's Mazed World.* Baton Rouge: Louisiana State University Press, 1977.

Hetherington, "The *Lears* of Peter Brook." *Shakespeare on Film Newsletter* 7 (1982): 7.

Hill, Errol. *Shakespeare in Sable: A History of Black Shakespearean Actors.* Amherst: University of Massachusetts Press, 1984.

Hodgdon, Barbara. "Parallel Practices, or the *Un*-Necessary Difference." *Kenyon Review* 7 (1985): 57–65.

Holmin, Lorrie. "Shakespeare in Sweden." *Shakespeare Quarterly* 31 (1980): 432.

Home Box Office. "Zeffirelli Directs *Hamlet.*" HBO, 1990.

Howell, Jane. Interviewed by Michele Willems, *Shakespeare a la Television.* Rouen: Universite de Rouen, 1987.

Horobetz, Lynn K. "Shakespeare in West Germany." *Shakespeare Quarterly* 12 (1971): 385.

Hortman, Wilhelm. "Shakespeare in West Germany," *Shakespeare Quarterly* 35 (1984): 215–18.

Hunter, G. K. *'Othello' and Colour Prejudice.* British Academy Lecture, 1967. London: Oxford University Press, 1967.

Jacobs, Tom. "Hamlet Is No Wimp." *Brunswick-Bath Times-Record,* 7 January 1991.

Jacobson, David. "The Subliminal on Television." *Portland Press-Herald,* 1 June 1991.

Jones, D.A.N. Review of the BBC-TV *I Henry VI. The Listener,* 6 January 1983.

Jorgens, Jack. *Shakespeare on Film.* Bloomington: Indiana University Press, 1977.

Kennedy, Andrew. "Shakespeare in Bergen." *Shakespeare Quarterly* 32 (1981): 374.

Kliman, Bernice. *Hamlet: Film, Television, and Audio Performance.* Madison, N.J.: Fairleigh Dickinson University Press, 1988.

———. "Branagh's *Henry V.*" *Shakespeare on Film Newsletter* 14 (1989): 1 and 9.

Koehler, Robert. "Peter Greenaway is Expert at Creating Film Tempests." *Los Angeles Times,* 2 December 1991.

Kott, Jan. *Shakespeare, Our Contemporary.* Garden City: Doubleday, 1964.

Leavis, F. R. "Diabolic Intellect and the Noble Hero," *Scrutiny* 6 (1937): 3–17.

Lindblad, Ishrat. "Shakespeare in Sweden." *Shakespeare Quarterly* 36 (1985): 460–61.

Litton, Glenn. "Diseased Beauty in Tony Richardson's *Hamlet.*" *Literature/Film Quarterly* 4, no. 2 (Spring 1976): 108–22.

Long, Michael. *The Unnatural Scene.* London: Metheun, 1976.

Maher, Mary. "Derek Jacobi's Hamlet: A Video View," with Elizabeth Leebron. Paper presented at the Shakespeare Association of America, April 1983.

———. "Kevin Kline's American *Hamlet:* Stage to Screen." *Shakespeare on Film Newsletter* 15, no. 2 (April 1991): 11–12.

Malcolm X. *Autobiography.* New York: Grove, 1966.

Mander, Jerry. *Four Arguments for the Elimination of Television.* New York: William Morrow & Co., 1978.

Marc, David. "Understanding Television." *The Atlantic* (August 1984): 33–44.

McLuhan, Marshall, *Understanding Media.* New York: McGraw Hill Book Company, 1964.

McLuskie, Kathleen. "The Patriarchal Bard: Feminist Criticism and Shakespeare: *King Lear* and *Measure for Measure.*" In *Political Shakespeare.* Edited by Jonathan Dollimore and Alan Sinfield. Manchester: Manchester University Press, 1985, pp. 88–108.

Mehren, Elizabeth. "College Town Becomes Lesbian Haven." *Portland Press-Herald,* 21 December, 1991.

Merchant, Moelwyn. "*A Midsummer-Night's Dream:* A Visual Recreation." in *Early Shakespeare.* Edited by John Russell Brown and Bernard Harris. Cambridge: Cambridge University Press, 1961.

Messner, Gerald, ed. *To Be Black in America.* New York: Harcourt, Brace and World, 1970.

Miller, Mark C. "The Shakespeare Plays." *The Nation* (12 July 1980): 46–61.

Mills, John. *Hamlet on Stage.* Westport, Conn.: Greenwood Press, 1985.

Miramax. "Prospero's Books." Miramax, 1991.

Mitford, Jessica. "Behind the Formaldehyde Curtain." In *The American Way of Death.* New York: Simon & Schuster, 1963. Reprinted in *The Norton Reader.* New York: W. W. Norton & Company: 1984, pp. 466–73.

Mordden, Ethan. "Rock and Cole." *The New Yorker* (28 October, 1991): 91–113.

Morris, Harry. *Last Things in Shakespeare.* Gainesville: University Presses of Florida, 1985.

Nardo, Anna K. "Hamlet: A Man to Double Business Bound." *Shakespeare Quarterly* 34 (1983): 188–99.

Neely, Carol Thomas. "'Documents in Madness': Reading Madness and Gender in Shakespeare's Tragedies and Early Modern Culture." *Shakespeare Quarterly* 42, no. 3 (Fall 1991): 315–38.

Nemerov, Howard. *Poetry and Fiction.* New Brunswick, N.J.: Rutgers University Press, 1964.

Nevo, Ruth. *Shakespeare's Other Language.* London: Metheun, 1988.

Newman, Karen. "'And Wash the Ethiop White': Femininity and the Monstrous in *Othello.*" In *Shakespeare Reproduced.* Edited by Jean Howard and Marion O'Connor. New York and London: Methuen, 1987.

Norris, Christopher. "Post Structuralist Shakespeare: Text as Ideology." In *Alternative Shakespeares.* Edited by John Drakakis. London: Metheun, 1985.

Ornstein, Robert. *The Moral Vision of Jacobean Tragedy.* Madison: The University of Wisconsin Press, 1960.

Ottaway, David B. "In South Africa, a Surge of White Resentment." *International Herald Tribune,* 4 February 1992.

Pall, Ellen. "Kevin Kline Discovers There's a Rub in TV Directing." *New York Times,* 28 October 1990.

Quinn, Edward. "Zeffirelli's *Hamlet.*" *Shakespeare on Film Newsletter* 15, no. 2 (April 1991): 1–2.

Roberts, Jeanne A. "Shakespeare in Washington, D.C." *Shakespeare Quarterly* 31 (1980): 236.

Rodman, Howard A. "Anatomy of a Wizard." *American Film,* November–December 1991.

Rosen, Carol. "Shakespeare in New Jersey." *Shakespeare Quarterly* 31 (1980): 204.

Rosen, George. "Orson Welles in U.S. Video Debut Scores Smashing 'King Lear' Triumph." *Variety* 192, 21 October 1953.

Rosenberg, Marvin. *The Masks of Othello.* Berkeley: University of California Press, 1961.

Rosenthal, E. M. "They've Helped Buchanan Make Bigotry Acceptable." *International Herald Tribune,* 15–16 February 1992.

Rothwell, Kenneth S. *Shakespeare on Screen.* Annabelle Melzer (coeditor). New York: Neal-Schuman, 1990.

Rowan, Carl. "David Duke Revives Racism." *Portland Press Herald,* 12 October 1990.

Simon, John. "Theater: Court and Courtroom." *New York,* 24 March 1986.

Smith, Peter D. "The 1966 Festival of Ashland, Oregon, and San Diego." *Shakespeare Quarterly* 17 (1966): 416.

Speaight, Robert. "Shakespeare in Britain." *Shakespeare Quarterly* 24, no. 4 (Autumn 1974): 389–94.

Spence, Gerry. *With Justice for None.* New York: Penguin, 1989.

Stavropuolos, Janet C. "Love and Age in *Othello.*" *Shakespeare Studies* 19 (1987): 125–41.

Stodder, Joseph and Lillian Wilds. "Shakespeare in Southern California." *Shakespeare Quarterly* 30 (1979): 239–40.

Taylor, Estelle. "Before Black was Beautiful." *Shakespeare Quarterly* 34, no. 4 (1983): 506–7.

Thompson, Ann. *King Lear.* Atlantic Highlands, N.J.: Humanities Press, 1988.

Tokson, Elliot H. *The Popular Image of the Black Man in English Drama: 1550–1668.* Boston: G. K. Hall, 1983.

Trewin, J. C. *Five and Eighty Hamlets.* London: Hutchinson, 1987.

Updike, John. "Facing Death." *American Heritage* (May–June 1992): 98–105.

Van Doren, Mark. Quoted in *Shakespeare's Critics.* Edited by A. M. Eastman and G. B. Harrison. Ann Arbor: The University of Michigan Press, 1964.

Waller, Gary. "Decentering the Bard: The BBC-TV Shakespeare and Some Implications for Criticism and Teaching." In *Shakespeare on Television.* Edited by J. C. Bulman and H. R. Coursen. Hanover, N.H.: University Press of New England, 1988.

———. "Review." *Shakespeare Quarterly* 43 (1992): 102–03.

Warren, Roger. "Comedies and Histories at Two Stratfords, 1977." *Shakespeare Survey* 31. Edited by Kenneth Muir. Cambridge: Cambridge University Press, 1978. 141–53.

Wells, Stanley. "Shakespeare Production in England." *Shakespeare Survey* 43 (1991).

Whitmont, Edward. *The Symbolic Quest: Basic Concepts of Analytical Psychology.* New York: G. P. Putnam, 1969.

Wiggins, Martin. "Review." *Notes & Queries* (December 1989): 506.

Willems, Michele, ed. *Shakespeare a la Television.* Rouen: Universite de Rouen, 1987.

Willson, Robert. *"Measure for Measure." Shakespeare on Film Newsletter* 14, no. 1 (December 1989): 8.

Wine, Martin. *Othello: Text and Performance.* London: MacMillan, 1984.

Wood, Robert E. "Shakespeare in Atlanta." *Shakespeare Quarterly* 34 (1983): 340.

Worthen, William. *"King Lear* and TV." *Shakespeare on Film Newsletter* 8, no. 1 (May 1983): 5.

Wright, Louis B. "The Significance of *Othello." Othello.* New York: Washington Square Press, 1957.

Zitner, Sheldon. "Wooden O's in Plastic Boxes: Shakespeare and Television." *University of Toronto Quarterly* 51 (Fall 1991): 1–12.

Index

Ackroyd, Peter, 26
Adams, Henry, 174
Adams, Val, 108
Afrikaner Resistance Movement, 157
Aldwych Theatre, 47
Ali, Muhammad, 145
Allen, Woody, 22, 40, 43
Alliance Theater, 143
All in the Family, 13
American Conservatory Theater, 25, 82
American Repertory Theatre, 33–50, 68
Anglo Saxon "Phoenix," 169, 170
Annie Hall, 22
Apeuleius, 33
Ardolino, Frank, 91n., 124
Aristotle, 149–50, 159, 166
Astaire, Fred, 42

Badel, Alan, 99
Baker, Sean, 150
Balaclava, 34
Baldwin, James, 142
Barber, C. L., 47
Bard Productions, 25, 53–54
Barker, Francis, 165
Barnet, Sylvan, 157, 161
Barton, John, 36, 37, 38, 49
Bass, Alfie, 42
Bates, Alan, 77, 118
BBC, 25, 91, 154
BBC *Hamlet*, 120–22, 123
Beckett, Samuel, 128
Beerbohm-Tree, Sir Herbert, 57
Bennett, Rodney, 64
Benson, Peter, 33
Berger, Thomas, 12-13
Bergman, Ingmar, 66, 116, 164, 166
Bergman, Ingrid, 164
Bergson, Henri, 47
Berkowitz, Gerald M., 38, 39
Bernhardt, Sarah, 57
Berry, Ralph, 38

"Black Adder," 28
Blessed, Brian, 89
Bogart, Humphery, 164
Booth, Edwin, 63n., 161
Boston Red Sox, 31
Botticelli, Sandro, 166
Bradley, A. C., 127, 129, 141, 147
Branagh, Kenneth, 32, 51, 93, 178
Brecht, Bertolt, 36, 167
Brissenden, Alan, 39
Brook, Sir Peter, 26, 36–37, 38, 46, 49, 96–100, 147, 179
Browning, Kirk, 80
Browning, Robert, 30
Brustein, Robert, 152
Bryant, Roy, 138
Burbage, Richard, 126
Burton, Richard, 57, 63, 69
Bush, George, 139, 153

Cabala, 170
Caine, Michael, 62
Caldwell, Sarah, 80
Camus, Albert, 128
Car 54, Where Are You, 31
Carteret, Angela, 22
Casablanca, 164
CBS, 29
Chamberlain, Richard, 57, 60, 63–64
Charleston, Ian, 121
Chaucer, Geoffrey, 33
Chopin, Fredrich, 19
Christ, 136, 177
Ciulei, Luivi, 35, 36, 37, 38, 39, 49, 86, 88, 90
Civil War series, 18, 19, 20
Clark, K. B. and M., 142–43
Clayton, Thomas, 35, 37
Cleaver, Eldridge, 142, 144–45
Close, Glenn, 32, 72, 73, 76-7
Cohen, Michael, 61, 121
Coleman, Ronald, 29

Coleridge, Samuel Taylor, 127, 139
Collins, Robert, 38
Connors, Nancy P., 79n.
Conrad, Joseph, 170
Cook, Hardy M., 91
Corbett, Jim, 168
Crosby, Bing, 42
Cross, William B., 143
Curry, Julian, 64

Daniels, Ron, 68, 179
Darlow, Cynthia, 44
Darrah, Thomas, 45
Davis, Desmond, 26
Day-Lewis, Daniel, 57
Delacorte Theater, 42
De Lillo, Don, 28
Dench, Judi, 25
Derrida, Jacques, 172
Dessen, Alan, 20, 21, 22, 154
Dexter, John, 150
Dobrowsky, Franz, 160
Donaldson, Peter, 180–82
Dukakis, Michael, 139
Duke, David, 127, 144
Dunbar, Mary Judith, 177

Eakins, Thomas, 174
Eastman, A. M., 175
Ebert, Roger, 172, 173, 175
Edsall, Thomas Byrne, 162
Edwards, Lee, 72
Eisenstein, Sergi, 11
Eliot, T. S., 71, 171
Ellison, Ralph, 144
Elsom, John, 162
Epstein, Alvin, 42, 49
Esslin, Martin, 29, 166
Evans, Maurice, 20

Fairy Queen (Purcell), 43
Faithfull, Marianne, 73–4
Father Knows Best, 13
Fellini, Federico, 12, 41
Fenwick, Henry, 70
Fergusson, Francis, 166
Ferrer, Jose, 41
Fiedler, Leslie, 146, 160
Fields, John, 163
Finlay, Frank, 157, 160
Finney, Albert, 29

First Corinthians, 170
Fitzsimmons, Ruby Robert, 168
Fludd, Robert, 160
Folger Library, 57
Forbes-Robertson, Sir Johnston, 57
Forbidden Planet, 164
Fordham, Frieda, 135
Foster, Julia, 179
Frazier, E. Franklin, 142
French, William M., 34
Freud, Sigmund, 129, 131, 136, 174
Friedlander, Larry, 179, 180
Frye, Roland M., 58
Fuller, Graham, 167, 176

Gardner, Dame Helen, 172
Garrick, David, 143
Gettysburg, 147
G.I. Bill of Rights, 165
Gibson, Mel, 32, 57, 62, 66–67, 72, 78, 116
Gielgud, Sir John, 59, 60, 61, 62, 164, 170, 171, 175
Giles, David, 34, 89
Gillespie, Arnold, 22
Godfrey, Patrick, 90
Goldberg, Jonathan, 127, 175
Goldman, Michael, 141
Gone with the Wind, 178
Goodfellow, William S., 40
Goodman, Benny, 67
Goodman, Walter, 81, 97–98
Goya, Francisco José, 91
Gradage, Michael, 155
Great Gatsby, 127, 151
Greenaway, Peter, 163–76
Gregg, Donald, 165
Griffin, Alice V., 97
Griffin, John Howard, 138, 139–40, 142, 143–44, 156
Guinness, Sir Alec, 57
Guthrie Theater, 35

Habicht, Werner, 40
Haddon Haines, Richard, 160–62
Hageman, Elizabeth H., 38, 43, 45
Hall, Sir Peter, 49, 171, 179
Hapgood, Robert, 42, 86
Hardy, Thomas, 33, 39
Harrison, G. B., 175
Hawkes, Terrence, 100, 127, 139

Hawthorne, Nathaniel, 33
Hearst, Stephen, 17–18
Heisenberg, Werner Karl, 29
Heller, Richard, 42
Herbert, T. Walter, 35, 169
Herlie, Eileen, 72, 178
Hetherington, Robert, 97, 99
Hill, Benny, 42
Hill, Bernard, 179
Hillerman, Tony, 33
Hodgdon, Barbara, 178
Hoffman, Dustin, 179
Holbein, Hans, 57–58
Holloway, Stanley, 60
Hopkins, Anthony, 73, 118, 126, 128, 150
Horobetz, Lynn, 38
Hortman, Wilhelm, 36, 37, 39
Horton, Willie, 139, 156
Hoskins, Bob, 101, 150
Howell, Jane, 23, 27, 28, 34, 87, 153, 162, 179
Huckleberry Finn, 40
Hulme, Peter, 165
Hunt, Marsha, 152
Huon de Bordeaux, 34
Hussein, Saddam, 131

Jacobi, Derek, 64–65, 84, 86, 89, 93, 123, 150
Jacobs, Tom, 60
Jacobson, David, 177
James, Henry, 151, 166
James, Peter Francis, 84
Johnson, Lyndon, 18, 19, 121
Johnson, Richard, 26, 72, 179
Jones, Cherry, 43
Jones, D. A. N., 27
Jones, James Earl, 74, 80, 142, 152
Jorgens, Jack, 41, 115, 118
Jung, C. G., 129, 133, 134, 135, 136, 137, 171

Kani, John, 157–61
Keach, Stacey, 57
Keats, John, 68, 159
Kemble, John Phillip, 57
Kennedy, Andrew, 38
Kennedy, John F., 18–19, 121
Kennedy, John, Jr., 189
Kingsley, Ben, 57

Kinnear, Roy, 62–63
Kliman, Bernice, 32, 60, 93, 114, 118, 123
Kline, Kevin, 61, 67, 80–92 passim, 120, 123–34
Koehler, Robert, 164, 174, 175
Kott, Jan, 36, 128, 129
Kozintsev, Grigori, 54, 63, 72, 114–15
Kurtz, Paul, 177

Laing, R. D., 72, 90
Lamb, Charles, 127
Lamour, Dorothy, 42
L.A. Story, 60, 67–69
Laurentis, Teresa de, 14
Lavallade, Carmen de, 45
Leavis, F. R., 152–53
Leigh, Vivian, 178
Leighton, Margaret, 73
Levin, Richard, 166
Lincoln, Abraham, 116
Lindquist, Frej, 74, 76
Litton, Glenn, 74
Livesay, Roger, 64
Lotman, Yuri, 100
Louis, Joe, 145
Lunt-Fontaine Theater, 62
Lyth, Ragnar, 60, 66–67, 73, 75, 77, 78, 120, 122–23

Magi, 136–37
Maher, Mary, 81, 85, 86, 87
Malcolm X, 142, 154
Malleson, Miles, 41
Malm, Mona, 73, 74–77
Mander, Jerry, 18
Marc, David, 27–28, 29
Marciano, Rocky, 67
Maris, Roger, 31
Markow, Marty, 161
Marshall, William, 25, 147, 148, 154, 155
Martin, Steve, 67–68
Mason, Brewster, 149
May, Rollo, 68
McEnery, John, 71
McGuire, Philip, 182
McKellen, Ian, 25, 49, 60, 64, 100, 150, 151–52, 153, 161, 166
McLuhan, Marshall, 18–20
McLuskie, Kathleen, 71

McNamara, Maggie, 29
Mehren, Elizabeth, 65
Mendelssohn, Felix, 42
Merchant, W. Moelwyn, 35
Meredith, James, 124–25, 162–63
Merriam, Kendall, 19, 121
Messina, Cedric, 23
Messner, Gerald, 142
Middlemarch, 35
Milam, J. W., 138
Miller, Jonathan, 23, 24, 33–34, 82, 157, 161
Miller, Mark C., 23–24, 88, 149
Mills, John, 60, 62, 63
Milton, John, 169
Minor, Worthington, 97
Mitford, Jessica, 59
Monmouth, Theater, 34
"Monty Python," 28
Moody, Ron, 25, 150, 153
Moranis, Rick, 67
Mordden, Ethan, 166
Morey Wheel, 168
Morris, Harry, 58, 146, 158
Moshinsky, Elijah, 23, 162
Munsters, 21
Muybridge, Eadweard, 168, 174

Nabokov, Vladimir, 166
Nardo, Anna K., 70
National Football League, 29
Neeley, Carol Thomas, 128, 129
Nemerov, Howard, 35
Nevo, Ruth, 171
Newman, Karen, 148
Newton, Sir Isaac, 43
New Yorker, 29
New York Giants, 30
New York World's Fair (1939–40), 175
Nixon, Richard M., 116
Noriega, Manuel, 165
Norris, Christopher, 170
Nunn, Trevor, 25, 34, 49–50n., 80, 100–104, 127, 146–57, 162, 179
Nyman, Michael, 173

Ohio Shakespeare Conference, 42
Olivier, Sir Lawrence, 34, 59, 60–61, 64, 78, 89, 93, 98, 114–15, 126, 147, 148, 149, 160, 161
Ornstein, Robert, 85

Oswald, Lee Harvey, 19, 20
Other Place, 147
O'Toole, Peter, 58
Ottaway, David B., 162
Ovid, 34

Pall, Ellen, 80–81
Papp, Joseph, 25, 42, 80, 122,
Paradise Lost, 46, 165
Paramount Films, 43
Parfitt, Judy, 73–74, 76, 118
Parker, Nathaniel, 77
Peacock, Trevor, 72
Pennington, Michael, 57
Playboy, 173
Plowright, Joan, 22, 34,
Plummer, Christopher, 59–60, 62–63, 101, 152
Poe, Edgar A., 13
Polanski, Roman, 163, 170
Powell, Colin, 145
Prospero's Books, 163–76, 181
Purcell, Henry, 42

Quinn, Edward, 82

Rackham, Sir Arthur, 37
Radzin-Szolkonis, Eliza, 72
Raiders of the Lost Ark, 21–22
Reagan, Ronald, 37, 165, 166
Redgrave, Sir Michael, 57
Rees, Roger, 89
Reifenstahl, Leni, 173
Reinhardt, Max, 42, 43
Renaissance Theatre, 25
Retallac, John, 179
Revelation, 28
Rich, Frank, 81, 92
Richardson, Tony, 31, 60, 63, 73, 77, 116, 117–18, 119
"Ring and the Book," 31
Roberts, Jeanne Addison, 40
Roberts, Marilyn, 69
Robeson, Paul, 126, 148, 150, 157–58
Rodman, Howard, 164, 167, 174, 167
Rogers, Ginger, 42
Rorschach, 37
Rose, George, 61
Rosen, Carol, 39
Rosen, George, 97
Rosenberg, Marvin, 126

Rosenthal, E. M., 161
Rothwell, Kenneth, 98
Rowan, Carl T., 144
Royal Shakespeare Company, 68, 80, 85n., 86, 90, 98, 115, 116, 146, 172
Ruby, Jack, 19
Ruth, Babe, 30
Ryan, Kenneth, 61
Rylance, Mark, 58, 70, 88

Samson Agonistes, 169
Scarsgaard, Stellen, 65–66, 68, 75, 123
Schaefer, George, 21, 33
Schell, Maximilian, 57, 62, 116–17
Schofield, Paul, 72
Scot, Reginald, 34
Seventh Seal, 164
Shakespeare, William: *Antony and Cleopatra*, 19, 22, 24, 25, 34, 65, 80, 154, 179; *As You Like It*, 42, 150; *The Comedy of Errors*, 25, 80; *Hamlet*, 11, 15, 16, 23, 29, 33, 57–70, 71–79, 80–92, 113–25, 154, 172, 178, 179, 180; *Henry IV*, Part I, 94; *Henry IV*, Part II, 28, 33, 57; *Henry V*, 93, 178; *Henry VI*, 23, 26, 87; *Henry VI*, Part II, 179; *Henry VI—Richard II* cycle, 34, 153, 162; *Julius Caesar*, 19, 97; *King Lear*, 16, 25, 26–27, 29, 80, 96–100, 154, 180; *Macbeth*, 21, 25, 80, 82, 163, 180; *Measure for Measure*, 15, 26, 65, 179; *The Merchant of Venice*, 15, 22, 33–34, 80, 149, 179; *A Midsummer Night's Dream*, 13, 25, 33–50, 80, 169, 170; *Othello*, 25, 29, 32, 100–104; *Richard II*, 24, 34, 95–96, 126–62; *Richard II—Henry V* cycle, 23, 34; *Richard III*, 93; *Romeo and Juliet*, 169; *The Taming of the Shrew*, 25, 80, 150, 182; *The Tempest*, 19, 25, 33, 42, 170; *Troilus and Cressida*, 147; *Twelfth Night*, 25, 42, 95, 150; *The Winter's Tale*, 23, 25, 26, 169–70
Shakespeare Centre (Stratford) 58
Shaw, George Bernard, 100, 163
Shelley, Mary, 158
Sherin, Edwin, 80
Simon, John, 89n.
Sinden, Donald, 160
Smith, Peter D., 35

Smith College, 71
Sommers, Joseph, 89
Sophocles, 128
Spanish Tragedy, 166
Speaight, Robert, 171
Spence, Jerry, 13
Spenser, Edmund, 169
Sports Illustrated, 164
Stanislavsky, Konstantin, 105
Stavropoulous, Janet, 132, 146
Stewart, Patrick, 121
Sting, 166
Stodder, Joseph, 39
Stratford, Canada, Shakespeare Festival, 80, 182
Stubbs, Imogen, 148
Sununu, John, 127
Suzman, Janet, 25, 157–58, 162
Swann, Robert, 121
Swanson, Gloria, 12

Taylor, Estelle W., 128
Tennant, Victoria, 67
Tennyson, Alfred, 34
Terré Blanche, Eugene, 157, 161
Theisman, Joe, 30
Thomas, Clarence, 153
Thompson, Ann, 129
Till, Emmett, 148
Tokson, Elliot H., 128
Tolkien, J. R. R., 171
Trewin, J. C., 116
Trick to Catch the Old One, 152
Tynan, Kenneth, 150

Ubersfeld, Anne, 181
Ucello, Paolo, 42
Updike, John, 58–59n.

Van Doren, Mark, 175
Variety, 97
Venora, Diane, 90, 122
Vermeer, Jan, 25, 44
Veronese, Paolo, 25, 166

Waiting for Godot, 64, 155
Waller, David, 36
Waller, Gary, 13, 17, 178
Wallgren, Pernilla, 75–76
Waltons, 13
Wanamaker, Zoe, 158

Warehouse, 26
Warner Brothers Films, 59
Warren, Roger, 37, 40
Wat, Servaas de, 161
Weinberg, Joanna, 160
Welles, Orson, 12, 26, 96–100
White Noise, 28–9
White, Willard, 148, 149, 155
Whitmont, Edward, 147
Whitten, John C., 148
Wiggins, Martin, 59
Wilber Theater (Boston), 42
Wilds, Lillian, 39
Willems, Michele, 23, 25

Williamson, Nicol, 51, 57
Willson, Robert, 23
Wine, Martin, 126, 147, 149, 152
Winfield, Paul, 143, 160
Winter Garden Theater, 95, 152
Wizard of Oz, 21, 22, 164
Wolfit, Sir Donald, 29, 57
Wood, Peter, 72
Wood, Robert E., 40
Worthen, William, 16
Wright, Louis B., 126–27

Zeffirelli, Franco, 32, 55, 66–67, 68, 71,
    72, 76–78, 82–83, 116–19, 166
Zitner, Sheldon, 12, 15, 23, 70